let us water the flowers

To: Rick

2011

let us water the flowers

THE MEMOIR OF A
POLITICAL PRISONER IN IRAN

jafar yaghoobi

Prometheus Books
59 John Glenn Drive
Amherst, New York 14228–2119

Published 2011 by Prometheus Books

Cover images © 2011 Media Bakery
Cover design by Grace M. Conti-Zilsberger

Inquiries should be addressed to
Prometheus Books
59 John Glenn Drive
Amherst, New York 14228–2119
VOICE: 716–691–0133
FAX: 716–691–0137
WWW.PROMETHEUSBOOKS.COM

15 14 13 12 11 5 4 3 2 1

Library of Congress Cataloging-in-Publication Data

Yaghoobi-Saray, Jafar.
Let us water the flowers : the memoir of a political prisoner in Iran / by Jafar Yaghoobi.
p. cm.
Includes bibliographical references.
ISBN 978–1–61614–449–4 (alk. paper)
1. Yaghoobi-Saray, Jafar. 2. Political prisoners—Iran—Biography. 3. Islam and politics—Iran. 4. Iran—Politics and government—1979–1997. I. Title.

DS318.84.Y35A3 2011
365'.45092—dc22
[B] 2010049902

Printed in the United States of America on acid-free paper

This book is dedicated to all political prisoners, prisoners of conscience, and to their families.

CONTENTS

Author's Note 9

Acknowledgments 11

Introduction: A Brief Political History of Iran 15

Part One: Resisting in Despair

1. Captured 29
2. The *Tavvab* Phenomenon 92

Part Two: Blindfolded Justice

3. Assayeshgah 107
4. Amoozeshgah 116

Part Three: The "Reform" Era

5. Quarantine 163
6. Group of 93 190
7. Unity against All Odds 198

Part Four: Islamic Inquisition

8. Welcome to Hell! 223
9. New Classifications 253
10. Let Us Water the Flowers 272

11. Survivors 317

Part Five: Not Many Survived Here
12. Kill, Release, and Deny 331

Part Six: Freedom
13. New Obstacles, New Horizons 341

Epilogue 367

Notes 377

Glossary 393

Resources 405

AUTHOR'S NOTE

This book is a firsthand account of events in Iran during the decade following the Islamic Revolution of 1979, when the theocratic regime of Ayatollah Khomeini consolidated itself through the suppression of all forms of opposition. The brutality and complexity of this repression are graphically illustrated through my own experiences as a political prisoner in the Islamic Republic.

I returned to Iran from the United States in 1979 after obtaining my PhD in genetics. Like many other revolutionaries of my generation, I wanted to help change Iran for the better. Postrevolution events in Iran did not follow the path we had envisioned. However, this was a much smaller shock for my generation than the brutality and criminality of the repression exerted by the Islamist forces, particularly in prisons.

I was imprisoned in 1984 and released into house arrest in 1989. Seven months later, I escaped to Turkey and then to West Germany. Soon after my family and I arrived in California, in 1990, I began to make notes from memories of my prison experiences. The notes grew into volumes only a little more than a year after my release from prison, while the events and memories were still sharp and fresh in my mind. Eventually I found work as a geneticist at the University of California in Davis. I began writing this memoir after my retirement in 2005, keeping a promise to myself in prison that if I survived I would one day tell the world what happened to us, a generation of Iranian political activists, at the hands of our Islamist extremist compatriots.

In writing this book, I have relied upon the hundreds of pages of notes I wrote in 1990, double-checking names and events with other fellow prisoners who now live outside Iran. I alone am responsible for any inaccuracies.

Memory has its limitations, and therefore some of the dialogue should not be taken as verbatim quotes of the actual discussions. I have tried to describe and reconstruct prison scenes and events as accurately as I could.

Despite the fact that the events described here happened twenty years ago, the brutal nature of Iran's regime is such that the safety and security of people who are mentioned in this memoir remain a major concern. Therefore, I have used the real names of prisoners and friends who were killed by the regime or have died of natural causes, to honor and perpetuate their memory. I have used fictitious names for all survivors, whether they live in Iran or abroad. For government authorities, agents, collaborators, and so forth, I have used their real names where known to me; otherwise, I have used the pseudonyms they were known by in prison. All fictitious names and pseudonyms have been put in quotation marks at their first appearance, to distinguish them from real names.

In a few instances, I have omitted details or have made minor changes in my presentation of the events, to protect friends and family members. These changes will be readily apparent to those involved without significantly altering the nature of events for the general reader.

I began writing my prison memoirs in Farsi (my first language), but soon American friends and co-workers who had heard me talk about my experiences in Iran convinced me to write in English. I share their hope that this book, written by a survivor of the mass killings of 1988, will help educate the public in the West about what happened then and shed light on the record and mentality of those who continue to have the upper hand in Iran today. May the book constitute both a source of pressure on the regime and a source of energy for the democratic forces opposing it!

ACKNOWLEDGMENTS

This book is written to honor the memories of all freedom fighters of the world, including tens of thousands of Iranians who have lost their lives or have endured torture and humiliation at the hands of the brutal Islamic Republic authorities in thirty years of struggle for freedom, democracy, and justice; particularly, it honors the memories of thousands of political prisoners who perished after 1981 and in the mass killings of 1988 and were buried in unknown mass graves. They shall never be forgotten.

Though this book tells of my experiences, and any shortcomings in its presentation are my sole responsibility, the true credit for its fruition belongs to my wife, Ketty, who is my true comrade, my partner, my best friend, and the love of my life. She suffered tremendously in our separation years during a period of loneliness and sorrow, but as a single mother she raised our daughter and never gave up hope. Her love and support through our life journey have been a source of positive energy, balance, and encouragement.

This book also owes its existence to our daughter, Bahar. The vision of her childhood innocence was with me throughout my difficult ordeal and was a source of hope, resistance, and survival for me. She was without her father for five years during her critical early childhood. I hope I have been able to compensate for my absence during those lost years. Her unlimited optimism and constant smile have helped me overcome the sadness and sorrow of those difficult prison years. I love her dearly.

I am indebted to my mother and father, all my siblings and their families, and my wife's family. My father, Bashir, passed away when I was young. My mother, Ashraf, raised eleven children. She had a son as a political prisoner during the shah's time, and two sons as political prisoners in the Khomeini era. She traveled back and forth to different prisons in her old age and suffered tremendously at the hands of the prison authorities. We can never compensate for her hardship and sorrow. I will always love her unconditionally. To my brothers and sisters, who supported me in all stages of my prison ordeal and then helped me settle down in my new life, I say I love you all.

In my short life, I have had the fortune of having many good friends. I am indebted to them all. To my American friends and co-workers at the University of California–Davis (UCD), who heard my stories over the years and showed tremendous interest and encouraged me to publish them, thank you for your support and friendship. My Iranian friends—those from high school and college in Iran, those from graduate school at UCD, those from the struggle years in Iran, those from prison, and those newly made here in America—are too many to list; they all know who they are and they have been a tremendous source of support for the completion of this work. Notably, I would like to express my deepest appreciation to my prison comrade Mehdi Aslani, whose friendship and humor helped me survive the hardship of prison and who has been a constant source of moral support during the writing of this book.

My first draft of this memoir was massive—three times the length of the present volume. The long and hard process of cutting and rearranging the manuscript lasted a whole extra year. Three ladies, dear friends, helped shape the manuscript into its final presentable form:

Lisa Zirin edited and commented on that long first draft. I am so sorry to have put her through that hardship. I am very grateful and will always be indebted to her and her husband, M.N., my dear old friend of close to forty years.

The second draft, a bit shorter, was read and commented on by L.H. She gave me good advice on where to cut and how to reorganize it. I also later had many fruitful discussions with her on different parts of the final manuscript, and her contributions were tremendous.

After many rounds of reading, rewriting, and cutting, I asked Margaret Arculus, a dear friend of our family for many years, if she would be interested in editing and commenting on my final draft. Her editorial work made the narrative flow well and the manuscript look presentable. I am deeply grateful to her and her husband, Lloyd Yu, my friend of so many years, for their time, effort, and enthusiastic love and support.

After all the hard work of preparing the manuscript, the publication process seemed so daunting. Finding a perfect match for the publishing of this book was not an easy task. Prometheus Books, publishers of thought-provoking, intelligent, independent literary works, saw the importance of publishing my memoir. I would like to thank Prometheus Books, and particularly my acquisition editor Mark Hall, PhD, who trusted my writing, saw the importance of its publication, and liked the narrative of my memoir from the very beginning. His support throughout the publishing process was priceless. I also would like to thank all those in the art department at Prometheus Books, particularly Grace M. Conti-Zilsberger for designing a wonderful book cover. Many thanks also go to Will DeRooy, who copyedited the book; his contributions were significant in making the text flow perfectly. Last but not least, my appreciation goes to all those in the production, sales and marketing, and publicity departments of Prometheus Books for all their efforts in making this experience, my first in literary book publishing, a tremendously enjoyable success.

I retired in 2005 and focused on the writing of this memoir. This was my first experience in book-length writing. I am a very disciplined person by nature, and I spent on average about two to four hours every weekday for a few years working on this project. As the saying goes, writing is a lonely process. This would be true in my case as well had it not been for the permanent presence of Chico, Olive, Koko, Bobo, and Tweety in my life. They were my companions during the day, as I was their caretaker, when my wife Ketty was at work. Chico and Olive were our two old Chihuahuas. Unfortunately, they both recently had to be put to sleep within the span of a couple of months. We miss them both terribly. Koko is our African gray parrot (age twelve), Bobo is our cockatiel (age sixteen), and Tweety is our parakeet (age ten). Without their lively and interactive presence I would not have been able to last those many years of lonely writing frustration. I thank them all from the bottom of my heart.

Introduction

A BRIEF POLITICAL HISTORY OF IRAN

Iran (the Islamic Republic of Iran), once known as Persia, is at the heart of one of the world's oldest continuous major civilizations. Over the past five thousand years, the region has developed a unique language and culture that distinguish Iran from its neighbors to this day. Even after the Arab conquest in 632 CE, when Persia's Zoroastrian population was forced to adopt Islam or be slaughtered, Zoroastrianism and the Persian language survived.

It was only in the sixteenth century that Shi'a religion became the dominant branch of Islam in Persia. The adoption of Shiism has been instrumental in maintaining the country's distinct identity within the overwhelmingly Sunni Islamic world. This choice also was an early marker of the tendency to use religion as a means of political control.

In the mid-nineteenth century, travelers and commerce introduced news and effects of Western social, technological, and political advances into Persia, stimulating the beginnings of an intellectual movement. At the same time, the unprecedented corruption and fanaticism of the Qajar dynasty (1794–1924) forced Persia open to the competing interests of the rising colonial powers of Imperial Russia and Britain. Known as "the Great Game," this period of contest between the two powers led to the Anglo-Russian Convention of 1907, in which Persia was divided into spheres of influence. Discovery of oil in southern Persia in the early

1900s led to increased British dominance. Nonetheless, Persia managed to maintain its sovereignty and was never officially colonized.

Influenced by the democratic and revolutionary trends of Western nations and Russia, respectively, Persian intellectuals began focusing upon two intertwined sets of demands: for democracy, freedom, and justice on the one hand; to maintain Persia's independence against growing pressures from external powers on the other. The embryonic middle class and destitute rural population, both suffocated by the tyrannical feudal system, together with bazaar merchants, workers, and progressive clerics, provided a base for the resulting Constitutional Revolution (1905–1911), the first of its kind in Asia. On August 5, 1906, the shah of Persia, Mozaffar-ul-din Shah, was forced to issue a decree permitting formation of an elected parliament (called the Majles) and the establishment of a constitution. Adapted from European constitutions, the constitution placed limits for the first time in Persian history on what had been the king's absolute power, and it established a parliamentary system in Persia. An active press emerged, together with a diverse range of political parties and associations. These developments led to the emergence of the first sense of nationhood among Persians. This nationalism involved a combination of three essential sentiments: antityranny, anticolonialism, and the rejection of any form of Islamist government.

Unfortunately, Persia's first experience of democratization was short-lived. While the constitution and the parliament survived, the spirit of constitutionalism was defeated. Contributing factors included the absence of essential social institutions, a lack of political consciousness necessary for democracy, political differences among the revolutionaries, the Qajar shahs' resistance to relinquish power to Parliament, the vested interests of the colonial powers, and the support provided to the monarchy and its colonial allies by a coalition of clergy, major landowners, and other powerful players.

The Bolshevik Revolution of 1917 in Russia shifted the balance of power in the region. Great Britain was now in a position to dominate Persia and secure its interests, particularly in the critical oil industry. Reza Khan, a brigadier general in Persia's only military force, the Cossack Brigade, was encouraged by the British to take control of the country. In 1921, he entered Tehran with a group of soldiers and was appointed commander of the military by the young and weak Ahmad shah of Qajar dynasty. Within a few years, after suppressing several rebellions in outlying regions, Reza Khan became the most powerful man in Persia. In 1923, Ahmad Shah appointed Reza Khan as prime minister and left for Europe to receive "medical treatment," which became an exile for him. When Ahmad Shah had not returned two years later, he was deposed by a specially convened assembly, who named Reza Khan, now known as Reza Pahlavi, as the new shah.

Reza Shah had an ambitious plan for modernizing Persia. He made huge strides in transforming the country from a preindustrial society to a semi-industrial and urbanized one by developing large-scale industries, building a cross-country railway system, establishing a national public education system, reforming the judiciary, establishing the University of Tehran, and starting many other major infrastructure projects. In 1935, he also officially changed the country's name from Persia to Iran.

Reza Shah ruled with an iron fist. During his first years in power, he waged successful military campaigns against regional and tribal leaders throughout Iran's far-flung regions, finally establishing the first strong central government over the entire country. This "King of Kings" and "Shadow of Almighty" had accumulated so much land and wealth by the late 1930s he was the largest landowner and the richest man in the country. Meanwhile, the vast majority of Iranians remained in abject poverty. The middle class, who sought freedoms and democracy, was alienated by his dictatorial policies. The religious establishment was outraged by his reforms of the education system, the judiciary, and law—the traditional domain of the Shiite clergy—in particular, his policy of forced removal of *hejab* (the veiling of women). Those who opposed him were brutally tortured and killed.

During the Second World War, Great Britain and the Soviet Union turned their attention once again to Iran. Reza Shah's strong ties with Germany worried Great Britain. The country's trans-Iranian railway provided a very attractive route for the transport of much-needed fuel, armaments, and goods to the desperate Soviets, who were under attack by Nazi Germany. Great Britain also wanted to secure the critical regional oil reserves. In August 1941 Britain demanded that Iran expel all German citizens, but Reza Shah refused. Britain and the Soviet Union reoccupied parts of the country, forced Reza Shah into exile, and crowned his son Mohammad-Reza Pahlavi as the new monarch.

With a new, young, weak shah in the anti-Fascist climate of the time, Iran enjoyed a period of relative political freedom. Political prisoners, most of them leftists and communists, were freed from prison. Journalism flourished, and many political parties and organizations soon formed. Of these, the Tudeh Party of Iran rapidly became the most influential. Formed mainly by released political prisoners and other intellectuals, it grew to become the largest pro-Soviet party in the region. At one point it had tens of thousands of members and sympathizers among intellectuals, workers, youth, women, and even military personnel.

In 1949, an assassination attempt against the shah resulted in the banning of the Tudeh Party and the expansion of the shah's powers. Increasingly, the shah intervened in government affairs and opposed or thwarted strong prime ministers. He also focused on reviving and rebuilding the army as the monarchy's main support base.

Under the leadership of Dr. Mohammad Mossadegh, the National

Front of Iran was formed in 1949 to uphold the 1906 constitution. Nationalizing the Iranian oil industry became its prime focus. Britain had exploited Iran's oil resources with little more than token benefit to Iran itself. In 1951, popular pressure influenced the shah to appoint Mossadegh prime minister. With the backing of the people, Mossadegh soon forced Parliament to nationalize the oil industry. Mossadegh, who fervently supported key institutions of democracy like Parliament and a free press, was also adamant about finding solutions to the country's dependence on Britain.

To Britain and to the United States—the new American superpower was rapidly superseding its old colonizer on the world stage—Mossadegh's nationalist policies set a dangerous precedent in the region. Collaboration between the CIA and MI6 (the British secret intelligence service) produced the 1953 coup, overthrowing the Middle East's first democratically elected government.

The Tudeh Party had initially opposed the oil nationalization strategy, arguing that Iran's oil should be shared with the Soviet Union. Their belated rally to the nationalist cause was too late to prevent the coup. The inaction and indecisiveness of the party leaders against the coup served only to expose their supporters to the crackdown that followed. After the coup, the shah, who had fled the country a few days earlier following the prior failed attempt by the army to arrest Mossadegh, returned, and the United States oversaw his reinstatement to total power. Thus, Iran's second attempt at democratization was thwarted by direct foreign intervention. Many hundreds of Mossadegh's followers and Tudeh Party activists were arrested, tortured, and imprisoned, and many were executed. Mossadegh himself endured three years of solitary confinement before being placed under house arrest, during which he died in 1967. Mossadegh became a hero and a symbol of Iran's struggle against dictatorship and against subjugation by external powers.

Within a year of the 1953 coup, operation of Iran's oil fields was turned over to an international consortium. Repression became institutionalized. A new secret police organization, the dreaded SAVAK, was established, trained, and equipped by the CIA and Mossad (the Israeli intelligence agency). American military and technological assistance, paid for with oil dollars, began flooding in. Over the course of the Cold War, the shah established himself as an indispensable ally of the West, particularly the Americans. To most Iranians, though, the shah was merely a puppet and a regional tool of the United States.

Under pressure from the United States to share power with the growing middle class, in 1963 the shah finally announced a reform program titled the White Revolution. Rather than initiating meaningful political change, however, the program opened the countryside to a market economy of imported goods and forced a flood of landless peasants into the urban areas, creating a cheap source of labor for the growing urban economy. The reactions to these reforms and the dictatorial police state of the shah came from the secular middle class, who sought democratic and political freedoms and rights, and, more forcefully, from a faction of the religious establishment (led by Ayatollah Khomeini), who feared a loss of their traditional power base and authority. Protests erupted into an uprising in 1963, which was ruthlessly suppressed. Khomeini was arrested, imprisoned, and sent into exile.

The events of 1963 were a turning point. A new generation of activists and freedom fighters, both secular and religious, concluded that peaceful protest and activity was futile; armed struggle, in their view, was the only way forward to remove the shah's regime.

The first armed action against the shah's regime was carried out by a group of secular leftist guerrillas in February 1971 in northern Iran. Although the action was defeated militarily and most of the participants were martyred, the survivors of this group joined another leftist group to form the Organization of Iranian People's Fadai Guerrillas (the Fadaiyan). Soon, an Islamic leftist group calling itself the People's Mojahedin Organization of Iran (the Mojahedin) proclaimed its existence through armed action as well. Dedicated to armed struggle, the two groups became the primary target of the regime's repressive apparatus throughout the 1970s.

The 1973 increase in oil prices and revenues spurred the shah in his ambitious goal of transforming Iran into a regional industrial power. It also provided the means to buy support of the military and parts of the middle class with his vast oil revenues. Meanwhile, SAVAK's ruthless repression of any sign of dissent continued unabated. Iranian society was prevented from developing even the most embryonic form of genuine secular civic or political institutions. The failure of the shah's land reforms had resulted in a massive migration of landless peasants and rural poor to the outskirts of the cities in search of work and other opportunities. In Tehran, more than two million people lived in shantytowns. Ironically, these same illiterate slum-dwellers played a critical role in the coming political/social changes of the country and the fate of the shah's regime.

As a result, when unrest started in 1978, the middle class and the working class, lacking political or trade union organizations, could not exert any form of leadership within the opposition. The only two credible political organizations in the country, the Fadaiyan and the Mojahedin, were underground guerrilla groups, many of whose members either had died—in street clashes, under torture, or through execution—or were languishing in prison. The traditional political parties of the 1940s and 1950s had been destroyed by SAVAK or were in exile, discredited, with no serious support base in the country.

The only opposition left intact were religious Shiite forces: the clergy, seminary students, religious university students and intellectuals, the traditional *bazaaris* (members of the bazaar), and, most important, the network of mosques throughout the country. Trapped in a cold war mind-set, the shah and his Western allies saw these religious forces and institutions only as a natural force against the Soviet Union and Iranian communists. This religious network became the organizational base for Ayatollah Khomeini, who from abroad in France assumed sole leadership of the opposition to the shah. Far from opposing Khomeini and his political Islamist views, Western powers actually accommodated them, expecting Khomeini and his followers would be a bulwark against communism. For their part, Iran's secular forces, particularly the Left, lacked a serious popular base and were themselves trapped in the "anti-imperialist" mind-set of a movement dominated by religious trends.

In February 1979, one of the largest popular revolutions in modern history ended the twenty-five-hundred-year-old monarchy in Iran. Khomeini had made many promises while in France so that he could achieve the widest unity possible among Iranians. But as he and his followers consolidated power, those promises were cast aside. Khomeini had his own vision for the country: establishing a Shiite theocracy ruled by the clergy. Khomeini relied on the religious network, on the *bazaaris*, and on the urban poor to achieve his goals. The Islamic republic he engineered combined Western concepts and institutions—like an elected parliament and elected president—with Islamic theocratic innovations. It was designed to ensure the dominion of the Shiite clergy. Key to this was establishment within the constitution of the position of supreme leader (*velayat-e faghih*)—a nonelected, lifelong position holding absolute power.

After the fall of the shah's regime and before consolidation of the new Islamic theocracy, for a short period there existed dual sources of power in the country. One came from below—from the masses, which had organized themselves in secular and religious associations, councils, and committees in neighborhoods and workplaces. The other came from the top—from Khomeini and the clerical system, the bazaar, religious activists, and part of the urban poor organized in a variety of Islamic militia and local committee groups. During this transitional period, many political parties, groups, and cultural associations were formed, and the press flourished. Briefly, freedom seemed to be within reach of the Iranian people.

Islamic ideology soon became a tool of domination and repression in the hands of the new rulers. In one way or another, any form of dissent was labeled anti-Islamic, and the crackdown started sooner than expected. Any gathering, organized activity, or demonstration by political opposition groups, the working class, Iranian ethnic minorities, or, particularly, by the secular women's movement was crushed by club-wielding vigilantes organized and led by the clerics or their agents. Soon, the regime's organized militia forces—the Revolutionary Guards, the local Islamic Revolution Committees, the Basij paramilitary forces, and others—took on this repressive role.

During and immediately after the Islamic Revolution was a period that held potential for democracy. For a time, a united front of all democratic forces in the country could have had a slim chance of changing the course of Iranian history. But such brief openings do not allow time for strong, visionary leadership to emerge and develop unity among a diverse, inexperienced opposition. Instead, the historical struggle of the Iranian people for democracy was once again defeated in the 1980s by reactionary forces bent on establishing an Islamic theocratic system.

The official and dominant religion in Iran has been Islam for centuries. At the time of the revolution about 89 percent of the population was considered Shi'a Muslim, 10 percent was Sunni Muslim, and Zoroastrians, Jews, Christians, and Baha'is formed the other 1 percent. But, a noticeable part of the overall population, maybe 10 percent, had become secular over the past decades prior to the 1979 revolution. This portion of the population formed the basis for the secular leftist opposition to the new Islamist regime.

Since the moment of capturing power in Iran, Khomeini and his followers have exploited every opportunity to crush the opposition. The American hostage crisis, the Iran-Iraq War, and particularly the actions of the Mojahedin in June 1981 became opportunities to purge the Islamic Republic of its opponents.

June 1981 was a turning point, at which Khomeini's forces moved to consolidate their power. The regime already had advanced plans to systematically destroy any form of opposition. In June 1981, Mojahedin followers and militia forces marched in the streets of Tehran and other major cities, providing an excuse for the regime to start its massive crackdown. During the ensuing mini–civil war between the Mojahedin and Khomeini's forces, hundreds were killed in street fights and tens of thousands were rounded up and thrown in prison. From 1981 to 1986 the security apparatus of the system methodically hunted down and destroyed any form of organized opposition to the regime. Political prisoners were brutally tortured, summarily tried in Islamic tribunals, and massacred by the thousands. For all practical purposes, the opposition within Iran was crushed.

It was during this period of turmoil in Iran that I was arrested in a Tehran street in October 1984.

“The free man is one who knows why he does what he does.”

Gottfried W. Leibniz (1646–1716)

Part One

RESISTING IN DESPAIR

Chapter One
CAPTURED

1

October 22, 1984

It all happened in a split second: a second that decidedly and irreversibly changed my world. Suddenly sensing the commotion and aware of people running up from behind, I dropped the tiny note from my hand before several armed security agents overpowered me. In that indescribable moment, I was both certain of what was transpiring and hoped somehow it was just a misunderstanding. The agents—there were seven or eight of them, in plain clothes—shouting and screaming, forced me to the ground while some of them worked the gathering crowd, telling onlookers that I had been selling illegal drugs to students. As soon as I was down, one agent forced my mouth open and another searched it, apparently looking for a suicide capsule of cyanide. The agents resorted to lies and diversions to mislead the gathering, curious students into believing that my detention was drug-related and not political. In those days, government agents snatched political opponents in broad daylight but made it look like the arrests were on drug-, sex-, or alcohol-related charges.

Having made sure that I was unarmed and had no cyanide capsule, the agents pulled me inside a small hardware store. The owner, an old man, was too shocked and scared to do anything but observe silently. The agents pushed me up against the wall while they did a full body search and emptied the contents of my pockets onto the store counter. A few agents were still busy controlling and working the crowd outside.

After the initial shock, I gathered myself and considered how to react to the situation. I did not want to reveal my political/organizational affiliation, because there was a chance that I really *had* been detained on suspicion of drug dealing. In that case I would be wise to keep the situation nonpolitical. On the other hand, my instincts were screaming at me that this was indeed a political arrest. I was in a dilemma and had only a few minutes to react. I decided to shout out and let the crowd of young people know that I had nothing to do with any drug dealing. Upon this, the agents quickly dispersed the gathering crowd. The contents of my pockets were put in a bag and taken away. I heard my car keys given to an agent to fetch the car. Up to this point, I had held a glimmer of hope that the whole incident could be a random mistaken arrest, but fetching the car without asking me for the make, model, and location indicated that they had already identified my car, had probably followed me to the parking spot, and maybe had even been waiting for me at the meeting site.

Handcuffed and hooded, I was led outside of the hardware store. Hooding, done apparently for security and intelligence reasons, in reality helps the agents to disorient, control, and psychologically dominate the detainee. They pushed me into the back seat of a Mercedes-Benz, which I was able to identify through the pores in the fabric of the hood over my head. Agents sat on both sides of me in the back seat, and many more entered into other cars, presumably to follow us. As soon as the car began to move, the agents in the back seat pushed my head down into my lap to prevent me from figuring out where they were taking me. While the two agents sustained the force on my neck and head, the agent in the front passenger seat kept asking me questions regarding my alleged involvement in drug trafficking and even in the killing of members of the Revolutionary Guards,[1] something that according to him had recently happened in the Iranian Baluchestan province. Then, he threatened me by saying that I should confess to everything before we got to the center, so that he could put in a good word for me. Otherwise, he said, I was going to be in big trouble. I told him that I had nothing to do with any drugs and that I was not going to answer any more questions in that regard. Then he immediately asked who were I if not a drug trafficker. I suddenly found myself in a very awkward and vulnerable position: If I stayed silent, I thought, it would be an admission of guilt. I had to either reveal my true identity or give them a false one. Either way could cause me problems. After a moment of hesitation, I decided to give them my true identity, hoping that it would help in the unlikely case that they were really suspicious of me for being involved in a drug-related offense. So I said, "My name is Jafar Yaghoobi. I am a geneticist and I work in the Ministry of Agriculture as a scientific consultant for poultry-breeding projects." This statement was met with hysterical laughter. I immediately started having doubts; had I done the right thing by revealing my true identity? Maybe I should have given them a false name. I felt I had made my first big mistake. But then I thought, revealing my true identity was helpful because whether I had been detained mistakenly or I had already been identified as an underground activist, it could not hurt if they knew who I really was in public life.

After the laughter was over, it finally got quiet in the car. At this point, though I was fairly certain that I had been followed and maybe even identified, my overall hope was that my detention was based either on mistaken identity or on my looking suspicious and out of place in the neighborhood. As I searched my memory for potential mistakes since that morning, events of the day flashed through my mind.

October 22, 1984, was a beautiful autumn Wednesday in Tehran. I had gone to work early that morning and left the Ministry of Agriculture building just before noon on an errand. My wife, Ketty Mobed, had long been asking me for a notarized power of attorney document, which would enable her to add our eighteen-month-old daughter, Bahar, to her passport. She was planning a trip to Europe to visit her parents.

I went to see my cousin "Aydin," who worked in a bank building located close to the official notary office. Aydin was my age and had been my friend since childhood. Since my return from America in 1979, I had kept in touch with and occasionally called on him. I knew he had connections in the governmental notary office. It would have taken me days to get a notarized power of attorney if I had gone on my own, but I did not have that kind of spare time. When I arrived at the bank, it was just past noon. Aydin took me to the notary office to one of his friends, and we were done with the process in fifteen minutes. I thanked them both and drove home. Connections and bribing have always been the fastest way of doing things in Iran.

I got home around one o'clock and gave the notarized form to my wife, which made her very happy and excited. I ate some lunch, gathered a few documents I needed to give to my contact in the organization, and composed a small note to myself listing what I needed to discuss with him. I kissed my wife and daughter good-bye and rushed out to make my two o'clock meeting with the contact. I hid the documents in a secret compartment under the hood of the car, carrying only the tiny note, which was small enough for me to roll up and conceal between my fingertips.

It took me about twenty minutes to drive from our home in west-central Tehran to the meeting location in the east-central part of the city. Following organizational safety guidelines, I frequently checked to make sure that I was not being followed and even used a couple of recommended safety tactics such as driving through long, quiet one-way streets to make sure I was not being tailed. In those days, the chance of being identified and arrested was very high. In the two years following the revolution (February 1979 to January 1981), the random arrest of opposition activists had been mostly sporadic. The clashes with Mojahedin (an Islamic leftist opposition group)[2] across Iran in 1981 had provoked a hysterical reaction from government security forces and the militia, although since early 1982 most arrests were now made systematically through sophisticated intelligence-gathering work followed by massive raids and strikes by the intelligence, security, and militia forces. The regime had successfully identified and destroyed many opposition organizations during the past three years. We had no doubt that they were actively working on destroying our organization as well.

When I got closer to the meeting location in the Nezam-abad area, I parked my car a couple of blocks away, left the documents in the secret compartment, and carried only the tiny note in my hand. Because I was late, I could not make the two o'clock meeting and decided to execute the two-thirty contingency meeting instead. I entered the designated meeting street and walked on the south sidewalk to the end of the block. Everything looked normal, as far as I could see. Then around two thirty I crossed to the north sidewalk where the meeting was going to be executed. We were supposed to pretend to be old friends running into each other after many years. We were then going to talk a little, maybe sit down in an ice cream shop, and execute our meeting.

I was wearing clean, neat trousers; a thin, sporty blue jacket; and a pair of nice-looking, shiny shoes. I was a bit better dressed than most of the people around me. Walking slowly and calmly, clasping the tiny note between the fingertips of my right hand, ready to swallow or drop it in an emergency, I got closer to the middle of the block. The local school had just finished for the day, and teenaged students were crowding the streets. I had passed the midpoint of the block but still could not see my contact coming from the opposite direction, as he was supposed to. Before I had a chance to make a decision to continue walking or to leave, I was apprehended by the security agents.

The day ended in disaster, but I was so glad I had gotten the notary document for my wife. I remembered her happy and excited face, the last image of her engrained in my mind.

2

After driving around for an hour in the city, partly because of the afternoon traffic but mostly to confuse me, the agents finally stopped the car. I had not been able to figure out yet where they had taken me. A gate opened; the car passed through it and parked. I was brought out of the car, still hooded and handcuffed. We went through a building into a triangular yard where I was led to a spot and ordered to wait. Once in a while, I heard people passing through that yard. It was obvious from their conversations that they were not detainees. After about half an hour, tired of standing in that manner, I began to protest. Someone approached who whispered in my ear in a serious tone, advising me for the last time, as he said, to confess to my relations with the drug-trafficking ring, adding that I ought to think about my family and my own life. I did not respond. He walked away laughing.

Though I was becoming convinced that there was no randomness or mistake in my arrest, my mind kept playing tricks on me. I thought maybe I had been reported to the authorities as a suspicious person in the neighborhood where we lived, causing them to follow me. But then I remembered how many plainclothes agents had been involved in my arrest. It was obvious that they had been waiting for me at that meeting location.

About an hour later, someone approached and asked my name and my father's name. He then grabbed my hand and walked me around for a while to further disorient me. When we stopped, he took my hood off and removed my handcuffs. I was in a small room in an office building. A man sitting behind a desk asked for my personal information and filled out a short form. He had a very distinctive, squeaky voice. An older man in a Revolutionary Guards uniform and a plain-clothed middle-aged man were also present in the room. These two men put me in a chair and one of them took photos for the form. The squeaky-voiced man asked me to sign the form. I tried to read it before signing, but he said that it was just an identification form to make sure that I would not get lost. They all started laughing. I signed the form, which basically documented that I had been booked on that day. Then the older man brought me a prison uniform consisting of a set of light-blue pajamas and a pair of sandals. They asked me to change and give them all of my personal belongings. Those were put in a bag and my name was written on it. Finally, the old guard gave me a pair of ugly, smelly gray blankets, a bag to use as a pillow, a plastic bowl, a plastic cup, and an aluminum spoon. At that point I asked why I was being booked. The old guard declared that I was in the detention center of the Revolutionary Guards until it became clear to the authorities that I was innocent, at which time, he added, I would be released.

Then they put a piece of thick black cloth over my eyes with a wide rubber band holding it at the back of my head. This was my own personal blindfold, which I was told I had to wear at all times. A guard standing outside of the door was called in to transfer me to the ward (a prisoner holding block consisting of many cells or rooms). He grabbed my uniform and led me into the yard. He walked me for a few minutes in different directions and up and down a few steps, and talked nonstop to distract me so that I would not know where this particular ward,

Ward 1, was located. Later I figured out that it was only twenty to thirty steps away from the office and it was the ground floor of a three- or four-story building.

We entered into a small *zir-e hasht* (foyer) and then we dropped a single step into the ward corridor. Later I would discover that this was called Ward 1. I could see the floor from under the blindfold—we were in a long hallway where detainees were sitting or lying on their blankets along both walls. The guard found an empty spot for me on the right-hand side and ordered me to spread my blankets and to sit down. Afterward, he whispered the rules and regulations of the ward in my ear: "Never contact other prisoners. Never look from above or below your blindfold. Never raise your voice, only raise your hand if you need assistance. When your name and your father's name is whispered in your ear, acknowledge only with a head gesture. Bathroom, only three times a day as scheduled. You will be harshly punished if you do not follow these rules!" In the prison system, the authorities identified a prisoner only by using his first name and his father's first name.

Reality started sinking in, and for the first time since my arrest I truly felt that I was in danger. I was also bothered painfully by the eerie silence dominating that corridor. I sat down on the blanket with my back toward the ward entrance. Gradually, my eyes got used to the lighting in the corridor. With caution, I raised my head a bit so that I could observe the corridor from under my blindfold. I did not believe what I saw at the very end of the corridor. My heartbeat shot up so fast that I thought my heart was going to explode. My dear old comrade Zeynolabedin Kazemi, whom we all knew as Abdi, was sitting on a blanket close to the end of the corridor. He was leaning against the wall with his head on his knees as though sad and distressed. Though I could not see his face, I was sure it was him—Abdi's large size was distinctive. Seeing that gentle giant there supported my strong suspicion that my arrest was not a random and isolated event. This made it fairly certain that a raid and strike against our organization in Tehran by the Ministry of Intelligence[3] (MI) or the security division of the Revolutionary Guards was under way. Abdi and I had worked together in the same section of our organization until his transfer to a different division more than a year ago. We were not positioned close enough in the corridor to contact each other. But seeing him there forced me to start thinking seriously about a strategy for dealing with the interrogators. I thought I would start by denying any involvement with the organization and thus force them to prove otherwise. This way, I thought, I would be in control, deciding what to admit and when to admit it. Basically I decided not to volunteer any information until I was sure they already had it or I was forced to admit to it under torture. At this point I was still thinking that I was the only member of my organization who had been arrested—besides Abdi, whose arrest could not have been related to me—and therefore I thought I could follow my own interrogation strategy. But how could I be sure no one else had been taken? I began to consider the grim alternative.

A guard started distributing the evening food ration. I could hear his footsteps and the sound of the metal food bucket hitting the floor. He soon approached me, put some food in my plastic bowl, gave me a few sugar cubes, and gave me a piece of *lavash* bread. He later poured some tea in my cup as well. The evening meal looked quite strange. It was supposedly *abgusht* (lamb stew) but contained only a piece of meatless bone, a small potato, some beans, and dried key limes. I really did not feel like eating anything. From the moment I had seen Abdi there, a fear had grown within me that others might have also been arrested and therefore I had to prepare myself for the worst. This realization made my guts churn. I tried to eat some of the bread and drink the tea, but I had no appetite.

The prison sound system started broadcasting the evening *azan* (call for prayer). The sound system was controlled from the prison office, with speakers located all over the hallways and each cell; it blasted religious chanting, ideological lessons, and official news programs into the cells a few times during the day and night. This helped us to keep track of the time.

Around seven in the evening a guard approached and whispered in my ear asking if I was Jafar son of Bashir, which I acknowledged. He ordered me to follow him and led me out of the ward into the small *zir-e basht*, into the small yard, and finally into the office building. We then took the steps on the left to go upstairs. On the second floor, he put me in a small hallway facing the wall. I stood there for about half an hour with feelings of powerlessness and anxiety like I had never had before. I felt I had no control over the events unleashed since that afternoon. I tried to focus on my strategy of going through the interrogation process. But it seemed as though I had lost control over my analytical thought processes and, in particular, I could not keep my mind calm and focused.

Someone grabbed my arm and whispered in my ear, asking if I was Jafar son of Bashir. He guided me into one of the rooms across from the stairs. He put me in the chair and left without saying a word. After a minute, having made sure that no one else was in the room, I checked it out from under the blindfold. It was a fairly small room. There was indeed nothing else in it except the chair I was sitting in. The wooden arm of the chair caught my attention. Names, slogans, poetry, and drawings were carved on it, mostly reflecting remorse, defeat, and despair, but there were a few poems and slogans of resistance as well.

The door suddenly opened and a few people entered the room. As they moved closer to my sides, my heart rate started rising. I could see the legs of two of them on my sides, but I sensed a third person and maybe even a fourth standing behind me. Then, they started rotating positions so that one from behind me was now on my left side. One stood in front of me and another on my right side. Whether there was still a fourth in the room, I could not tell. The one standing in front of me was wearing some type of pajamas and looked a bit chubby from what I could see of him. The interrogator standing on my left side started politely with regular greetings and then asked, "Mr. Yaghoobi, do you have any idea why you have been detained?"

"No, I really don't. Apparently, they had suspicion that I was involved with drug traffickers, in drug dealing or something of that nature."

"Were you involved?"

"Of course I wasn't. I have never had anything to do with any drug dealing or drug trafficking."

"I agree with you 100 percent. You do not look like the sort."

"So, why have I been detained, then?"

"Well, we just had a few questions we wanted to ask you, if you don't mind."

"Not at all—whatever you need to ask."

"What were you doing in the Nezam-abad area where they arrested you today?"

"I was on my way to visit my sister when I started having car trouble. So I turned toward that area to find an auto-repair shop."

"Did you find one? Did you show your car to a mechanic?"

"I was walking and looking for one when I was attacked and arrested for the ridiculous charge of drug dealing."

"Do you have any political interests and activities?"

"Of course I do. Everyone does in Iran today."

"So, what is yours?"

"Why do you ask me this question? Have I been arrested for political reasons?"

"No, I am just curious. If you do not want to answer, you do not have to."

"I am a supporter of the revolution. I support the rights and demands of the Iranian people for justice, independence, and freedom."

"Have you read any publications of any political parties, particularly from the Fadaiyan[4] organization?"

"Yes, I have read some."

"Have you read from all different factions of them?"

"I do not know what you mean."

"Oh, you don't? Then let me update you on what has happened to the Fadaiyan, since you may not have read about them recently. A split in the Fadaiyan organization in 1980 yielded two different groups: one calling itself the Fadaiyan Majority and the other the Fadaiyan Minority. The majority organization split again, in 1981, into two parts known as the Fadaiyan Majority and the Fadaiyan Sixteenth of Azar."

"I don't know much about these groups and events."

"So, you are claiming that you have never read anything from the Fadaiyan Sixteenth of Azar group?"

"Yes. I know nothing about that."

"So you have never had any relations with the Fadaiyan Sixteenth of Azar organization?"

"I have never had any relations with any political organizations."

"Mr. Yaghoobi, I think we have had enough of this bullshit game playing—"

"Haj-Agha, these guys are not human!" the man in pajamas standing in front of me exclaimed angrily. (He was addressing the one who was asking the questions; "Haj-Agha" is generally an honorific title of respect.) "They are like animals and we need to treat them as such. We need to make them understand who is in charge here. Let us take him downstairs and prepare him, so that he would respond to your questions seriously."

But the lead interrogator continued with what he had been about to say before his associate interrupted him: "I want to put two courses of action in front of you, before things get serious and ugly. I am going to give you a half hour's time to ponder these two paths, because you seem to be a nice guy. After a half hour, when we return, things are going to get real nasty if you do not start being cooperative and straight with us. But first, let me inform you that we have arrested you in relation with the Fadaiyan Sixteenth of Azar organization. This organization has been involved in antirevolutionary and anti-Islamic activities against Imam Khomeini and the Islamic Republic of Iran. Now, one path in front of you is honesty and cooperation with us. In this case we will be kind, compassionate, and forgiving toward you. The second path for you is to keep doing what you have been doing so far; to have a malicious and impure heart, to be dishonest, to keep playing games, and to continue being an enemy of the Islamic system and the path of Imam Khomeini. If you do choose this so-called path of resistance, as you people like calling it, then we will treat you accordingly in a way that either you will not survive or if you do survive you will never be relieved of the consequences. I am going to give you plenty of time to ponder these options, and when we return you will see how different and nasty things can get here."

As they turned to leave the room, the third interrogator, who was standing on my right side and in full Revolutionary Guards uniform, whispered this in my ear: "You should be wise and act responsibly. You should think about your life and the future of your family. We have already collected critical intelligence on your activities. Your leaders have already been detained and they are all here and collaborating with us. We are only going to test your honesty and character here. This is not about extracting information from you at all. Believe me, we already have collected or have obtained necessary information from your top leaders. If you choose the cooperation path, we would be willing to bring some of your leaders to meet you, so you know that they are indeed cooperating with us."

After they left, in the dead silence of the room I could hear my heart pounding away crazily. My mouth was dry and my breathing heavy. I tried to pull myself together to focus on how to approach the interrogation and the torture soon to follow. If it was true that the top leaders of the organization in Tehran had been arrested, then my arrest and others' as well was part of an extensive, systematic raid by the security forces attempting to destroy our organization. I needed to figure out how extensive the arrests were and how much the interrogators really knew about my activities in the organization. To be able to achieve this goal, I had to refine my strategy. I decided that for me, under the circumstances, the best course of action would be a middle path. I was not going to have myself tortured to death. But I was not going to surrender and collaborate with them either, to betray my values and corrupt my moral character. I made up my mind I would resist to a reasonable degree and try to figure out as much as possible about what the interrogators knew or did not know about my activities. And only then would I try to relieve myself from unnecessary torture by admitting, agreeing, or providing bits of information and disinformation. Of course, like anything else in life, this was easier said and thought than done. One thing was clear to me. I was not going to be pushed by the interrogators to one of the two extremes. From a practical point of view, I decided to make my decisions during the interrogation very pragmatically. If I knew they had a piece of intelligence and just wanted me to admit to it, then I was not going to be stupid and put my life on the line. If I thought they knew nothing on an issue, I was going to resist as much as I could and when I could not resist anymore I was going to provide them with false intelligence to buy myself more time. After a half hour of analyzing and strategizing, I felt strong and at peace with myself. My only real worry at this time was about my wife and daughter, not knowing what had happened or might happen to them.

It was about nine o'clock when the interrogators returned. The lead interrogator, the one who did the actual questioning, stood behind me this time. I learned he was called "Haji Mahmood." The other two were standing to my right and left, where I could see only their legs. The one called "Ibrahim" was still in his pajamas, while the other was still in Guards uniform. Haji Mahmood started:

"God willing, I hope that you have chosen the correct path for yourself. For starters, tell us about your relations with the organization."

"What organization?"

"What organization? So, you have chosen the resistance path. Get up, you stupid antirevolutionary! I will show you what organization when we get to the *ta'zir* room." (*Ta'zir* is a category of crime and punishment in Islamic law.)

As they grabbed my arms and shoulders to take me to the torture chamber, Ibrahim intervened: "Haj-Agha, with your permission, I would like to have a few moments alone with him before we take him down. He seems to be a nice guy but just does not know what he is getting himself into." They argued back and forth for a minute, but finally Haji Mahmood agreed to leave the room and the Guards member followed him out. I was left alone with Ibrahim. He started talking to me in a soft voice: "Do you know what happens to guys who try the so-called resistance path here? Do you really want to go through with it? I know that you are a distinguished and educated person. I normally don't do this, but I feel sorry for you, and I advise you to be reasonable and wise about this. We know everything about you and the organization. We know your status and your responsibilities in the organization, and we know who was above you and who was under you. Your whole organization is in the palm of our hand at this point. We put everyone to the test to determine who is still antirevolutionary and evil and who has had a change of heart. The only thing we really want from you is to admit to your organizational relations and to your antirevolutionary activities. We are not concerned with your ideological beliefs at all. I should not have told you all this, but I feel sorry for you. If Haj-Agha knows that I have discussed these issues with you, he is not going to like it. When he returns, if you still act like before, you will be in a great deal of trouble. Not only have we ascertained the true identity of each one of you, we even know your pseudonyms. To show you that I am not playing games, I am going to give you this last bit of information: your pseudonym in the organization is 'Babak.' I hope that you finally make the right decision."

He then left the room and I was alone again. It was as though someone had poured a bucket of ice-cold water over my head. My body temperature dropped and I started shivering. I tried to take control of my body but I could not. How did they know my pseudonym? This meant that they might have other information as well. One possibility was that they had found out my pseudonym from the documents I had hidden under the hood of my car. In that case, not only were they aware of my relations with the organization but also they were aware of all the other information in those reports. The alternative possibility was that someone was talking or even collaborating with them.

The pseudonym by itself was not a very important piece of intelligence, but it meant that I could not continue on the path of complete denial. They knew of my relationship with the organization, and probably more, and therefore I had to adjust my responses accordingly. I did not want to put myself in a position of danger over something that they already knew.

When they returned, Haji Mahmood, who sounded like he had no more patience left, started by asking angrily, "Are you ready to write and admit to your political and organizational activities?"

"I am ready to answer your questions, but admission depends on the subject."

"Why are you still not giving straight answers?"

"I am giving you straight answers, but I have to know what I am admitting to."

"Do you have organizational relations with the Fadaiyan Sixteenth of Azar group or not?"

"Yes, I am a sympathizer of that organization."

"What is the name of the person in charge of you in the organization?"

"I do not know his name."

"That is it. No more of this stupid fucking bullshit. We are going to take you down and beat the hell out of you, so you know that we mean real business here. And it is going to hurt you even more because I am going to tell you right now what the name of your contact in the organization is. I have this information because he is sitting in the next room, you stupid fuck, and he has been collaborating with us on everything since before his arrest. His name is 'Djalal'; he is one of the leaders of your organization in Tehran; your name is Babak and you certainly are not just a sympathizer. Get up, you stupid American spy. I am not going to accept any excuses from you anymore, because I think you have decided to resist and we are going to break you down."

Ibrahim intervened again and asked me if what "Haj-Agha" just revealed was incorrect. I quickly reviewed the situation. If they knew the name of Djalal and his position, and also that he was my contact in the organization, then I should not deny all this and get tortured for nothing. So, I shouted back, "I don't know his name, I only know him by his face. But if you say it is Djalal, then so be it because it doesn't make any difference to me anyway."

"So then, who were you in charge of in the organization and what were their names?"

"I was not in charge of anyone. Nobody was under me in the organization. My connection with Djalal was limited to providing financial support and receiving organizational publications."

As soon as I said this, all hell broke loose. The interrogators attacked me from all directions: punching, slapping, and kicking. They were shouting and swearing while beating and pushing me down the stairs. I tried to protect my head and to keep my balance so that I would not fall down the concrete stairs; not an easy job blindfolded. When we got to the first floor, one of them grabbed my uniform and pulled me through a door across from the stairs. He led me through a large storage room full of clothing and other junk until we got to another door. A man was sitting in a chair in the vicinity of this door. I could see only his legs. We passed him as we entered through that door. It was a small chamber. There was a torture bed with tools on one side of the room. One of my escorts pushed me down onto the side of the bed. Haji Mahmood also entered the room. The third agent was out talking to the man sitting in the chair, but I could not hear what they were saying. Then they pushed me face-down on the torture bed and strapped my wrists and ankles to both ends of the bed. Haji Mahmood started talking to Ibrahim, though his words were meant for my ears:

"This guy is a stupid one who needs to be flogged before he comes to his senses. Some are smart and start talking as soon as they get here, while others want to be lashed to prove to themselves and to others that they are resistant and combatant. But the latter are the foolish ones, not understanding that everyone eventually talks here. The judge has ordered seventy-four lashes for him for his lying. Administer it while I talk to the judge on other issues about this guy. I also need to get *kubl* number 7." He then left the room.

A *kubl* is a length of cable covered in rubber, used for flogging. Ibrahim took a *kubl* and stood at the bottom of the bed. He asked if I was ready to write and admit to my antirevolutionary activities. I did not respond. The third agent held me down at the back and shoulders. Ibrahim started by reciting verses from the Koran, and then came the flogging. The first few strikes were really painful, but I gradually adjusted to the pain. Once in a while the pair would stop to talk to me to see if I was ready to write and sign. I basically ignored them at this point. The way it was going, I thought, I could handle it for a long while. After he finished the seventy-four lashes, Ibrahim started talking to me.

"You stupid fool, I have told you once and I have told you a thousand times, we have all the information we need about all of you. We have arrested all your leaders and every one of them is collaborating with us, as you will see in the process. Why are you putting yourself in harm's way for no reason? Isn't your pseudonym Babak? Isn't Djalal your contact person in the organization? Didn't the executive committee of your organization in Tehran have three members with the pseudonyms of Djalal, 'Samad,' and 'Hossein'? And finally, were you or were you not in charge of a few people, including one with the pseudonym of 'Mamad'? Is this not enough to bring you to your senses?"

The revealed intelligence hit me much worse than the lashes of the *kubl*. How could they know all this? Was someone really collaborating? Why was Ibrahim telling me all this? I was very confused and disoriented. I was being overwhelmed with the extent of the intelligence they were throwing at me, which was rather unconventional. Organizational training had not prepared us to deal with a situation where we might be confronted with vast amounts of information revealed by the interrogators. It was creating serious problems for me. It was clear that they had information about our organizational structure from the top, and they also had intelligence about our pseudonyms. What I was not sure about was whether they had really arrested anyone else besides Abdi, whom I had seen in Ward 1, although the interrogators were probably not aware of my knowledge of his arrest. I had to resist my interrogators until I could somehow figure out the extent of the arrests. I was hoping that with the rate of their disclosure of information, I would soon find out who else had been arrested.

Therefore, I declared that I had already admitted to my involvement with the organization but that I knew nothing about the other names mentioned.

Haji Mahmood entered the room and asked Ibrahim whether he had administered the seventy-four lashes and whether I had come to my senses. He responded that I had not and that I was still being stubborn and resisting. Haji Mahmood shouted at me angrily, "You think that was the real *kubl* strike? We were just giving you a chance to save yourself. I am going to treat you to the real thing now. I have gotten a verdict from the judge for three hundred counts with *kubl* number 7 for you, for lying, concealing information, and resisting facts." Then he turned to his assistants. "Come on, open him up and drag this American counterrevolutionary out of here. We need to level with him once and for all."

"What do you want from me?" I cried out. "I already admitted to my relations with the organization. What else do you want?"

They were paying no attention to me at this point. Haji Mahmood was still shouting:

"Come on, you American fool. I am going to show you why you should not have chosen the resistance path, as I had advised you. Djalal is talking, telling us everything, cooperating with us, and so is Samad. But you want to play games with us! You think we need your information? We know everything. We are trying to help you skip the pain and suffering. But no, you have to prove your bravery and resistance. Come on, let's go."

He led the way out of that room, and the others followed, dragging me along, because at this point I was barefoot and my feet were swollen and in pain. We passed the man still sitting in his chair outside the room; we passed through the large storage room; and we went through the hallway and the triangular yard. We then entered the small *zir-e hasht* where the entrance to Ward 1 was located. We didn't go to the ward, however; we passed through another door. As soon as I stepped into that next room, I sensed the real danger. The other torture room had been only a preview. This medium-sized, darkly lit room, its walls covered with a strange material, was the main torture chamber. There was a torture bed and there were chains, hooks, metal brushes, and a variety of *kubl* and clubs. The air smelled of sweat and blood.

My heart started pounding crazily. I tried to control my fear and anxiety, but there was no way I could calm myself down or concentrate. They sat me on the side of the bed. All three were in the room, and they closed the door tight. It was probably after midnight now. I think they interrogated and tortured at night on purpose. Night exerts extra pressure and fear on the victims. After they sat me on the edge of the bed, Haji Mahmood said, "For the last time, are you ready to admit to everything?" I intended to bargain with him, but nothing came out of my mouth. Suddenly they pushed me face-down and tied my ankles and wrists to the bed. I still tried to say something, to stall them somehow, but either I had no voice or they were not listening anymore. They put pillows and blankets on my back, neck, and head. One of them sat on my back, and the other held down my arms, shoulders, and head. Ibrahim started talking to me, but I could barely hear him because of the pillows over my face and head and because of the loud, rhythmic religious song that started blasting in the room. I felt like I was going to suffocate before any serious beating had even started.

I could barely hear Haji Mahmood reciting some religious verses, and then came the first strike with the so-called *kubl* number 7 on the soles of my feet. It would be difficult to describe what really happens with such a strike. Besides the excruciating physical pain, it was like a high-voltage current passing through my whole body. Some torture victims have described it as feeling like two tiny birds entering your body from the feet, flying through your body, and pushing themselves out of your ears, all in a matter of seconds. I imagined I had jumped so high as a result of the first blow that I had broken the straps that held me to the bed. The pain was unbearable. My brain was still reeling from the first blow when a second strike, harder than the first one, hit under my feet. It was so hard that I thought the bones in my feet had shattered. I was suffocating and screaming, and the strikes kept coming.

After about thirty counts, I felt nothing anymore. Whoever was wielding the *kubl* had stopped so that Ibrahim would talk to me. I barely understood him because of the religious song they had on at what seemed like full blast (apparently they played these songs both to provide themselves with moral support and to increase pressure on the prisoner). I understood him saying that if and when I was ready to write and sign, then I should open and close my fists to indicate that I had had enough. They put the pillows back on my face and head and held me down again. I attempted to stop them to buy myself some time but they did not give me a chance, on purpose, because they knew I was still resisting and also that my feet could still take some more strikes. They wanted to make sure that I would request a pause *during* the striking.

Strikes continued. I resisted until I could not take it anymore. I opened and closed my fists. I had no sense of my feet being attached to my body. When my torturers raised me to sit I noticed my feet for the first time. Each one had turned into a small, round pillow. Another few blows would probably have torn and ruptured both feet, which seemed to be something these men did not want to happen yet. They made me stand up and forced me to walk and even jump on my swollen, tortured feet. They reasoned that if I did not walk on them right then and there, it could create serious medical and health problems. Ibrahim kept talking to me.

"Why do you like to do this to yourself? Why don't you listen to my hints and advice? Were you not in charge of three people in your cell? Was your pseudonym not Babak? Was your contact in the organization not Djalal? Did you or did you not give this written report to him a while back?" He then started reading from the report, which was about a member of the organization named "Ehssan." We had received it from Ehssan's sister through a channel in our branch of the organization. I had made a note on it and had given it to Djalal about three weeks ago.

Ibrahim continued, "Were you in charge of Mamad, 'Asghar,' and 'Nader,' or not? You see that we have everything we need, as we told you before, but in return your behavior has been nothing short of stupid and stubborn. Now, do you want me to bring in Djalal to face you, so you know that he is really cooperating with us?"

At this point, as a result of the overwhelming information they had disclosed and the possibility of one or more people talking or maybe even collaborating, I thought it was useless for me to continue getting tortured. But I did not want to see Djalal, fearing that it might weaken my morale and resistance to see that he was truly cooperating with them. I needed to buy some time. Therefore, I said, "I do not want to see Djalal or anyone else. Yes, I was involved with the organization, and I am ready to admit to that."

They sat me on the side of the bed. Haji Mahmood, who had stepped out of the room, returned with some official interrogation forms. He said that he was going to write questions and I should answer them honestly, then he threatened that for every lie there was going to be another seventy-four strikes like what I had just been served. Then he wrote a question and put the form on my lap. I read it from under my blindfold:

When, where, and why were you arrested?

I wrote: "I was arrested on Wednesday around 2:30 PM in Nezam-Abad Avenue while executing an organizational meeting."

Write down your organizational position, your responsibility, and the names of people you were in charge of.

"I was in a committee with three other members, named Mamad, Asghar, and Nader, and I was the contact person of our committee with the organization."

Up to this point I had only repeated information already revealed by them. I was expecting the big question to come next. We had been trained in the organization that the main goal of an interrogation was to discover the particulars of upcoming organizational meetings and therefore that we should resist as much as we could and then provide the interrogators with false information about those meetings to delay the process and to mislead them. I had been thinking about how to respond to this particular question since I was arrested, and now it was time to see if I could stick to the plan as I had played it in my mind.

Write down all of your meeting appointments, including times, locations, signs, and directions.

Without any hesitation, I started writing a false time and location for my appointment with Mamad. As soon as he saw what I was writing, Haji Mahmood shouted, "Strap this traitor American spy to the bed! He needs to be taught more lessons in this business!"

I shouted back, "What do you want from me? Why do you enjoy torturing me?"

"We do not torture here," he declared. "It is prohibited in our faith. You receive punishment decreed by *hakem-e shar'* (an Islamic judge) for your lies and for concealing important information from us. Do you take me for a fool? You met with Mamad regularly in the Amir-abad area, did you not? Are you trying to write a false appointment?"

This piece of information revealed by him, because of my attempt to write a false appointment, told me clearly that extensive surveillance had been carried out on us in the past months. Fortunately, in my last meeting with Mamad, because of the recent security issues we agreed to change our meeting location in the city. Unfortunately, I had written the new meeting information on a package that Mamad had given me, which I had placed in the secret compartment under the hood of my car. I did not know whether they had already discovered that package or not. In any case, keeping in mind what he had just revealed and hoping that they had not yet found the evidence from under the hood of my car, I admitted that I was confused. Then I wrote down false information for my meeting with Mamad in the Amir-abad area. The interrogator apparently was satisfied, because he did not object to it. I was not sure whether he was playing games with me or he really did not know about what was under the hood of the car. Then, I wrote false information for my meetings with Asghar and Nader as well. I tried to write them all in such a way that I could reproduce them exactly when asked, which I was pretty sure Haji Mahmood was going to demand soon. I wrote the meetings for the following Saturday for Mamad and Monday for Asghar and Nader.

Haji Mahmood had me sign the forms, then took them and left the room. The assistant in the Guards uniform followed him out. Only Ibrahim stayed. He forced me to walk around some more and even jump up and down, which was very painful. Haji Mahmood returned after about half an hour. It must have been around four in the morning. He put a new interrogation form in front of me.

Write down all of your organizational appointments, with all details.

I wrote them down just as I had done the first time. He took the paper and checked to make sure they matched the first set, and then he wrote another question.

Write down your organizational position, rank, and all your responsibilities.

I wrote: "I was a member of the organization, had been assigned to the youth section leadership committee in Tehran, and was the contact person from our section to the highest leadership committee in Tehran."

He did not like my answer and started shouting again. "Strap him to the bed! He doesn't seem to be the kind of person who knows his limits."

My screams for time-out did not get any response. They tried to tie me up and I resisted it this time, now that I had tasted the real *kubl* beatings, but the three of them overpowered me, forced me down, and tied me up again. Before the beatings started anew, Haji Mahmood said, "We know you are either a full or a consulting member of the leadership committee of your organization inside the country. Therefore, when you are ready to admit, open and close your fists."

I was in a very tough situation on this one, because I could not give them false information to escape torture. I was not a member of the leadership committee inside Iran, but the only way to end the torture was either for me to confess to being part of the committee or for Djalal or someone else in the leadership to corroborate my claim that I was not. But I could not confess, because that would have put me in a very vulnerable and dangerous position as far as the continuing interrogations were concerned, and it would have made the case against me weightier. Such cadres had more responsibility in the organization, were naturally under extraordinary pressure during the interrogations, and would eventually pay a higher price for their positions and responsibilities. I did not know what Djalal might have already revealed regarding this particular issue. I wondered if he could even corroborate my story, one way or the other, given that we had not known each other very long.

They again put the pillows on my back and head, and they held me down. The torturer started the *kubl* strikes again, which, given the condition of my swollen and bruised feet, were more painful than before. He was hitting very hard, though with longer intervals between consecutive blows. It seemed they wanted me to feel the pain to the fullest possible extent but were worried about the condition of my feet as well. If my soles cracked and burst open, they would have probably had to stop, and they didn't want that to happen at this particular juncture. They were hoping that I would confess soon. Meanwhile, I was thinking that I had to stop this from continuing or else I would be dead or crippled soon. Strikes kept coming until I felt nothing; I had passed out. They brought me back by pouring some water on my face. They untied me and forced me to stand up, but I could not put my feet on the ground anymore because of the pain and shock. Ibrahim and the man in the Guards uniform wedged themselves under my arms to support me and forced me to walk. The air was so stuffy and thick with the smell of sweat and blood I felt like I was about to suffocate. Also, it felt like my face was contorted as though I had had a stroke—like my lips and cheeks were deformed.

"So, Mr. Yaghoobi, are you finally ready to admit, or do you want us to continue? There is a definite end to this as far as we are concerned. We will continue until either you confess or you die. So think about yourself and your family."

"I have never been a full or a consulting member of the leadership committee. If you enjoy torturing and killing me for no reason, then go ahead, but you should know that you are wasting your time and my life."

"We are not fools, and we do not punish you for pleasure. We have succeeded in breaking up most of the opposition organizations and have arrested their leaders and members, as you know very well. We have their organizational charts posted on the walls of our intelligence room. In all of these cases—every one of them—a person with your organizational position and responsibility is either a full or a consulting member of the central or leadership committee. How then can we accept that your case is the only exception to this rule?"

I saw the predicament I was in and felt completely helpless. Our central and executive committee leadership members had left the country for security reasons. Of the three members of the leadership executive committee in Tehran, I had never met two of them, and the third, Djalal, who was my contact, had known me only the last six months. Therefore, even Djalal probably did not know everything about my status and situation. I was stuck in a tough position. I needed to buy some time to see how I could get out of this predicament. Therefore, I said, "Before you torture me more, and for no reason, why don't you go and discuss this issue with the three leaders that you say are in your custody and you claim are all cooperating with you? They will tell you that I have never been a member of the organizational leadership committee in any capacity."

"I don't need to do that right now. Write down what you claim you were in the organization, and I will figure it out one way or another."

"I was a member of the leadership committee of the youth branch of the organization in Tehran, and recently I had become the contact person of our committee with the organizational leadership executive committee in Tehran."

"You are lying again. I know for a fact that you were one of the active cadres of this organization, and at the very least you were a member of the newly formed leadership committee inside the country and in charge of the youth branch of the organization nationwide, and not in Tehran alone, as you claim."

"Believe me, that was not the case. Whoever told you this was lying."

"Write down what you were."

I began to write: "I was a member of the organization." He hit me on the head with the *kubl* and told me to open parentheses to put "organizational cadre" after the word "member." I did, then continued. When I had completed, the statement read "I was a member (organizational cadre) of the organization. My position was in the youth branch leadership committee in Tehran, and I was the contact person of this branch with the leaders of the organization in Tehran." He had me sign every page of the interrogation forms. Then, with disgust in his tone, he said, "You stupid fool. We have all of the information about your old organizational structure, and we have the new reorganization chart as well. We knew you guys were transforming the organization and preparing to resort to armed activities. You thought we would let you recruit our youth in your treacherous and subversive ways to put their lives and our lives in harm's way. You were in the process of forming independent base-units and committees. You had formed a secret special unit and were in the process of going completely underground. But we were always one or two steps ahead of all of you. We had all of you under surveillance, and when the right moment came, we swept all of you from top to bottom."

Some of his points were news to me, especially the "secret special unit." I had no idea what he was talking about. At this point, it seemed highly probable that our organization inside the country either had been completely destroyed or had at least taken serious blows.

He continued, "Now we come to the main issue. We have established that you were in charge of the youth branch of the organization. I have in my possession the chart of your branch, in your own handwriting with your pseudonym Babak signed under it, which you provided to Djalal a few weeks earlier. I am going to show it to you later on, so you know that we really have it. But before I do that, I want to know if you have changed at all through this whole process or if you still are an antirevolutionary, evil-hearted *kafar* (nonbeliever). Put down your branch's chart with all of the subcommittees and the names."

"As I said before, it was only me and three others. And you have all of the names. There was no one else."

He ordered his assistants to strap me to the bed again for more flogging. They forced me onto the bed and tied me up again. He threatened but did not strike immediately, probably due to the fact that there was not much room left on my soles for more beatings. Ibrahim intervened, seeming sympathetic, and asked Haji Mahmood to give me a few minutes to think it over. He accepted and left the room. Ibrahim unbound my hands and feet and talked to me.

"We know everything about your organization. You are putting yourself under unnecessary pressure and in danger of serious harm. Part of the information we have revealed to you tonight comes from your own reports in your own handwriting that you had given to the organization and that we have in our possession, and part of it comes directly from Djalal and others who are in our custody and are cooperating. If I were you, I would start being honest and smart, because we are entering the judgment phase and this will determine your fate."

The information they had on us clearly indicated that we had been under surveillance for a long time, and maybe that they had even infiltrated our organization, or at least had had some people collaborating with them before we got arrested. There was also the possibility that one or all of the three leaders were cooperating. I was under a great deal of pressure physically, mentally, and politically. Haji Mahmood returned and asked, "Are you ready to write what I asked you?"

"I only remember a few pseudonyms that would have no value for you."

"OK—we will help you to remember them all."

He ordered his assistants to pull me up. Within a few minutes my hands were tied behind me. Then, suddenly, I was yanked up at the wrists by a chain. The pain of my arms being wrenched backward was unbearable. Soon I was completely suspended in that way, and I imagined feeling my arms breaking off of my shoulders. I do not remember what happened next, because I passed out. I do not know how long I was suspended. When they brought me back to consciousness by spraying water on my face, I was lying down on the torture bed. I was actually feeling not much pain. I could not concentrate or focus on anything. I had lost my analytical and tactical ability. They sat me up on the edge of the bed, and Haji Mahmood put the paper and pen on my lap.

"Write down the chart of your branch."

My hands were shaking so badly that I could not write for several minutes. Then I wrote my pseudonym and those of the other three members of the committee and put a couple of pseudonyms under each of them.

"Is that it? Come on, finish it up."

"This is all I can remember."

"OK. I will read to you from your own report and you fill in."

From a page that he was holding, he read some names and asked me to add them to the chart. He then continued, "Now you see that we had it all and we really just wanted to test you." Then in a tone of disgust and sarcasm, he said he did not even need me to write anymore.

What he held was indeed the original chart and all of the information in my own handwriting. I had provided the final version of our reorganization chart to Djalal a few weeks prior to the arrests, and now it was in the hands of the interrogators. I was not sure at that moment what was worse: to be beaten and tortured physically and psychologically, or to be hit repeatedly with our own supposedly secret intelligence, which was sacred to us in the organization but was now in the possession of the police. It seemed they truly had the upper hand.

It was almost morning when they finally stopped interrogating me. The two assistants lifted me up, carrying me under my arms, and walked me back to the ward where they delivered me to the ward guard, who put me on my blanket in the corridor.

3

In our organization we had never imagined facing this particular scenario. We had prepared and trained for other types of circumstances and threats to our security, but we had never seriously considered the possibility that we might be arrested collectively, facing an overwhelming amount of intelligence, which would make resisting very difficult. You always assumed that you would be arrested individually, or with another comrade during a meeting, or, at the most, with a few others in a meeting. But when the form and nature of the struggle for freedom and democracy changed after the revolution, and previously small underground groups became massive political parties, the new regime could not limit itself to arresting opposition activists one at a time. The security forces were forced to centralize, change, and adapt to the new situation to make their intelligence work more efficient. In contrast, the opposition lacked resources and creativity in countering the militia and intelligence services of the regime. We did not prepare ourselves for a situation of massive organizational arrests, even after a few other opposition groups were destroyed with sweeping raids and strikes by the government security forces. Besides our ignorance and poverty of vision, I should add that many of the small organizations within the fractured opposition were no match for the government security and intelligence apparatus with regard to manpower, technology, finances, and other resources.

My body was in pain, and my mind was under tremendous pressure. I was angry, frustrated, and horrified. I examined my feet closely for the first time and found them to be in pretty bad shape. Each one was the size of a small pillow, with blisters as well as bleeding bruises and cracks all over it. I raised my hand to get the guard's attention. He finally approached and said that the medical aide would do his round in two hours and could check them out for me then. I tried to rest a little, but my mind was going crazy. I thought I would check to see if Abdi was still there. But I could not locate him in the corridor anymore.

Then I heard a very strange rustling noise. The noise came closer. Soon, I saw it was made by a prisoner walking to the bathroom. His tortured feet had been bandaged and then put in plastic bags to prevent infection and to protect the ward floor. Some tortured prisoners pulled themselves on the floor, dragging their feet in plastic bags behind them. There were two bathrooms at the end of the ward, one on each side. When I carefully checked from under the blindfold, I saw no cell doors in the corridor but only a few openings in the walls on both sides. I figured out that cells must be located in the small hallways through those openings. Then I heard a new footstep approaching. When you are blindfolded, your hearing quickly dominates the other senses. You keep track of every voice, noise, and sound. A coughing stranger approached and sat in front of me. He put his box of medical aids on my blanket and started treating and wrapping my feet. He gave me two plastic bags and said that I should use them whenever I went to the restroom. Soon it was my bathroom turn. Moving was very painful, but I knew I had to use the bathroom to wash my dishes and to clean up. I wrapped the plastic bags around my feet, took my items, and dragged my tortured body to the bathroom. The guard followed and watched me go in and then he closed the door. It was a pretty large room, with three toilet stalls and two sinks. After a while the guard opened the door and led me to my blanket. I tried to rest and calm myself down, knowing that they would soon come for me again.

A couple of hours later I heard the same footsteps that had taken me to interrogation the first time. As soon as I heard them, my heart rate went up high and I started to shiver. I could not control my fear and anxiety. The agent approached and asked my identity in the usual way. He ordered me to follow him. I managed to get to my feet with difficulty. I slowly and painfully followed him on my bandaged feet. I was guided to the interrogation building again. The agent took me upstairs and put me in a corner in the hallway. It was so quiet in there that I could hear my own heartbeat. I started shivering again. To overcome this feeling, I started talking to and arguing with myself. After I calmed down a bit, I tried to focus on the issues at hand. Someone grabbed my sleeve and guided me into the interrogation room. He put me in the chair and started talking to me. It was Ibrahim, who was wearing pants, shoes, and an overcoat now. He shouted that if I thought it was over, I was dead wrong. He said that it would never be over as long as I was alive in prison. He put an interrogation form and a pen on the arm of my chair and asked me to write down again, in detail, all my appointments. I protested that I had already written them twice before. He insisted that I write them once more. I put down what I had written before. He looked at the form and gave me a new order: "Write down all your political activities from the beginning till now." Then he left. He did not return for more than an hour.

I had doubts about where and when I should start in my description so that I would not create problems for myself either way. I debated for a while and decided to be a bit cautious. I wrote a paragraph indicating that while studying abroad I had taken part in the student movement against the Iranian monarchy. About my activities after the revolution, I wrote that I started to sympathize with the Fadaiyan Majority organization in early 1981 and then sided with the Fadaiyan Sixteenth of Azar group in the fall of that year.

Then the three interrogators all came into the room. Haji Mahmood took the page, looked at it, and asked, "Did you have any secret hiding place for your stuff in your home?"

"No, I had nothing to hide. I only had books, newspapers—"

"We have already gone to your home and have brought back everything we could find. For every lie, you are going to get seventy-four lashes. Remember that when you answer."

I had some items in a few hiding places in our home. My wife was aware of them. I was hoping that when I did not come home last night, she had taken care of them according to our mutual plan. But then, I could not be sure that she had had the chance. There was a possibility that they had detained her in the house at the same time they arrested me in the street, and therefore they might have already brought everything as they claimed. I had to take a cautious route so that I would not be tortured more.

"As I said, I only had some unimportant items there."

"So, where did you hide these unimportant things?"

"They were in my work desk."

"Did you have any cyanide capsules, guns, copy machines, printers, typewriters, and things like these?"

"No."

"What have you done for the organization in your workplace?"

"I have done nothing. Nobody in the organization even knew where I worked."

"Come on! You take us for fools? A member of the organization with your status, who does not try to infiltrate, spy, or help his organization? That is just bullshit. We know everything, and you better think seriously before you answer."

"My profession had nothing to do with the organization. I did not try to infiltrate or spy."

"OK. If you were not trying to infiltrate or spy, then what were you doing in the Majles (Parliament), and why and how were you involved with the elected representatives?"

This last point shocked me speechless. Nobody arrested with us could have known about the contact I had had with a representative in the Majles; only my then organizational contact person, who was now abroad, had known about this connection. This certainly proved to me that they must have been following me before my arrest. I had to give a convincing reply or expect the worst. I said, "I have a childhood friend who now represents our hometown, Tabriz, in the Majles. He tracked me down through family and friends, and I met him in his home in Tehran. He insisted that I help him in the agricultural committee of the Majles, which he led. I did take part in one committee meeting as his guest, but afterward I did not accept any role in the committee. You can go and ask him if you wish."

"OK. We will do that, and we will find out soon. And you'd better be right, or else you are going to be in a big load of shit on this one. I am sure you know what we do with the infiltrators."

He then went on to give me a lecture: "In essence, your organization aimed to overthrow the Islamic regime. You had hidden weapon caches and other necessary resources and tools to use against the regime. You had infiltrators in the revolutionary institutions and governmental offices. You had formed a secret terror and confiscation unit, which planned and carried out some operations. We have arrested all of you including the top three leaders and all layers of organizational cadres and active members. We have everyone in custody, and most of the key figures are collaborating with us; not just because they are afraid they are going to be hanged but mainly because we, the dedicated soldiers of Imam Khomeini, spent days and nights planning and collecting intelligence on all of you so that when the arrests were made, none of you would have a way to escape the crushing facts."

The lecture lasted a whole hour. He then emphasized that they had a very heavy case against me and that if I chose to cooperate with them, they would put in a good word with the judge on my behalf so that I would get a lighter sentence. Otherwise, he said, only God could save me. They then left me alone there for a while. I was exhausted and confused. It was almost afternoon when a guard took me back to the ward. I lay down on the blanket and felt depressed and sad. I had not slept and had had almost nothing to eat or drink since my arrest. My body and mind were aching. It was after the lunch hour, but some rice was on my plate and a cup of cold tea had been left for me. I forced myself to eat and drink, but nothing went down easily; it felt like something was blocking my throat. I felt sick.

4

I had apparently dozed off, because the noise of dragging feet wrapped in plastic bags startled me. I sat up and leaned back against the wall. It was late afternoon, and prisoners were once again hauling their own tortured bodies along the corridor. Until evening not much happened in the corridor. This period of quiet gave me a chance to figure out more about the ward. There were three openings in the left-side wall and then a door at the end opened directly into the corridor. Then came one of the bathrooms. There was a kerosene-burning stove at the end of the hall; it was the only source of heat for the whole ward. The right side mirrored the left side. Each opening led to multiple cells. Overall, there were twenty-two cells and two bathrooms in the ward. Later, I figured out that some cells held one prisoner and others two. There were always some prisoners kept in the corridor. I also later learned that Wards 1 and 2 served as processing units for mass arrests. Afterward, prisoners were gradually transferred to other floors to clear space for the next mass arrest. Organizationally related prisoners were kept in different wards or at least were positioned in the ward in a way that limited contact and exchange of information among them. Usually, prisoners with higher organizational rankings, who had more responsibilities and therefore more intelligence, were either not kept in the corridor at all or were kept there for just a very short time.

From late that night until the next morning, blindfolded in the corridor, I drifted back and forth between sleep, dreaming, and being awake. Around nine o'clock Friday morning, the guards came for me again. We went through the same routine and I ended up in the same interrogation room, waiting. Haji Mahmood walked in and followed up on his talk from the previous day. He emphasized again the dangers I was facing. He then asked if I was willing to cooperate to save my family and myself. I had prepared the previous night how to respond to this question. I had made my peace with myself that whatever the consequences, there was a red line that I would not cross. I had decided that under no circumstances would I agree to become a traitor, a spy, or a snitch for them. So I said I did not understand how I could help.

He said, "We are trying to save the young people whom you and your leaders have exploited and corrupted. We are trying to bring them back to the ranks of the Islamic Revolution. We need help to be able to achieve this goal."

I replied firmly that I could not and would not help them with that. I said it was against my character, beliefs, and principles.

"Get lost. You think I really need your help? I was just testing you. Djalal and Samad are already doing it, and others are standing in line. You want to become a martyr and a hero, go ahead and be my guest!" he shouted angrily and left the room. The assistant put an interrogation form and a pen on the arm of the chair. This one read, *Write down all you know about the activities of your wife and her position in the organization.*

About forty-eight hours had passed since my arrest. They had not asked a single question about my wife until now. I was not sure about her fate, whether she had already been arrested or not. Maybe she was in the next room or in one of the cells. This was the toughest point in the interrogation for me, emotionally and psychologically. My answer could put Ketty in danger of arrest if she had not already been taken. And if she had been arrested, then she could face more pressure and torture. Somehow, I thought, I had to divert the responsibility to myself. Even if she had been arrested and had admitted to some activity with the organization, at the worst they would torture me some more for concealing information or lying. I was fine with that as long as I could protect her. I put down a single sentence declaring that my wife had never had any connection with or undertaken any actions for the organization.

The interrogator returned, looked at my answer, and said only, "We will find out soon if you are right. Get lost—go to your ward." To me this indicated that either Ketty had not been arrested yet or she had been arrested and had said the same thing as I had. This gave me a jolt of relative relief.

It was midafternoon when they returned me to the ward. I rested a bit, hoping that for the rest of that day they would leave me alone. I fell asleep but soon awoke to the sound of dragging plastic bags. That night, I had some quiet time to ponder the interrogation. There was the issue of the false appointments I had written for Saturday—tomorrow—and Monday. Another issue that seriously haunted me was about my wife and daughter and their fates. Lying down on my blanket in the absolute silence of the ward, I was wondering where they were. Suddenly the screams and cries of a woman broke the silence. I jumped up and sat on my blanket. I saw from under my blindfold that other prisoners in the corridor had done the same. The screaming continued for a while; it sounded like she was being tortured. I could not think or concentrate anymore. My head hidden between my arms and knees, I was tortured along with the woman prisoner. Was she my wife? I pulled the blanket over my head. Powerless to do anything about it, I quietly cried. It was always harder to witness the torture of others. Her torture finished after about an hour, but I was so shaken by the incident that I could not sleep that night either. My mind was out of control and I was cramped with worry.

The guards always started the morning bathroom round long before sunrise. They wanted to encourage morning prayers and to give a chance to anyone interested in them to be able to prepare. Also, it took about two hours in every round to send everyone in the ward to the bathroom, and they wanted to have everyone ready before the morning office hours. This morning, the shift guards started sending the corridor prisoners first to the bathroom. Because I had not slept at all and my mind was still going crazy, this was a welcome change for me. A few minutes without the blindfold in the bathroom were a big relief. I returned to the blanket somewhat refreshed. I had to prepare myself mentally for a difficult day ahead. For breakfast we each got a piece of *lavash* bread, some feta cheese, and a cup of tea with a few sugar cubes. For the first time since my arrest I ate and drank it all.

Before two o'clock an agent came to fetch me. He wore a nice suit, and his shoes made a distinct noise when he walked. He asked my name and my father's name and then ordered me to pick up all my things and to follow him. I painfully followed him, pulling my sleeping gear behind me. Later, I learned this man was called "Jalali" and apparently was in charge of moving prisoners within and between wards. Of course, the final decision on the matter was with the lead interrogator; Jalali merely executed those decisions. The majority of the names used by the guards and authorities in the prison system were aliases; I assume this was the case with Jalali. He took me through the first opening on the left side of the corridor into a small, narrow hallway, where he opened the door of a cell at the end and told me to enter. He then closed the door and left.

The cell was about seven by five feet. It had a metal door with a small, round peephole covered from the outside. Knocking on the door was prohibited and punishable by flogging. There was a piece of long, narrow cardboard that you had to insert in the peephole if you needed help. A small window, about one square foot in size, was located at the top of the wall opposite the door. From the cell I could hear the yard noise but could not see much except the legs of people walking there, which meant that the ward floor was below the yard level. The tiny window was protected with a metal mesh and a clear plastic cover on the inside, and with metal bars on the outside. A weak, yellowish light bulb in a metal mesh enclosure hung from the tall ceiling; it was controlled from the outside but was kept on day and night. The cell was dirty, damp, and dark. Worn-out, dirty carpeting covered the floor, but the cell was otherwise empty. I put my blankets down and examined the thick walls, which were full of carvings, writings, and drawings. It looked like guards had made a halfhearted attempt to clean up parts of it but had given up.

I was absorbed in examining the walls when the cell door opened. The guard warned me that any time the door opened I must put on my blindfold and face the opposite direction. He then ordered me to follow him out and delivered me to a group of agents in the *zir-e hasht*. I realized then that they were going to take me out to the meeting with Mamad, which I had written for that afternoon. Blindfolded and handcuffed, I was seated in the back of a car between two agents; they pushed my head down on my lap. A few minutes later, after we were out of the area, they took my blindfold off and told me to sit up straight.

After three days of torturous ordeal, I was outside again where people went about their normal lives and the traffic seemed as heavy as it always was in Tehran. I tried to watch, hear, and absorb as much as I could. I also saw the faces of these agents for the first time. They were all young and in civilian clothing. The one sitting in the front passenger seat, who apparently was their leader, pulled out his handgun and pointed it at my forehead, saying that if I tried anything brave, he would shoot me on the spot.

They drove toward the Amir-abad district, to the area that I had indicated as my meeting place with Mamad for 4:00 and 4:30 PM. The leader of the group revealed that they already knew Mamad from the surveillance work and that they even had taken photos of us in our previous meetings. They all got out and took positions, except their leader. The first half hour passed and of course there was no sign of Mamad. We stayed there until a few minutes to five, when they all returned to the car and we headed back to the detention center. On the return journey, I focused on the directions to figure out where the detention center was located. After a few minutes, they put my blindfold back on and pushed my head down on my lap, but I had already realized we were going to the infamous Komiteh detention center.[5]

I prepared myself for more torture after they had failed to arrest Mamad due to my false meeting information. But instead they took me straight to my cell. After a few minutes the guard came back for me. I thought he was going to take me for interrogation, but instead he sent me to the bathroom. When I returned to the cell, he was distributing the dinner ration, which was a bowl of chili and some bread. It was about seven or eight o'clock, and they had not come for me yet.

Generally speaking, as a prisoner, you do not want to be taken for interrogation. But at times like this, you want to know what they are going to do to you so that it will be over and done with. I started pacing back and forth, though my feet were still in excruciating pain. In that small cell I could take only four steps in one direction, then turn. I kept pacing until I was not conscious of the place or the time. It was like I had been chanting or whirling like a dervish for a long while.

When I came back to myself, I noticed that the prison sound system had ended its radio broadcast, meaning that it was after 9:00 PM.

Exhausted from pacing for almost an hour and a half, I sat down to calm myself and tried to prepare for a possible late-night interrogation session. I was so worried and anxious that I could not sleep, so I started pacing again. It must have been another couple of hours before I came to my senses. I had to try to get some rest. I spread my blankets and arranged for my head to be near the door so that I could hear the footsteps better. I dozed off, but I would jump up every time I heard any noise. I do not know how much time passed before I fell asleep.

Sunday went by and nothing happened. That night I had a hard time falling asleep again, but I finally did after exhausting myself with pacing. I thought I was hearing the footsteps of the interrogator in my dream, but I awoke to the realization that he was walking in the ward corridor in the eerie silence after midnight. I was startled and sat straight up. The footsteps got closer and closer. He turned into the little hallway and got closer to my cell. The guard opened the door lock. I turned my back and put my blindfold on. The cell door opened. My heart was beating out of my chest. The guard told me to keep my head down. Then he stepped back and the interrogator entered the cell and stayed behind me.

"So, Mr. Yaghoobi, you gave us a false appointment, did you not?"

"I did not give you a false appointment. I always had meetings with Mamad in that area, as you know."

"That is correct. But you forgot to mention the fact that in the last meeting with him you had decided to change it to a new location."

"I do not remember doing that."

"We will help you remember it, because we have in our possession this change of meeting location in your own handwriting, but, more importantly, we were able to find Mamad today on our own. We are going to deal with your lies separately at another time. If you think you can protect your fellows, you are mistaken. As I told you before, we have all the information we need to arrest anyone we wish."

They had arrested Mamad and had been busy torturing him, and that was the reason they had not come for me earlier. Either they had located my documents hidden in the secret compartment under the hood of my car, or they had found Mamad on their own as the interrogator claimed. With Mamad arrested, many more issues occupied my mind. I could not get any more rest that night. Instead, I paced like a caged tiger.

The interrogation resumed in the morning by Haji Mahmood and one of his assistants. First they asked me questions about Mamad, then they turned to the issue of the false meeting information. I had prepared myself to stick to the two remaining false appointments I had given them, even if they beat me up some more. Instead, Haji Mahmood declared again that they had enough intelligence to arrest anyone they wished, even if my meeting information was false. But he added that if it were false, it would cost me heavily in the sentencing stage. I insisted that the information was what I truly remembered. After some threats, they both left the room.

Someone new entered the room, brought a chair, and sat behind me. I could not see him at all. He started turning pages of a file, read from a report, and asked me for some clarifications and details. I soon figured out he was reading from the surveillance reports that they had done on me. It was clear that at least from a month and a half before the arrests they had detailed reports of all my movements and meetings. They knew the location at which Djalal and I had regularly met until three weeks prior to the arrests. They had found my sister's home and the home of my friend who was a representative in the Majles. From this interrogation and the ones to come over the next couple of days, I realized an important shortcoming of the surveillance reports: they contained basically no information about any nighttime happenings. This agreed with the reality of my movements and activities, which was always during the day except for a few rare cases, when, because I was very busy, I arranged some important one-on-one meetings with members in their homes at night, where I would stay until early morning. There was no mention of these cases in the surveillance reports. This was encouraging, because I could keep those people out of harm's way. No one but me had that information.

As today was Monday, they took me out again for the appointments I had written for this day. First we went to the location I had written for the meeting with Asghar. Of course he did not show up. The lead agent, "Khossravi," was very upset and threatened that I would really be in big trouble if we returned empty-handed. Then we went to the other meeting location, for Nader, which was in another part of the city. It took us about an hour in afternoon traffic to get to the location, and I enjoyed every minute of watching the city and the people. The agents, however, were very edgy and angry. We waited until 5:45 and then they decided that it was all nonsense and took me back to the detention center.

This time, I expected a harsh reaction from the interrogators, and they came for me that night. They beat me up as much as I could take, but I still insisted that those were the real appointments and that I had no other way of reaching those two people. They said that *they* had other means of reaching them, and Haji Mahmood promised that they would have both of them in custody soon. He emphasized again that this was going to cost me dearly. After a couple of hours, they sent me back to my cell.

5

Interrogations on different aspects of our organization continued for the next couple of days. Thursday was a relatively quiet day in the ward, and one week after my arrest I finally found some quiet time to focus more on my family. Were my wife and daughter in this prison? What was going to happen to them? What would I do if I faced a situation where they were being held as hostages? Thoughts of this nature took me on a depressing ride that day. I ended up pacing in my cell maybe ten hours that day. I was so exhausted after dinner that during the broadcast of the eight o'clock radio program I collapsed and was motionless for a while.

Around 9:00 PM, it was announced through the sound system that they were going to broadcast the "Du'a-ye Komeyl" (Repentance Supplication) ceremony from a mosque in Tehran. Being a nonreligious person and relatively uninformed about these matters, I had no idea what this meant. I assumed it would be like any other of the religious programs that dominated the airwaves day and night. But I was wrong. Through suffering it involuntarily I learned that this was a *du'a* (supplication, call out, or summon) in Islam for repentance and remorse in which a professional performer spent about one and a half hours crying in repentance, making his listeners cry and repent as well. I had never experienced such psychological, emotional, and ideological pressure before. It was overwhelmingly depressing, especially for a secular person who had been arrested and tortured and was under tremendous stress in solitary confinement. It threatened to break down my mental resistance and drive me crazy.

After the *du'a* was over, it took me hours to stabilize my mind and to calm myself down. If this was going to be the regular ration of Thursday nights, then I needed to prepare myself mentally to deal with it. For the following Thursday, I practiced ahead of time to block the whole thing out by doing physical activity and engaging in mental exercises—talking to myself, practicing my English, reviewing genetics. Though I tried my best, it was difficult to ignore the broadcast as long as I was alone in a cell. Generally speaking, I think most prisoners experienced the "Du'a-ye Komeyl" as one of the worst pressures of solitary confinement in the

Islamic Republic prison system, but it was particularly difficult for secular or leftist prisoners.

Friday, the official weekend holiday in Iran, was my first real day of quiet. Except for new arrests and emergency cases, the interrogators did not work on Fridays. In the following days, I started demanding basic rights and necessities. Whenever they took me to interrogation for whatever reason, I protested that with all their claims of Islamic values and compassion, why would they not let us shower or provide or sell us health and sanitation necessities? Finally, two weeks after my arrest, they gave me some of my money back and allowed me to buy whatever the "prison store" had for sale on a weekly basis. Also, I was told that I could use the shower once a week when it was our ward's turn.

The "prison store" was in fact a guard who pushed his little cart through the wards once a week to sell his limited goods to prisoners who had money and were permitted to shop. He sold underwear, toothpaste, toothbrushes, towels, packaged dates, and dried figs. Cigarettes were sold to smokers but as a rationed item, only five cigarettes per day (thirty-five weekly). You had to indicate from the beginning that you were a smoker to get on the list. In general, if you had no money on you when you were arrested and your interrogator did not permit you to get money from your family, then you were in a very tough situation. Interrogators used these so-called luxuries to reward or punish prisoners.

There was camaraderie and solidarity of the highest level among the prisoners. Prisoners who had money and could shop would watch their fellow prisoners to see if they were in need of anything and then smuggle across these items at an opportune time. Prisoners in the corridor who had been there for a long time and basically had nothing would ask for different things from prisoners who were walking to the bathroom. Some people would then drop off items for them on future bathroom trips. In any of these cases, if you were caught, you were punished in whatever way the guards chose, such as by beating, by having your privileges terminated, by being sent to interrogation, and even by lashing.

One early morning, there was a great deal of commotion in the ward. Cell doors were being opened in no particular order. Soon my cell door opened as well, and the guard ordered me to get ready for the bathhouse. I quickly took a plastic bag, put new underwear and a towel I had bought in it, and got ready. The guards led us to the lobby and then into a round yard to the left of the ward building, where there were more guards waiting for us. They took us through one of the doors in that yard into a long hallway, where we were ordered to wait for our turn. The guards continuously screamed and threatened that if anyone tried to communicate with others in any form, he would lose his shower privilege and would be severely punished. Nonetheless, it was in that bathhouse line during those minutes of waiting that I seized chances to exchange bits of information with other prisoners. I recognized a few of my organizational comrades in our line and in the line coming out, which seemed to be from a different ward. After a few minutes, our line started moving forward. When we got to a desk we each received a ration bar of soap, a set of winter underclothes, and a fresh prison uniform. We were ordered to leave the dirty prison clothes behind when we left the bathhouse. About twenty of us moved inside the bathhouse, and each was put in front of a shower stall. The guards barked that we had fifteen minutes only. When they started the time, it took me a couple of minutes to get ready just to go in the shower. The water was pretty cold at first, but it did become warm, barely.

I heard someone coming to the shower stalls and asking prisoners if they needed any Vajebi (depilatory paste). I had used this paste only two or three times in my life—when I was in college in Iran in the 1960s. I thought I should use it, but I could not risk losing precious shower time. So I decided that I would try it next time, when I would be more prepared. We needed to use the depilatory paste because they let us shower only once a week, and we were wearing very warm winter woolen underclothing against the cold in the cells. All this made conditions favorable for fungus growth or parasitic infestations in the hairy and warm private areas of the body. The dirty, ugly, dark gray prison blankets were the main source of all kinds of skin diseases and body parasites, but because of the cold winter, we had to use them.

6

My first days in solitary were difficult and depressing. In the beginning, I could not eat or sleep well. I was jumpy and anxious. But gradually I adapted to eating and sleeping under stress. I paced the cell regularly, talked to myself continuously, and attempted to block out some of the minor irritations. In the process of adjusting to the solitary lifestyle, I was molding myself into a changed and stronger person.

As a means of continuous torture, the isolation of solitary confinement probably ranks at the top of the list. Solitary confinement with no resources, no access to the exercise yard, and no contact with other prisoners causes deterioration of your memory, concentration, and focus. At the same time, it enhances your daydreaming and imaginative abilities. Gradually, you develop a form of dual personality, most notably the pessimist and the optimist. This may be a natural adaptation and survival response to isolation. It seems to be a relatively reversible condition depending on the length of the solitary experience, the foundation and strength of the character of the prisoner, and the severity of the torture and abuse during the solitary period. But all of us were affected by the solitary confinement to a certain degree.

Initially, there was nothing in the cell and I had not developed a plan to keep myself busy, active, and relatively productive. Gradually, as the frequency and intensity of the interrogations decreased, I had more free time in the cell, and soon I realized that I would go crazy without a plan and some discipline for my life in solitary. I started to organize my daily life by dividing my free time among pacing, practicing English, reviewing genetics, exercising three times a day, examining the carvings on the walls, and practicing Morse code. Morse code tables had been carved and drawn on the cell walls in many different formats by previous prisoners.

One day while cleaning the cell carpeting, I lifted a corner of it, and to my surprise I discovered a folded newspaper underneath. I could not believe my eyes! I was so excited that I jumped up and down in the cell for a few minutes. I immediately covered it up, to examine it later. It was a whole page from a daily newspaper, but more importantly, the page contained the crossword puzzle. I had previously smuggled in a pen from the interrogation room and had hidden it in the cell. I had the necessary tool to try to solve the puzzle, but I needed to do it when it was safe. I did not want to lose the treasure I had found.

At night, after the last bathroom turn and when silence had settled over the ward, I cautiously brought the newspaper out and copied the crossword puzzle onto a paper bag that I had kept. I then slowly and methodically solved the copied puzzle. That way I could copy and solve the puzzle many more times, saving the original still untouched. This became a secret source of diversion for me during those long, lonely nights.

The evenings in solitary were tougher than the days. I could set up routines to keep myself busy during the daytime, but evenings were lonely and depressing. Outside, family or friends got together in the evenings, and I had gotten used to that. Here, nothing happened after dinner, and the isolation and silence were overwhelming. It was wonderful to find something to help pass the evenings and also to help exercise my mind in a positive and productive way. I solved that puzzle every other night for several weeks.

Singing, talking, and noise of any kind were prohibited at all times. However, some prisoners, during the shifts of "nicer" guards, would whistle or hum a tune or a song. Eleven o'clock at night marked the time of mandatory silence and bedtime. I would usually lie between two blankets and try to think and dream about my loved ones until I fell asleep. As I mentioned, the guards woke us up very early, before sunrise, for the morning bathroom round. They claimed they were obligated to provide us with the opportunity in case we had a "change of heart" and wanted to wash up and prepare for morning prayers. Sometimes they woke us as early as four in the morning. Though they knew that none of us prayed, they kept up this practice. I considered it another form of torture and abuse, like Thursdays' "Du'a-ye Komeyl" broadcast.

The frequency and intensity of the interrogations decreased dramatically in weeks five to six, when I was taken for questioning perhaps only once a week. One Thursday afternoon in early December, I was again called for questioning. Thursday afternoons were normally quiet times unless something important came up. Standing blindfolded in a corner in the second-floor hallway of the interrogation building, I wondered what could be so important a month and a half after my arrest that they would have to bring me for questioning on a Thursday afternoon. Many thoughts ran through my mind. I could not think of anything new or important that they could have discovered this late in the game. I was taken to the interrogation room and was seated as usual.

After a while, someone entered the room and asked me to keep my head down. He pulled up a chair behind me and sat down while putting his briefcase by the side of his chair; I could see it and his legs because of my head being down. He introduced himself as "Haji Mojtaba" and started talking in a polite way, mostly chatting with me about my days abroad when I was a student in California. It was clear that he knew much about Iranian students' activities abroad in the 1970s. He talked to me for about ten to fifteen minutes and then said good-bye and left. Later, I learned that he was the person in charge of the division handling our arrests and interrogations. His real name was Seyyed Kazem Kazemi, one of the founders of the intelligence section of the Revolutionary Guards and the Ministry of Intelligence, and he had previously been a member of the Islamic student association in California in the 1970s before the revolution. I did not know him personally, but maybe he knew of me from that time.

7

One of the ward guards, an old man called "Haji Karimi," would have long discussions with Hossein Sadrai (a.k.a. Hossein Eghdami) in Cell 5, who was an outspoken, combative prisoner and a member of our organization. Karimi would open Hossein Sadrai's cell door and they would talk about the Islamic Republic, the opposition and our organization, regime policies, the Iran-Iraq War,[6] Islam and Marxism, and more. Karimi apparently had lost two sons in "the Iraqi-Imposed War," and war was a very sensitive topic for him. Karimi defended the policy of the regime regarding the war while Hossein Sadrai criticized and rejected it, and they had passionate and heated discussions about it.

Haji Karimi was an interesting character among the guards there. He had a mellow personality, was generally nice to prisoners, and was very flexible in administering the ward regulations. He would allow prisoners emergency bathroom visits more often than other guards. He had a small, battery-operated radio that he would carry with him and would turn on when the prison sound system was off. Sometimes, he would increase the volume so that we could also hear it.

There were basically two types of shift guards. The first type consisted of fanatical fundamentalist extremists, whose mission was to torment, beat, degrade, and create hell on earth for the prisoners. They did not believe in any compassion and kindness or in any rights as human beings for the prisoners. Some of them would openly say that the interrogators and authorities were wasting their time and the resources of the Islamic system on the prisoners, and that instead they should just take them out, hang them, and be done with it. An old guard called "Haji Zanjani" and another called "Mosslem" were the leaders of the abusive guards there. On the other hand, there were guards who were relatively kind, who would treat prisoners like semi-human beings. Haji Karimi and a man called "Tehrani" were among this group.

One of the surprising features of being blindfolded for so long was that my hearing gradually took over and I became sensitive to the slightest of sounds and noises. Every sound became significant. I began to be able to distinguish different footsteps, for example: was that a guard's, an interrogator's, or maybe a newcomer's? Different sounds relayed different information to us: the sound of a cell door opening and closing, screams, the rattle of the prison store cart, the sound of a Morse-code message, the whispers of prisoners in the corridor, and the clatter of food buckets and teakettles. More than anything else, the sounds related to the metal food buckets and teakettles would become meaningful to us.

After the early, torturous interrogation weeks, prison life in solitary or the corridor was very isolated and routine. The fixed points in our existence were the food, tea, and bathroom rounds. The sounds of the cell doors came more frequently. These sounds held meaning for us. You wanted to know which cell door was opening or closing. And after a while, it felt like you had control of what went on in the ward. I tried very hard to master this skill of recognition, which took me about a month to achieve. After that, under normal conditions, I could with certainty tell which cell door had opened or closed at any given time. Then, from the sounds of the openings and closings, and the duration of time the cells were left open, I could determine what was happening in those particular cells. Gradually, I figured out the patterns for the bathroom rounds, for the food and tea distribution, for the bathhouse, for the yard privilege, and so on. When a single cell door opened, it meant the prisoner was going to the interrogation/administration building, or something of that nature.

One of the cell-door patterns that I had a hard time figuring out was when some doors would open only for a few seconds every day around three or four in the afternoon. It took me two months to figure out that this brief opening of the doors was for the delivery of newspapers and magazines to certain cells. Getting newspapers in solitary was like finding water after being lost in the desert for a long time. Not only was it crucial politically, but more importantly, it was crucial psychologically. It provided the only means of connection, albeit indirect, to the outside world. It brought the prisoner out of complete isolation. Besides, with new stories and topics, it brought change and variety to the monotonous solitary life. The day I was allowed to receive newspapers and magazines in solitary, after about four months, must have been one of the happiest days of my prison life. The daily newspaper was free, and magazines were sold weekly. After months in complete isolation in solitary, my life suddenly got a new meaning.

There was another cell-door pattern that took me a while to understand. Once in a while, some cell doors in the ward would open and prisoners would be taken out. I could hear from the voices of the guards that these prisoners were lined up in the triangular yard, and then one or two at a time were taken into the administration/interrogation building. Later, I found out that this was for phone call privileges provided to prisoners. The agent in charge of this function was Khossravi. The phones were located on the first floor of the interrogation/administration building.

It was at about the same time that I got newspapers that I was allowed to have phone privileges as well. The first time, I gave Khossravi the phone number of our landlady, "Mrs. Hamidi." She told me that my wife had moved out of the house because it was too big and too expensive for her. I asked if she could ask Ketty to be there for my next phone call. Mrs. Hamidi said that she would try to find her. Khossravi jumped into the conversation and said, "He will call in three days at ten in the morning." Three days later, we called again. My wife was waiting there for my call. After about three months of hell for both of us, we finally heard each other's voice. Both of us were extremely emotional, and it took a while before we were able to start talking. In her voice, I could sense her loneliness and the pressure she had experienced during this period. But at the same time, her voice radiated hope and joy from knowing that I was still alive. In the end, I told her that I was allowed to call every other week. She said she did not have a phone at her new place, but that Mrs. Hamidi had kindly offered her the use of her phone. Then she added that, because she felt alone and without support, she was planning to go live with her parents. I told her that she should go wherever it would be better and easier for her to raise and to provide for Bahar and wherever she thought they would have a productive life.

Ketty's parents lived abroad, and this was her way of telling me that she had decided to leave the country. I was fine with that. Even though I was going to lose the chance of being able to see her and Bahar, it would ease my mind if they were safely out of reach of the regime. She said she would let me know if she decided to go. Then I talked a little bit with my daughter, who was just twenty-one months old at the time.

A couple of weeks later, in another phone conversation, Ketty told me that she was ready to go and stay with her parents. She said that they had tried very hard to get a visit with me but had not succeeded. It was late February when she informed me she would probably leave soon. I said good-bye to her and to my daughter over the phone. I did not know if I would ever see them again. When I was returned to my cell, I cried quietly. I was so sad, depressed, and bewildered that I could not eat or sleep that day. That must have been one of the lowest points of prison life for me. But in my heart I was relieved that they would be out of reach and out of danger. I knew that my infinite love for them would provide me with strength and hope to survive, to be able to see them again another day and under better circumstances.

Two weeks later I called my older sister's home. My brother answered, probably sitting by that phone waiting for my call. He immediately said that he had taken Ketty and Bahar to the airport himself and that they had gone to her parents' and had arrived there safe and sound. Khossravi, who was listening, asked me later where they had gone. I said that they were abroad. The following week when I was in the interrogation room, Haji Mahmood asked where my family had gone and I said that they were abroad. He claimed that they knew she was going abroad and they wanted to let her go. I was not sure if he was bluffing or not. But, either way, the issue of my wife was not brought up again as long as I was in the Komiteh detention center.

8

In early February, I heard some cell doors opening one at a time at about twenty-minute intervals. Eventually, a guard opened my cell door as well and ordered me to follow him out. We went up the stairs located next to the round yard, a route that I had never taken before. We passed the third floor; the stairs ended in front of a door. The guard opened that door and let another prisoner out. He put that prisoner in a corner and grabbed my arm and directed me through the door. After I entered, he said that I should be ready after fifteen minutes. He closed the door and left. I took my blindfold off and could not believe my eyes. I was on top of the prison building. This was where *havakhori* (recess; taking fresh air; yard privileges) in the Komiteh was provided to prisoners. They had walled off a space the size of a large room and had covered the top with wire mesh. I could not see the city, but I could hear the street traffic. And I could see the sky. There were signs posted all over the walls saying that writing and carving was prohibited, but still prisoners had written slogans and poetry on them. There were two plastic balls for playing, but I preferred to walk, to watch the sky, and to listen to the sounds and noises of ordinary life outside. I noticed that most of the graffiti were in Armenian. It was a real surprise to me that they might have many Armenian prisoners in the Komiteh. The yard privilege, after it was granted for any prisoner, was supposed to be a weekly event, but it did not happen regularly. Over the next four months, I was only allowed up there maybe three more times.

Escaping from the Komiteh, I thought, would be very difficult if not impossible, and for the most part that was true. Committing suicide, especially during the interrogation period in a detention center, was more common than escape attempts. The conditions were so inhumane and brutal that some prisoners preferred to kill themselves rather than go through the tortures. Often it was during the early parts of the interrogation that prisoners looked for means of killing themselves, when they were under tremendous psychological pressure because they either had already betrayed their organizational secrets and comrades under torture or feared they would do so.

Forcing prisoners to repent and to collaborate was an ideological and political policy stemming from the top of the system. Under this policy, simply providing information to interrogators was deemed unsatisfactory. Prisoners had to prove to the authorities that they had genuinely repented politically (from their political positions regarding the regime) and ideologically (from their worldview, comprehensive vision, or philosophical outlook) and were ready to collaborate, to prove in practice that they were prepared to do whatever was demanded. Repentance after arrest, particularly for the top cadres of opposition in general, and for most followers of the radical/militant groups, was the only option of survival presented to them by the authorities. If they rejected this option, they would suffer extreme torture and, finally, execution. Pressure on prisoners to provide information, collaborate with the authorities, and spy on other prisoners was the fundamental cause of the majority of the suicide attempts in the Islamic Republic prisons. Suicide attempts were either calculated decisions or the result of serious nervous breakdown. Some of these attempts succeeded, while others resulted in serious injury.

In the Komiteh, from what I heard or observed, certain methods of suicide were prevalent. One of the most common ways was swallowing the depilatory paste. Another was setting oneself ablaze. This was possible only in the fall and winter, when the heating stoves were in operation in the corridors of the wards. When I was in Ward 1, a prisoner in an opportune moment on his way to the bathroom poured kerosene from the stove over himself and opened the stove to catch fire. He was like a ball of fire, running in the corridor and in the yard screaming, "You killed me, you killed me!" But the most common and easiest method was to cut your wrists, to bleed to death. Many tried this method, using different objects like blades, broken aluminum spoons, broken glass or mirrors, or a piece of a metal object. Some tried to throw themselves down the stairs or off any high place to get killed. Others tried to hang themselves. And finally some tried to throw themselves in front of moving cars when they were taken out of prison for a variety of reasons.

9

It was also in February when the interrogators first asked me if I would like to have a cellmate. They knew exactly what prisoners yearned for after being kept long in solitary. A few days later, Jalali came and told me to get ready with all my belongings. I wrapped up all I had in my blankets, put my blindfold on, and followed him into the corridor. He turned toward the end of the ward and we entered into the tiny hall containing Cells 13, 14, 15, and 16. The door to Cell 16 was ajar and Jalali told me to enter. No one was in the cell at the time, but some items were already in there, indicating that someone else was living in it. The cell looked different from my previous one. It had photos of children and pictures cut from magazines on its walls, and there were books and newspapers all over its floor. There were nice, colorful home blankets and extra clothing, which certainly did not belong to the prison. It was obvious that whoever lived there must have been in prison for a long time.

A few minutes later, a young man walked in. He took his blindfold off and his jaw dropped in surprise. He kept staring at me. We shook hands and then he held and hugged me like I was his long-lost older brother. Neither of us could say a word for a while. Finally I introduced myself and then he said that his name was "Ruben." He was an Armenian arrested a year ago in connection with the Armenian Secret Army, a group formed by Armenian youth during the revolution of 1979 to fight against Turkish government interests in Iran. The militant wing of their organization had attacked the Turkish embassy in Tehran with grenades and hand-made bombs in protest against the April 1915 massacre of the Armenians by the Turkish army, during which, they believed, more than one million Armenians had lost their lives. He immediately emphasized that their group was against the Turkish government and not against the Islamic Republic of Iran.

We both noticed that we were still standing. Ruben was happier and more emotional than I was because he was much younger and had been alone longer. He told me that he was twenty when he got arrested and had been involved with only the political division of their organization. I asked him how he, and their group in general, had been treated, given that they had done nothing against the Iranian regime. He said he was taken to the torture room but never beaten. Then he added that the experience was so horrifying that the trauma still had not left him after a long year. He said he was sure that members of the armed wing of their organization had been treated differently. Then, he bent close and whispered in my ear that they had developed a system of communication with each other via the restrooms, the bathhouse, and the *havakhori* yard. I was surprised that he felt no caution or inhibition in telling me that. He then asked me to talk to him about myself.

I told him a little bit about my education, my political affiliation, and myself. His jaw really dropped when he heard that I had a PhD in genetics and that I was educated in America. He said genetics was his favorite subject. He insisted that I talk to him some about genetics. I told him that we would have many long hours to kill in the future and that there was no need to rush.

We were so busy that we did not even notice when the guard had come and gone twice to give us our dinner and tea rations. It was after seven and we had talked nonstop for two hours. We decided to eat and drink and then continue. Hardboiled eggs with bread and cold tea were sitting behind the cell door. We grabbed them and sat down to eat. I told him that we needed to calm down and develop a plan for the coming days, so that they would be productive. We both were so excited, upbeat, and happy.

He was telling me about the photo of a child on the wall when suddenly we heard footsteps approaching. We both stopped and listened. They sounded like Jalali's footsteps. The footsteps got closer and closer.

The cell door opened. Jalali appeared behind the door and ordered me to come out with all my belongings. I looked at Ruben, who was staring at me. We did not say a word, but our eyes connected in disappointment. I started getting my things together. Then I said good-bye to him. We had known each other for only three hours, but that short time in the Komiteh under the circumstances meant a lifetime. He was so sad that he could not even say good-bye to me. He only hugged me and cried quietly. I whispered in his ear that they were trying to pressure us and we had to cope with it and stay strong.

I put my blindfold on, came out of the cell, and followed Jalali into the main corridor. I thought he was going to transfer me to another ward now. We walked toward the ward door, but then he entered the small hallway and sent me back into my own previous cell. He closed the door and left. I took the blindfold off, put my stuff in the middle of the cell, and sat down on it in absolute silence and shock. Regardless of the pep talk I had just given to the young Ruben, I was so shaken by the experience that I sat there for hours, motionless. Then, I got up, spread out my bedding, organized my things, and started pacing again. I knew what I had to do. I slept, and when I woke up in the morning I followed my old routine and tried to forget all about the incident.

It was also during this period that guards one night turned on all the extra corridor lights in the middle of the night and there was a great deal of commotion in the ward. Cell doors started opening and closing. I jumped up and listened to figure out the pattern. Why were they opening the cell doors at this time of the night? My cell door also opened, and the guard ordered me to put my blindfold on and to face the wall. Someone entered the cell and stood behind me. He brought a driver's license in front of my face and asked if I knew the person. I looked at the name. I knew him. He was a member of our organization named "Azad." I said I did not know him.

"In the morning, we will find out if you are lying or not. If I were you, I would not create more problems for myself," the interrogator said.

"But I do not know this person. Do you want me to lie?"

He closed the door and left. I kept listening to the footsteps. He opened Cell 5, Cell 6, and a couple of cells on the other side and then left the ward. The extra lights were turned off, and silence prevailed once again.

I guessed that either they had arrested some new people from our organization or they were about to do so. Nothing happened in the morning, but a couple of weeks later I found out that the Ministry of Intelligence had indeed arrested some more people from our organization. In a press conference, Mohammad Rayshahri, the Minister of Intelligence, announced that they had crushed the "antirevolutionary" organization of the Fadaiyan Sixteenth of Azar and that they had arrested many leaders, cadres, and members. Although most of us had been arrested months earlier, they had delayed the public announcement until they had arrested everyone they wanted and also until after they had finished the intelligence-extraction portion of the interrogations. In his press conference, Rayshahri leveled many charges against us, including conspiracy against the Islamic Republic, attempting to overthrow the regime, organizing armed activities, concealing caches of weapons, and membership in an illegal underground organization.

Over a decade or so prior to the revolution of 1979 I had come to believe, like many others, that the only way forward for Iran was through a revolutionary transformation. Like many others, when the revolution of 1979 happened I supported it. But my views, as a secular leftist, and my dreams for a democratic and eventually a socialist and just society soon came to a clash with the reactionary, autocratic, and oppressive system of government that the Islamist forces, who had captured power, forced on the Iranian society. I joined a revolutionary secular leftist opposition group (the Fadaiyan Sixteenth of Azar) to fight for my views and ideals for Iran and to prevent the reactionary forces from taking Iran back into the darkness of the past.

Chapter Two

THE *TAVVAB* PHENOMENON

1

March 1985

Pressuring prisoners to repent and to turn into collaborators, to the extent of betraying their fellow prisoners to the authorities, has been one of the continuing major policies of the prison system of the Islamic Republic. As I mentioned, this pressure was one of the main reasons for the majority of the prison suicides. The authorities continuously elicited prisoners' cooperation through physical and psychological torture, intimidation, taking family members hostage, threatening to destroy the prisoner's credibility and honor, and many other means. Prisoners who succumbed to these pressures and, in the authorities' view, repented, were referred to as *tavvab*. *Tobeh* literally means to repent, and a *tavvab* is a person who has repented. This is a concept that dates back to early Islam. In the eyes of the prison authorities, everyone arrested had strayed from "true Islam" and needed to repent and to return. Therefore the authorities continuously pressured prisoners to repent and to become *tavvab*. Not all who declared their intention of becoming or being *tavvab* actually collaborated with the authorities. Many used this tactic, though temporarily, to escape torture and death, and others used it to obtain a reduction of their prison term. But cooperation and collaboration were expected of genuine *tavvab* prisoners. Many of them committed horrendous acts against their fellow prisoners. The *tavvab* phenomenon was one of the most complex issues of the Islamic Republic prisons, and it was a constant source of conflict for all of us.

One day in early March, I was once again ordered by Jalali to come out with all of my belongings. This time he took me up the stairs to the third floor, to Ward 5. He sent me into Cell 1. The new cell was larger and there were already two prisoners in it. One was a member of the pro–Soviet Union Tudeh Party,[7] and the other was a sympathizer of our organization. Soon after my arrival, they both stood up for their daily praying. Since both belonged to secular leftist groups, I immediately deduced that they had repented and retreated from their ideological and political positions. This was my first direct exposure to the *tavvab* phenomenon in the Islamic Republic prisons. While they were praying, I had to decide how to deal with the situation. As long as they did not bother or act against me, I thought, I would try to have an ordinary, human relationship with them. I did not want to create problems for myself with them in the cell or with the interrogators. I just had to be very careful around them regarding intelligence and political matters. Most probably, the interrogators were hoping either that these people would have a "positive" influence on me or that they would find out information from me that was still of interest to the interrogators. Whether these prisoners had agreed with the interrogators to spy on me I was not sure at the time, but later I learned that this was indeed what was expected of true *tavvab* prisoners.

The very first night, when we were arranging our bedding, "Jasem," the sympathizer of our organization, quietly shared his story with me:

> I was a sympathizer of the organization, and many months ago I was put in contact with someone called Djalal. We agreed that he and a

couple of his committee members would hold occasional meetings in our apartment. I really had no idea who they were and in what level or capacity they were involved in the organization. Starting in early 1984 they held a few meetings in our home. There were usually three of them, whom I knew as Djalal, Samad, and Hossein. Prior to their arrival and during their stay in the apartment, I was supposed to be alert about security issues and to notify them if there were any problems in the apartment complex or outside. On the meeting day, they would start coming one by one in the afternoon, starting at three or four o'clock, and at least half an hour to an hour apart from each other. Then they would start their meeting in a room, and my wife and I would do our own thing. They would usually break their meeting for dinner and then would continue as long as necessary, sometimes until midnight. In the morning we would have breakfast and then they would continue their meeting, if needed; otherwise, they would start leaving one at a time, and again at least half an hour apart. They had devised two levels of safety signs and signals for coming to the meeting. One was for the safety of the house, and the other indicated the safety of each arriving person. I had to make sure that the surroundings were safe and then I would put up the house safety sign in a way that was visible from a distance. They had to check the house safety sign before coming to the meeting. They also had to provide their own previously agreed-upon safety signal over the phone before ringing the doorbell.

On October 17, 1984, I put up the house safety sign after checking everything inside and outside of the apartment complex. First, Hossein called, gave his safety signal, and after a few minutes rang the doorbell. I opened the building door using the remote door opener. We lived on the second floor. Hossein came in and said everything looked normal outside. After about an hour Samad called. He also gave his safety signal and then after a few minutes rang the doorbell, and I opened the door. He came up and said things looked normal as well. We all sat down in the living room, chatting and having some fruit and tea while watching a soccer game on TV.

Djalal was supposed to come around 6:00 PM. He called and gave his safety signal, then said that he was stuck in traffic and would be a little late. It was about 7:00 PM when Djalal called again and said that he had finally arrived and was in the public phone booth in the neighborhood. The building doorbell rang after a couple of minutes. It was Djalal. I opened the building door with the remote door opener and we waited for him to knock on our apartment door. Suddenly the door was busted open, and armed agents poured in. None of us had any chance to react. All four of us were pushed to the floor and were searched for weapons and cyanide capsules, which none of us had. Then, we all were handcuffed. A couple of the agents searched the rooms. I saw them coming out of the meeting room with a plastic bag full of papers and documents belonging to Samad and Hossein. We were all shell-shocked. I guess every one of us at that moment was wondering about Djalal and his strange 'arrival behavior,' which was very suspicious, to say the least. I thought Djalal either had been arrested or was free and was watching this whole thing unfold. The agents searched the apartment for an hour and asked me some questions, such as whether there were any guns, cyanide capsules, printing equipment, or "illegal" stuff in the apartment. Then they took us one by one downstairs and put us in separate cars parked in front of the building. I saw Djalal sitting in one of those cars. The question in my mind was answered, but I could not tell if he had been arrested right there upon his arrival or if he had been arrested earlier and then brought there. We were taken straight to the Komiteh prison.

I figured out from the beginning what a huge mistake I had made in getting involved in all this. I cooperated with the interrogators and became a true *tavvab*. My wife was released after three days. I saw Djalal, Samad, and Hossein in the interrogation building area only on that first night, and I have not seen them since.

This was how Jasem described the arrests of the three leaders of our Tehran organization on that fateful evening. Was this the version the interrogators had ordered him to volunteer to me, or was this really how it had happened? I had no way of knowing at the time.

Jasem also shared with me that on the anniversary of the Islamic Revolution in February, the prison authorities had taken him to his home for a supervised visit with his family. Jasem added that they had treated him with kindness and also that he had not been tortured. He said he had truly repented and had become a *tavvab*, and if released, he was going to follow an ordinary, nonpolitical life and remain a devout and practicing Muslim. The interrogators had promised him that they would try to have him released when he faced the Islamic judge in Evin. They had said that even if he got a two-year sentence, he would be free in one year at the most.

The following morning, he was moved out of the cell. I figured that the interrogators had wanted him to tell me what had happened on the night of his arrest in his home before moving him out.

2

"Hoorang," my remaining cellmate, was a veteran Tudeh Party cadre. From what he revealed later, in party life he was a member of the editorial board of the official organ of the party, Mardom (People), and politically he was in contact with Noor-al-Din Kianoori, the secretary general of the Tudeh Party. Apparently, in his public life he had been a member of the editorial board of the daily newspaper *Kayhan* as well. He had worked for the *Kayhan* during the previous regime and had been arrested once by the shah's secret service, SAVAK. The Fadaiyan, soon after the revolution, declared that, based on the documents they had confiscated from SAVAK offices during the revolution, Hoorang apparently had been collaborating with SAVAK over the years. The Tudeh Party defended Hoorang by claiming that he had "infiltrated" SAVAK under the directive of the party leadership. Anyhow, he had been arrested this time around in the beginning of 1983, along with the leadership of the party. When he told me that he had been in the Komiteh for two years, I could not believe it. Ruben had been there a year and Hoorang two years. This seemed to indicate that my previous assumption of a few months in the Komiteh was unrealistic.

It was now just Hoorang and me in the cell. Neither of us could really trust the other. A few days passed while he did his own thing and I did mine. We had an enforced polite relationship, given the confined situation and the fact that there were only two of us in the cell. If either of us wanted to converse, we had to initiate the discussion, which he did more often than me. The only things I volunteered to talk about were my education and my experiences in America. About my political affiliation, I just said that I had been arrested in relation to the Fadaiyan Sixteenth of Azar group. He shared with me that he had really had a radical change in his belief system, truly had become a devout Muslim, and would stay one as long as he lived. He prayed regularly and did the dreadful "Du'a-ye Komeyl" (Repentance Supplication) on Thursday nights. He had friendly relationships with most of the guards—partly because he had been there for such a long time, but also because he was a charming guy.

Of hundreds arrested along with Hoorang from the Tudeh Party, apparently only three or four had been kept in the Komiteh. The other two or three had been infiltrators in the Revolutionary Guards or in the "Ideological-Political Sections" of different branches of the military. Hoorang understood why the other ones were still being kept there after two years, but he did not understand why he was being kept there that long. He was very frustrated at this time. I thought he was angry both at himself and at the interrogators because he had become a *tavvab* and had done whatever he could, as he had done under the previous regime with SAVAK, but he was still being kept in the detention center while most of the other members and even the party leaders had already been transferred to Evin. He thought that the longer he was kept in the Komiteh the lower would be the chances of his survival. But I thought that the interrogators were retaining him and others like him longer because they were still using and exploiting them for some purpose.

It was on the eve of the Iranian New Year, Nowruz (First Day of Spring), when they moved Hoorang out of the room. Later, I found out that he had been moved to a cell in Ward 2 and not to Evin prison, as he had hoped.

At the same time, they brought a new prisoner to the cell, carrying two plastic bags full of books. A balding man of medium height with a strong build and a full-grown beard, he was probably in his mid-thirties. We greeted each other and then sat down to get acquainted. He turned out to be another *tavvab*, but this one really knew his religious stuff and surely could not have learned it all in prison. His books were mostly about Islamic theology, history, philosophy, mysticism, and morality. He looked and sounded much like a hardcore Islamic theology/philosophy student.

He introduced himself to me as "Bagher Rezai" and said that he had been in charge of the Shiraz branch of Rah-e Kargar[8] at the time of his arrest in 1983. He apparently was interrogated and kept in the Shiraz jail for a year, then was transferred to the Komiteh in October 1984, the same time as my arrest. In Shiraz, he was beaten, but that was nothing compared to what they had done to him here in the Komiteh. After being lashed for days, he was then hung for three more days, on and off, until he broke down and agreed to cooperate. Nothing could have saved him, he declared, and he believed there was no choice left for him but to give up resisting and to cooperate in order to survive.

When he stood to pray for the first time that afternoon, I noticed how horrifying the soles of his feet had become as a result of the *kubl* (flogging cable) beatings. They had been torn apart, and though the flesh had healed, it was completely deformed. He had been through hell and back, but all that meant nothing at this moment because he clearly admitted he was cooperating with the authorities, and therefore I had to be very cautious. I told him only who I was, about my education, and that I had been arrested in connection with the Fadaiyan Sixteenth of Azar organization.

Bagher, if that was really his name, turned out to be an interesting person. Though he admitted to being a *tavvab*, his behavior was contradictory. Of the three *tavvab* that I had met in this room so far, he was certainly an outlier. For one thing, he exercised extensively, something that broken *tavvab* prisoners did not normally do. Furthermore, and more important, when he talked about some of the veteran fighters martyred by the previous or even the current regime, he did so with utmost respect and with fire in his eyes. Again, this was something that a true *tavvab* would not do. Therefore, I was very much intrigued by him, and we developed a good relationship over the coming days.

He paced in the cell for a couple of hours every day, talking to himself and repeatedly saying, "It is going to be fine. It is going to be fine!" Once, I asked him what he meant by that. Later, in the silence of the night, he talked to me: "I feel I have lost every opportunity in my life. I am very angry with myself that I have not done what most people do in life, like going to university, getting married and forming a family, traveling, and so forth. I feel that I have not taken enjoyment in life's pleasures, and I am very disappointed that I may never get another chance again. I am especially disappointed that I never got married. Even if I survive—a very unlikely event—it would be too late for me anyway." I will never forget his sorrow when he said that. I was starting to like the guy, though I was very cautious about political and intelligence issues. He seemed very smart. I felt sorry that he had gone through such a torturous, inhumane ordeal, resulting in his breakdown and forcing him to become a *tavvab*—or to pretend to be one.

From these early experiences, I started forming an opinion on the phenomenon of *tavvab* in the Islamic Republic prison system. Basically, I felt that every activist had begun with honorable intentions and ideals and none had volunteered on arrival at the prison to become a *tavvab*. The fact of the matter was that almost all *tavvab* prisoners were broken under intense physical and mental torture or ideological pressure, lured or forced to choose the so-called salvation path mainly out of fear of real or perceived life-threatening danger. It was true that they made this choice while others resisted, and even died, rather than submit. Circumstances, character, personal strengths and weaknesses, the type and degree of pressure, and the extent and severity of torture all played a role in the process. Certainly, people's weaknesses played a big role in their selection of the *tavvab* path, but the blame and responsibility rested first and foremost on the shoulders of the torturous regime, and only then on those of the *tavvab* prisoners. Of course, this does not absolve *tavvab* prisoners from the responsibility for their actions, particularly regarding their treatment of their fellow prisoners. If they spied on their fellow prisoners, if they helped the authorities in mistreating other prisoners, if they participated in any action against other prisoners, then they were and are responsible for those actions and should answer for them.

3

On the fifth of April another *tavvab*, "Shahang," was brought to the cell. He had been arrested in connection with a Maoist organization called the Ranjbaran Party of Iran (a.k.a. Ranjbaran). While a student in California at the same time as I was, he had been active in the Confederation of Iranian Students Abroad. Now, he was completely broken; not only his politics and ideology but his spirit and character had been torn apart. He thought of his interrogator as God and seemed to be under his absolute control and domination. He believed that the interrogators were the most intelligent people he had ever met in his life. He had a bizarre case of a defeatist mentality. Bagher and Shahang naturally forged a relationship because they were both *tavvab* prisoners and therefore they prayed, discussed books, and did the appalling "Du'a-ye Komeyl" together. For about two months, I lived in that room with these two *tavvab*.

The morning of Thursday, May 1, I was called out of the cell. I was taken to the Komiteh gate area, where many other blindfolded prisoners were waiting. Some of us were then boarded onto a minibus. We were handcuffed to the metal seat bars and threatened against trying to communicate. The guards were really nasty and forced us to put our heads down on our knees, even though curtains were pulled over the windows and we were blindfolded. There were other vehicles packed with more prisoners in the gate area as well. As the bus headed north, we guessed we were being taken to Evin prison. Once we arrived in Evin, after about an hour drive, we were taken quickly up some stairs into a temporary-type structure, where our blindfolds were collected before we entered the building. It was the first time since our arrests that we were in such a large group without the blindfolds. It was a very strange feeling. As soon as I looked around, I noticed many familiar faces, and soon we figured out that we were all from the same organization, maybe thirty of us in this group alone. Everyone was chatting with each other in small groups of two or three. I had positioned myself next to Abdi and Hossein Sadrai. While we were talking, the guards called us one by one and lined us up behind a high curtain in the middle of that salon. They gave us a talk explaining the rules, emphasizing that we had to end the visit and go behind the curtain when ordered. This was when I realized that we were here to visit with our families. Whether other prisoners here had had visits before I did not know, but my guess was that it was the first time for most of them as well. Then we were ordered to pass through the curtain and stand behind a glass partition in designated stalls.

There was nobody on the other side of the glass yet. We would not be able to touch or embrace our loved ones through the glass, but on either side was a telephone handset. At least we could speak with them. Certainly our conversations would be monitored and recorded by the authorities; we would have to resort to sign language and lipreading to communicate any private or secret messages.

While we waited, I realized we were all unshaven, pale, thin, and dressed in the depressing prison uniforms. I thought about our poor families and how horrified they would be to see us in this condition after six months or more.

A door opened on the other side of the glass wall, and the families rushed in. There were greetings, cheering, crying, screaming, and kids running around. It was a different world on that side of the window.

My oldest sister had come to my visit. At the time of my arrest she had been abroad. For a couple of minutes, neither of us could say a word. She was, of course, shocked to see me in that condition. I could see fear and sadness in her eyes. We had only fifteen minutes, so I encouraged her to talk. She repeatedly asked about the prison conditions and the status of my case. And all I asked about was my wife, my daughter, my mother, and all my other relatives. Those fifteen minutes were over very quickly. When it was time to say good-bye, sadness returned, but now we were both stronger—or we pretended to be.

The guards shouted that the visit was over and ordered us behind the curtain, where we were given our blindfolds. As though it had been only a dream, we were back in the reality of prison life again. We were taken back to the Komiteh. I had finally seen a family member, albeit from behind a glass wall. It made me happy, charged, and hopeful, on the one hand, and created turmoil in me, on the other hand. Turmoil was due to the fact that I had tried hard to adapt to the separation from my family, and now seeing one of my relatives had triggered all sorts of emotions and memories in me.

4

In late May, the Islamic month of Ramadan started. The prison went into the fasting routine. Meals were given before sunrise, which was very early in the morning, and then again only after sunset. The authorities naturally encouraged fasting, but in those days in Tehran prisons they did not force nonreligious prisoners to fast. So if you wanted to eat during the daytime, you could—you just had to eat the early morning meal cold for breakfast or lunch.

There were basically no Mojahedin or other religious prisoners kept in the Komiteh at this time. Fasting prisoners in the Komiteh were mostly the *tavvab*. My roommates practiced fasting very religiously, but people like me, who made up the majority of the prisoners in the Komiteh and who did not fast, had a very tough time during Ramadan. The guards woke us all up in the early morning regardless of whether we were fasting. They said they wanted to make sure that we used our bathroom turn, because they were not going to send us during the morning hours. After a week or so, I decided to stay awake at night until the meal was distributed, which was about three in the morning, eat the hot food and then sleep until late in the morning. If I were to be called for interrogation early in the morning, it would disturb my sleep; but the interrogators, because of fasting, usually started their work very late in the day unless there were new arrests or some important intelligence emergency came up.

It was about the same time when I decided to stay up late that we noticed one day that the corridor was suddenly full of new prisoners. That same day I was called for interrogation. Haji Mahmood and others came into the interrogation room, and Mahmood claimed they had arrested the remainder of our organization. Then he said that I would get punished and might even lose my life for my lies and concealment of intelligence. After the setup, he said that he was going to give me one last chance to come clean. He wrote an instruction and then they all left the room:

For the last time, reveal all your information about your activities.

I pondered for a few minutes and concluded that if they really had arrested everyone, as they claimed, then they did not need my old intelligence. If these new arrestees belonged to another organization, then I had nothing to worry about. Therefore I wrote only a short sentence: "I have nothing new to reveal."

When they returned, first they made some noise and threats, but then the only point they pressured me about was whether my wife had been active in the organization. My answer was negative, as before. They made me sign a paper accepting responsibility if they found out someday that she had been active. I was then returned to the cell.

In the coming days, we figured out that the new arrestees were from the south Tehran branch of the Rah-e Kargar organization. Most of them had been severely tortured. From our cell, I could hear the dragging of their injured feet wrapped in plastic bags when they walked or pulled themselves to the bathroom or to go to interrogation.

Part Two
BLINDFOLDED JUSTICE

Chapter Three

ASSAYESHGAH

1

June 1985

One morning during the second week of Ramadan, guards poured into the ward and ordered everyone to pack up. We quickly took our plastic bags and blankets and were soon ready. In the last seconds, the guards said that Bagher had to stay behind. We said good-bye to him. That would be the last time I ever saw him.

When the line of prisoners from our ward arrived downstairs, we saw that lines of prisoners were coming out of other wards as well. In the back yard by the gate, buses were waiting. We were loaded into the buses, into minibuses, and even into cars. We assumed that this exodus meant they were closing down the Komiteh for good, but later we learned that the Ministry of Intelligence was still using it. Our personal belongings (clothing, shoes, documents, etc.) were delivered separately to our next destination, the notorious Evin prison.

In Tehran and the immediate regions around it there were four main prisons: Komiteh and Evin were within Tehran, while Ghezelhessar and Gohardasht prisons were just outside Tehran close to the city of Karaj. Besides these prisons, there were smaller detention houses in the local Islamic Committees and many secret interrogation places all over

Tehran for the intelligence forces. The army also had its own detention center in Tehran. Provinces had their own prison systems, usually a main prison in the capital city and others in every major provincial town.

Evin prison is located in a residential and commercial area known as Evin village, at the foot of the Alborz mountain range. The National University of Iran is nearby. In 1971, the modern Evin prison was built. By 1977, it had expanded to house more than fifteen hundred prisoners; "Ward 209" was for political prisoners. A two-story building, Ward 209 had interrogation and torture chambers on its first floor. On its second, there were ten wards, each with eight solitary cells plus a bathroom and a shower. Evin also contained four communal political-prisoner holding blocks, an administration building, a clinic, a kitchen/dining area and sports facility, an execution yard, a courtroom, and separate blocks for women and nonpolitical prisoners.

After the revolution of 1979, the Islamic regime turned the administration building into holding blocks, turned the dining facility into a *hosseiniye* (place of worship), covered the pool in its basement, and turned that into a workshop. This new prisoner-holding facility was named Amoozeshgah. From 1981 to 1983, Assadollah Lajavardi,[9] the Islamic Revolution Public Prosecutor (IRPP, a.k.a. the Revolutionary Prosecutor, or the Prosecutor) of Tehran, with the help of *tavvab* (repenter) prisoners and forced labor from others, built a large facility with two four-story buildings: one with a few hundred solitary cells, named Assayeshgah; the other belonging to the offices of the prosecutor. The Amoozeshgah and Assayeshgah buildings are perpendicular to each other. Lajavardi and his *tavvab* prisoners also built a swimming pool in the open area in front of these blocks. A visiting salon was built in Evin prison during the Islamic regime as well. In the Islamic regime, Evin housed the courts and release office of the whole prison system in Tehran, so this was where prisoners were taken to be tried and sentenced or, alternatively, executed or released.

In its early years, during the shah's regime, Evin prison was known worldwide for its political prisoners' wings and for its torturous practices. Under the Islamic Republic, besides those practices, it is notorious worldwide for its Islamic tribunals, its obtaining of forced confessions and interviews, and its mass torture and killings.

When we got to Evin, we were taken into the Assayeshgah building, and a cleric with a list at hand administered the cell and section assignments based on our assignments in the Komiteh. Shahang and I were put in a cell on the second floor. Most of the cells were for solitary or had two prisoners in them, but there were some larger rooms, which accommodated up to fifteen or more prisoners. When we were moved to Assayeshgah, it was a new structure, maybe only two or three years old. It had a wide corridor with cells on both sides. Our cell was a typical one, about seven by five feet. A toilet bowl and a sink were in one corner, and large metal pipe—a crude radiator—ran along one side of the cell. The metal door had a small peephole at the top and openings for food delivery at the bottom. The cell was very clean and modern, with no sign of writing on its walls. There was a small, high window opposite the door that looked outside to the compound. From that window, when we climbed up onto the heating pipe, we could see a large clock, which belonged to the National University of Iran, where I had worked as an assistant professor after the revolution until the universities were shut down during the so-called Cultural Revolution. The Cultural Revolution was a period following the 1979 Islamic Revolution when the regime attempted to purge academia of "Western and non-Islamic" influences to bring it in line with Islam. We also could hear the street vendors selling fruit and vegetables in Evin village.

The guards would light cigarettes for smokers only twice a day: after breakfast and after dinner. They gave tea three times a day, once after each meal. There was a switch in the cell to turn on an outside emergency light to call the guard's attention. Knocking on the door was absolutely prohibited. You had to turn your back immediately when the door opened, or else you were punished. Total silence was enforced in Assayeshgah at all times. Once in a while, you might hear a prisoner coughing, humming, whistling, or whispering very quietly. Prisoners with mental or psychological illnesses were the only ones who made noise, like the one in the cell above us, who would scream loudly once in a while. Otherwise, prisoners were severely punished for talking, singing, or sending messages in Morse code.

Shahang and I passed most of our time analyzing and anticipating what was going to happen to us. We had some old magazines and a couple of poetry books with us, but we were not given newspapers anymore. Silence was the real killer in Assayeshgah. It was so bad that it could easily drive anyone insane. The name "Assayeshgah" in the Iranian culture has always been associated with a kind of mental hospital, a psychiatric ward. Warden Lajavardi certainly had chosen that name on purpose, as was indicated by his statements on the subject in many occasions: "There are no political prisoners in Islam. In reality either you are people who have drifted, for one reason or another, from the true path of Islam, or you are infidels. You have been infected with ideological and cultural agents and diseases of the East or the West. What needs to be done is to help you get cured, and the best way is with solitary confinement, so that you are forced to confront your demons and find your true Islamic nature. If you repent and become a *tavvab*, then you will be cured and will be saved. Otherwise, you shall all be killed according to sharia." So, he named the new building Assayeshgah, a place where ideologically "wicked and sick" people would get cured or eventually be eliminated.

The food in Evin, compared to that in the Komiteh, was terrible, both qualitatively and quantitatively. There was very little meat in the weekly ration. The plates of rice were flattened going through the opening in the door, and most of the rice was lost. Commonly, a meager ration of plain rice was all we had for lunch, and dinner consisted of a small loaf of bread and one hard-boiled egg or bread and cheese with some unwashed greens and herbs.

2

About two weeks after arriving in Evin, I was called out. They loaded me, blindfolded of course, along with a few others into a minibus and took us to the Sho'beh, one of the interrogation buildings in Evin. A guard led me up the stairs to the third floor and put me by the side of a door in the hallway. Soon I heard screams and shouting close by, and then came the sound of a *kubl* (flogging cable) strike. My heart was pounding crazily and my body started shivering uncontrollably. Everything here reminded me of my early days in the Komiteh. But Evin provoked extra fear in people because of its notoriety. I could hear the conversation between an interrogator and a prisoner. The interrogator spoke slowly and clearly to the prisoner, asking, "Are you ready to write?" He apparently did not get an answer back. I could hear him strike the prisoner a few more times with the *kubl*. The screams of the prisoner were maddening. I felt sorry for him while worrying about my own fate. Why was I there? I tried to analyze my situation, but under the circumstances I was unable to figure out what could possibly have brought me here almost seven months after my arrest.

The interrogator asked the prisoner again if he was ready to write. Apparently he heard a positive reply this time. Then he threatened the prisoner, saying that if he saw bullshit on the paper when he returned, he was going to kill him. He then left the room, closed the door, passed in front of me, and opened another door—probably his office—and went inside. For ten minutes or so, silence prevailed in the hallway. I heard the opening and closing of a door again. The interrogator passed in front of me, then opened and closed the other door. Moments later he shouted, "You fucking asshole, are you playing games with me? I will teach you a lesson you will never forget!" Then he started striking the poor man with the *kubl* many times. The prisoner's screams drove me crazy.

A guard approached and asked if I was Jafar, son of Bashir, then took me through the door next to us. We entered a long room where a man was sitting behind a desk in one corner. I was taken in front of him. He told me to go sit on the chair close by, facing the wall. It was very quiet in the room. I could hear him turning the pages of a file. Then he got up and walked toward me. For a moment my heart stopped beating. He put an interrogation form in front of me, pulled my blindfold up a bit so that I could see the form, and said that I should write a precise response to the question, not too long but not too short. Then he went back to his desk. His voice and demeanor, for some odd reason, did not strike me as threatening. I looked at the question. It was the same old question asked so many times before:

Write all your political activities, with dates and locations.

I raised my hand and said that I had replied to this many times before and had nothing new to add. He replied that this time it was for a different purpose and I should do as instructed. I started writing what I had written on every other occasion. After a while, he took a look at my writing and asked me to sign the form. He asked a couple more questions. About an hour passed, and the questioning still continued.

Suddenly, the door opened and there was a commotion in the room. I was facing the wall, but I could sense the presence of many more people in the room. They brought two women prisoners over to put them next to me. I peeked from the corner of my eye. They were covered head to toe in black *chadors* (shapeless cloaks, the traditional Islamic cover for women in Iran, part of the *hejab*). From the questioning, I figured out that there was another male prisoner on the other side of the room. A few interrogators were also present. I could not hear the whispers between these other interrogators and the official who had been questioning me, who seemed to be a head interrogator or maybe an examining magistrate in Evin.

I had lost my concentration. I was curious to know who these prisoners were and why they had been arrested. One of the interrogators approached and questioned one of the women sitting next to my chair. He told her that she had planned a party to take place after an explosion at the Friday prayer to celebrate the killing of innocent people by a bomb that her brother had hidden in a rug. She replied, while crying, that she had no knowledge of what her brother allegedly had done. She then said, "He arrived from Kordestan saying that he was in the carpet business, buying and selling local rugs. He had brought a few rugs that he later took to show somewhere. He returned in the afternoon and said that he had sold them. He was happy that he had made some money. I already had planned a birthday party for my son and had invited some friends and family over. I had no knowledge of the planning or the execution of the alleged bombing."

"Are you saying that while he was staying in your house during the last few days and kept the explosive rug in your home, you had no knowledge and had no role in all this?" the interrogator asked.

"Believe me, brother, I had no knowledge of what he allegedly has done," the woman replied.

"We will soon find out how much of the money was your share and how much involvement you had in all this," said the interrogator. He then left and went to the head interrogator. I could not hear their conversation, but I had already found out what these other prisoners were accused of.

The head interrogator put to me another question:

What is your opinion on Marxism?

This was the first time since my arrest that I had been asked this question in writing. I knew I had to be very careful in answering this type of ideological question in the Islamic prison system. Defending Marxism from a philosophical standpoint could have been taken as proof of *ertedad* (apostasy), which would be punishable by death according to sharia. Depending on the political climate of the country and the prisons, defending Marxism from a socioeconomic or political standpoint was tolerated at times, at least in the Tehran prison system. At other times, defending Marxism in any way could result in death.

After pondering for a few minutes, I decided not to give a straightforward answer. I just wrote a few simple sentences about the political and social aspects of Marxism without admitting to anything.

Then the head interrogator wrote the following:

Mr. Yaghoobi, you are charged with:
Conspiracy to overthrow the Islamic regime.
Membership and activity in an illegal and clandestine organization.
Activity in corrupting the Islamic youth.
Activity in opposition to our just war against aggressors, nonbelievers, and corrupters of the world.
Activity under a pseudonym.
Do you have anything to say in your defense?

I accepted some of the charges and rejected others. When he looked at my answer, he shook his head. He then asked if I had any requests. I replied that I did not. He called a guard to take me back to my cell. The guard put me outside, by the door again. While I was waiting there, an interrogator brought one of the women out of the room and led her toward an elevator across from where I was standing. He told her, "Very soon we will make you admit if you were really involved."

I heard screaming continuously in that hallway. A guard finally came and took me downstairs, then I was escorted to Assayeshgah and to my cell. Shahang was waiting anxiously. He asked me where they had taken me. I told him it looked like they were preparing my file to send me to court. He was upset at his interrogators because he had been expecting to go to court before me. But there was no order or logic in what they did in that chaotic system.

Chapter Four
AMOOZESHGAH

1

June 1985

A few days later, a guard ordered me to move out. I said good-bye to Shahang. He was very disappointed at losing me as a cellmate. I hoped that I had had some positive influence on him. I took my blankets and my two plastic bags and followed the guard out. He got a prisoner from another cell as well and walked the two of us to the front office of the Assayeshgah building. I heard someone telling the guard to take the other prisoner to the prison clinic and to take me to Amoozeshgah.

I did not know where Amoozeshgah was, but hearing that name caused me anguish, just as the name of Assayeshgah had, simply because of its ominous literal meaning. Amoozeshgah means "learning center" or "training center." I worried that the authorities had decided to send me to an indoctrination center. We walked a very short distance and entered a building that seemed to be attached to Assayeshgah. The *zir-e hasht* (lobby) of the Amoozeshgah building was a large hall. The guard sat me on a chair next to the door. Another guard approached and asked me some questions to fill out the registration form for Amoozeshgah. This guard barked like a dog and mistreated me as much as he could. Another guard, who was checking my belongings, nagged and barked, then he confiscated almost everything I had. The guard filling out the form inquired about my political/organizational affiliation and then asked if I still was a *mortad* (apostate). I said I didn't understand what he meant. He asked if I had repented and prayed or whether I still held to my *kafar* (nonbeliever) views. I replied that I did not pray and had never been religious. He then asked if I was willing to participate in an "interview" condemning my "malicious activities." I said no.

He finished completing the form, hit me on the head a couple of times, cursed at me, and finally called another guard to take me to "Salone 3." He gave me one of my plastic bags containing a few permitted items, and I took my blankets and followed the new guard. He took me to the left corner of the *zir-e hasht*, where there was a large closed door. He knocked on the door and delivered me to the ward guard. This guard said his name was "Abbas Hemmat." He closed the door behind us. I saw from under my blindfold a long corridor with many thick curtains hanging on both sides, apparently covering doors to rooms. Abbas Hemmat stopped in front of "Room 64" and pulled the curtain aside. The door was ajar behind the curtain; he pushed it open and told me to enter. As I entered the room, Abbas Hemmat pulled the door back to its original position, still ajar, and closed the curtain behind me. The door was ajar for a bit of ventilation in the summer heat, as I would learn later on.

I was worried to death about what I was going to find here behind the curtain. I took my blindfold off, and it took my eyes a minute or so to get used to the lighting. I was in a fairly large room (about twenty-two by fifteen feet) with about thirty prisoners calmly and curiously standing around. The first thing that struck me was that they all had clean-shaven faces and looked pretty neat in their own personal clothing. I, on the other hand, was wearing a prison uniform, had not had a shave in over a month, and must have looked pale and disoriented.

Other things I noticed were a TV set sitting on a stand to my left side and a metal bunk bed to my right. Finally, I said hello and introduced myself. A few prisoners immediately approached me, while the rest remained standing. One took my plastic bag and put it aside, while others started asking me questions. When I said I was with the Fadaiyan Sixteenth of Azar organization, everyone else in the room stepped closer and surrounded me as well. I was still a bit cautious and suspicious, and so were they. They did not know whether I was a *tavvab* (repenter), and I was not sure whether this was a *tavvab* room.

One of them took a risk and asked if I would like to have a shave to get cleaned up. At first I thought he was joking, but then I asked if they had the tools to do it. He replied that they did. I said I would love that. This was a bit reassuring to both sides. One man, "Mansour," brought the tools, and another, "Mehran," tied a cloth around my neck and handed me the reflective lid from a powdered-milk container, to use as a mirror. Mansour cleaned up the manual hair-clipper, sat in front of me on a stool, and started shaving my face. He explained that they did their own haircuts and shaving with those primitive tools, the only ones they were allowed to have. He said he had been in Evin since 1980 without any charges being brought against him and without being sentenced.

From what I had seen so far, I thought this could not be a *tavvab* room, but I was still a bit cautious. I told Mansour a bit about my arrest and where I had been in the last eight months. Someone came closer and sat down. He introduced himself as Jamshid Sepahvand. I had heard of him; he was a cadre of the Fadaiyan Sixteenth of Azar. I was very excited that this room held a member of our organization. I got up and we embraced. Another prisoner came closer as well and introduced himself as "Yashar," a sympathizer of our organization. We chatted while Mansour continued to shave me. I told them a bit about the arrests in our organization. Yashar said he had been arrested in February, when part of the remainder of our organization in Tehran was rounded up. Mansour finished shaving me, and my face looked clean and shiny. I could not believe that with those primitive tools someone could do such a fine job. We got up and gathered in a corner of the room and talked some more about the room, the ward, and the prison.

I learned that Assayeshgah was indeed attached to Amoozeshgah, which through its lobby was attached to Evin's *hosseiniye* (place of worship) facilities. In the basement of the *hosseiniye,* there were workshops where *tavvab* prisoners worked. These prisoners also did most of the work in the wards. *Tavvab* prisoners were very organized, and they collaborated with the authorities in suppressing the non-*tavvab* prisoners. In return, they benefited from more privileges than the rest. Amoozeshgah was the largest prisoner-holding structure in Evin prison. It consisted of two three-story buildings connecting to each other in the *zir-e hasht.* While prisoners did not wear blindfolds in their rooms or wards, they had to wear them as soon as they exited their rooms or wards before entering the *zir-e hasht.* To the right of the *zir-e hasht,* a three-story building contained Salones 2, 4, and 6. To the left, another three-story building contained Salones 1, 3, and 5. We were in Salone 3. Most *tavvab* prisoners in Amoozeshgah currently were kept in Salones 2 and 4, and some were kept in 6. Salone 5 held prisoners who had given a positive reply to the question of praying and a positive reply or a "maybe" to the question of willingness to do an interview. They were a mix of *tavvab,* tactical *tavvab,* and "passive" religious or secular leftist prisoners.

An open-door policy prevailed in those four Salones (2, 4, 6, and 5), meaning that the room doors were always open and the prisoners were free to move around within the ward. For Salones 2, 4, and maybe 6, there was even an open-yard policy, meaning that when the yard was available, the door stayed open and the prisoners came and went as they wished. Salone 5 got more yard privileges than Salones 1 and 3 overall.

In contrast, a closed-door policy prevailed in Salones 1 and 3, meaning that prisoners of different rooms were not allowed to have any contact with each other. They got very limited yard time. Salone 3 had thirteen prisoner-holding rooms and two combination toilet/shower rooms. The small lobby at the other end of the ward had stairs going to the lower level and the yard. There were three yards for our side of Amoozeshgah. Prisoners were allowed the use of a ball, volleyball net, and two small soccer goals in each yard, so the space could serve as either a volleyball court or a mini soccer field. At that time, on average each room in Salones 1 and 3 held about twenty-five prisoners. In previous years (1981–1984), there could be more than fifty to sixty prisoners in each room. In those days, people slept packed like sardines in these rooms. If someone got up in the middle of the night and returned to sleep, he would not be able to squeeze in and would have to stand in a corner until morning.

I asked Jamshid if praying was the only or the main criterion for assigning prisoners to different Salones in Amoozeshgah. He replied:

> It can't be the main or the only criterion, because we have a room in our Salone containing followers of the Mojahedin. They are religious and pray, but because they are deemed combatant prisoners, they are kept in this ward. We even have a Mojahedin prisoner in our own room. He has been sent here, among the infidels, as a punishment for him. But Salone 3 holds mostly secular leftist prisoners. Salone 1 has some secular leftist rooms and some for religious groups, mostly the Mojahedin. Most of the rest of the Mojahedin prisoners in Evin currently are in Salones 2, 4, 5, and 6. One room in Salone 3 (Room 61) is currently dedicated to *tavvab* prisoners. Until a few days ago, every room in this ward had two or three of those *tavvab* prisoners. They were distributed among the rooms to spy and help the guards control us. Then one day, as a result of recent policy changes, they were gath-

ered together and put in Room 61. After the removal of Lajavardi and his gang from Evin late last year, *tavvab* prisoners were also gradually consolidated into their own wards. But in a policy reversal from about two months ago, the authorities again brought back a few *tavvab* prisoners to each room for tighter control of the non-*tavvab* prisoners.

Life became difficult when *tavvab* prisoners were in the room. No one was allowed to talk or even whisper. The TV had to be turned off when they were praying, and it had to be on for all the religious programs and so forth. They would call the guards in for any infraction, and each time certain prisoners or the whole room would be punished. There were a lot of fights between *tavvab* and non-*tavvab* prisoners. In one room, the non-*tavvab* prisoners decided to bring the matter to a final conclusion, whatever the consequences. Someone picked a fight with one of the *tavvab*, and suddenly the rest of the room attacked *tavvab* prisoners. They were beaten so badly that they had to be hospitalized. The guards pulled everyone out of that room, beat them all, and kept them standing the whole night outside in the cold. The guards portrayed the incident as a riot and got a judicial order for flogging. Pairs of combatant prisoners from that room were taken to different rooms in the Salone, were lashed in front of the other prisoners, and were left there. This way, the authorities thought they had taught a lesson to all prisoners in Salone 3. Two weeks after the incident, news reached Salone 3 that a new warden had taken over Evin prison. A coordinated plan was made throughout Salone 3 to start fights with *tavvab* prisoners in all the rooms. This forced the authorities to make a decision about the policy of distributing the *tavvab* prisoners among the rest of the prison population. When the new warden came for a visit of the Salone 3 rooms, prisoners complained, requesting that *tavvab* prisoners be removed. Later, the warden ordered that this be done. In Salone 3 they were gathered together in Room 61.

The policy of controlling combatant prisoners with the help of *tavvab* had backfired this time around. The times had changed, and the efficiency and power of the *tavvab* phenomenon had diminished. *Tavvab* prisoners were a bunch of broken beings that had lost everything, including their dignity. They were not taken seriously even by the prison authorities, let alone by the non-*tavvab* combatant prisoners. They were treated like dirt by the interrogators and guards and were not liked or trusted by the other prisoners. During previous years, they had been protected by the prison system, and in return they had helped control and suppress non-*tavvab* prisoners. But they had lost their best guardian, their "godfather," Lajavardi. It was truly the end of an era for the phenomenon of *tavvab* in the Islamic regime prisons. When news arrived that Lajavardi had been sacked, one of the top hardcore *tavvab* prisoners in Salone 6 had said, "We lost our father and our protector."

Bathrooms were good locations to make contact with other rooms and to exchange news and information. From the time a room door was opened by the guard, it took a few minutes for all of the twenty to thirty occupants to reach the bathroom. Those who were the designated contact persons would rush in first and stand on the bathroom floor, which was raised relative to the ward corridor, so that they could see into the opposite rooms through the windows on top of their doors. Communication took place using Morse code, lipreading, and other forms of signing. The three rooms (62, 63, and 64) across from the bathrooms served as a center for the dissemination of news and information to all rooms in the ward.

The room had organized a rotation so that each day a new pair of prisoners was responsible for the daily chores. Before dinner, the two daily workers asked everyone what they wanted as their support food. Support items were prepared using provisions that we could purchase with our own money. This was necessary because of the low quality and limited quantity of the edible portion of the prison food ration. Prisoners signed up for support items like canned fish or eggplant, yogurt, tomatoes, halvah, and honey. The daily workers took the orders and prepared the side dishes. Then, they spread *sofreh* (dinner cloth) in two rows and set up the silverware, bread, and other items. People sat down, and the workers served them their side dishes, while bowls of prison *aash* (thick soup) were placed between pairs of prisoners sitting across from each other, a bowl to each pair.

One elected person—the *mass'oul-e senfi* (food service representative)—supervised the whole dining process. He was the one who ordered and bought items for side dishes. He was also in charge of the consumption of bread—the staple food for prisoners and a sensitive issue for the guards. If prisoners did not eat all their bread, it created problems with the guards. Wasting bread has always been discouraged in the Iranian culture, but because of the ongoing war at the time the guards were especially touchy about this. Disposing of any uneaten food, for that matter, posed a serious problem. Once, we had some extra *aash* that we needed to get rid of because it was full of beans and not suitable for many prisoners with digestive problems. We were caught, and all twenty-five of us were taken to the *zir-e hasht*, where we were teased, abused, and punished. Disposing of bread would result in more serious punishment. The person in charge of the bread and the two daily workers would soak the extra bread and any leftover food in a bucket of water, which they would cover with dirty dishes to smuggle it to the bathroom for disposal. It was always a risky endeavor.

After dinner and cleanup, the elected person in charge of the room—the *mass'oul-e otagh* (room representative)—would turn on the TV set for the evening news. Each room had a TV set, which was always a source of friction with the authorities. If they wanted to punish a room, they would disconnect its TV. While it was connected, we could select between two governmental channels. There was agreement in our room on which programs had priority. News programs had top priority. Then came political and social programs, interviews, and finally movies and sports. If none of these were available, we voted on what to watch. It was helpful and useful for prisoners to have TV, but the main reason for its presence in the rooms was political propaganda and ideological brainwashing. The prison authorities would interrupt the regular programming whenever they wanted to broadcast their own religious programs, interviews, and propaganda lessons from Evin. A network of TV and radio broadcasting had been set up in Evin in 1981 to "educate"—brainwash—prisoners. From nine in the morning until noon, prisoners were forced to listen to or watch ideological propaganda and political exposés. This was also the period when prisoners were bombarded with propaganda and other programs from *hosseiniye* recantation shows, which were shown on closed-circuit TV and broadcast over the prison sound system, blasting into cells, communal rooms, and even solitary.

After the night bathroom round, it was time to sleep. I noticed that everyone had bedding of about six by one-and-a-half feet, made out of prison blankets but covered with nice, clean fabric from shirts, pajamas, or even linen gotten from families. Most people also had colorful non-prison blankets. Pillows consisted of a clean bag or pillowcase filled with extra clothing. Everyone had his own assigned spot to sleep. People set up their beds in two rows, with their heads against the walls and their feet against each other. That first night, all I had were the ugly prison blankets. Jamshid informed me that there was some spare good bedding left from previous prisoners stacked on the top level of the lone bunk bed in the room. I grabbed one set, and Jamshid gave me a clean sheet. I set up my bed close to the door. The top level of the bunk bed was used for storing the bedding every morning. Mansour was in charge of organizing the beds. Then he himself slept on the top bunk. There was a rule in Evin at this time that only one person could sleep on each bunk, though previously, during the crowded period, three had slept on each bunk. At 11:00 PM, the TV was turned off and everyone had to be in bed.

Gradually, it became quiet in the room. But I could still hear prisoners from other rooms in the corridor going back and forth to the bathroom. I had a hard time falling asleep because of the change in my circumstances. Maybe around two in the morning, after the corridor noise had subsided, I finally fell asleep, but soon two loud bangs on the door of the room made me jump out of bed. It was 4:00 AM and the guards were calling us for the early morning bathroom round. Later, they gave us the morning Ramadan warm meal. We ate the food and immediately got back in our beds and slept. Going to early morning bathroom was mandatory here. Only two days were left of Ramadan. Everyone in the room was counting the days and hoping for the resumption of the normal prison routines.

At about eleven in the morning, our room was told to prepare to go to the yard for *havakhori* (recess). One elected person was in charge of the sporting activities. *Havakhori* was only twenty minutes long for each room in Salone 3, so everything needed to be organized ahead of time. Not a moment of precious yard time could be wasted. Four soccer teams of four players each had already been organized to play matches. Each pair of teams was going to play an eight-minute game. If there was any time left after these games, it was considered *vaght-e melli* (nonassigned extra time) and people who still wanted to could play. That first day I was not part of any team yet. I only walked around the yard and enjoyed myself. The center of the yard, where the sport was played, was a large pavement, but there was also a long, narrow dirt strip by the yard wall for gardening, although nothing had been planted in it.

2

The ward had a specific schedule. For store supplies, we were asked to provide our shopping list every Saturday morning. After collecting the lists, a guard would take them to the store located between the doors for Salone 1 and Yard 1 downstairs. Then he would take the room representatives one by one to pay for and bring back their room's items that were in stock in the store. Other items like fruits, vegetables, packaged milk, and yogurt were sold when available and normally were brought and delivered to the rooms. *Tavvab* prisoners ran the store. The bread ration was delivered to the rooms every other day. Evin had its own bakery where was made a certain kind of bread that was tasty when fresh but became difficult to chew, like rubber, later on. A very small breakfast ration of feta cheese was given weekly. Tea was given three times a day. What I am describing of course did not apply during the month of Ramadan.

Meal portions for lunch in Evin were very small. At the best of times, the standard allotment was one regular plate of cooked rice and about two spoonfuls of any *khoresht* (stew) between two people. According to prison ration protocol, one whole chicken was supposed to be allotted to eight to twelve people for one serving, but we got only about half a chicken for twenty-five to thirty people. Someone, using his fingers, would separate, bone, and clean the portion of chicken. He would then shred the edible parts completely and mix them into the rice, to make the meal easier to divide. Dinners were even worse—just thin or thick soups (*aash*), chili beans, cooked lentils, feta cheese with tomatoes or cucumbers, or boiled potatoes with some butter. Only on Friday evenings did we receive two eggs per person and a whole bar of butter for the room. *Tavvab* prisoners later took these supplies, room by room, to make us scrambled eggs. These Friday dinners were the best dinners that we would have in Evin prison.

Fruits and vegetables, when available, were bought and consumed on a daily basis either with the meals or as a snack around four o'clock. The two daily room workers were responsible for preparing food, setting up, cleaning and washing dishes, dividing food and tea, putting down and collecting the sandals when we all went out of the room for any reason, and more. One of the daily workers' most difficult duties was cleaning the carpet three times a day, every day. First, they would sweep the floor after each meal. Then they would wipe the carpet using damp cloths to collect the *porze* (lint) produced by the ugly prison blankets. This extensive procedure had been decided by earlier prisoners and had become part of the room practices. Later on, we revolted against it, reducing the frequency of this chore to once daily, after breakfast. When it was time for our long bathroom turn, some of us would have time to take showers. At 4:00 PM we would have our tea, which we kept warm from lunchtime in a covered kettle. Then some people would watch TV, while the middle of the room would be kept free for people who wanted to walk. When possible, we tried to vary our routine life with fun and entertainment at night, which we called *carevan-e shadi* (something like a happy hour). The form and content varied depending on the general prison conditions, but *carevan-e shadi* could include singing, dancing, telling jokes and funny stories, staging a short play, imitating mullahs, and reading poetry.

Room members in periodic general meetings decided all room policies if conditions allowed such meetings to take place; otherwise, the elected people in charge of activities decided them. The *mass'oul-e otagh* (room representative), elected in the room-wide meeting, was in charge of contacting the guards on behalf of the room, conducting the meetings, keeping a waiting list for the prison clinic, and keeping the room funds, and he had the internal control of the TV set. Every two to four weeks, we had a room-wide meeting where all new suggestions and concerns were raised, discussed, and resolved. Every three months or so, new elections were held for the people in charge of activities.

The most important issue for prisoners in detention in any community was to decide if they were interested in living as a *komon* (commune), living independently of each other, or some form of community in between. There were periods when any sign of communal living was suppressed and punished by the authorities in the Tehran prisons. Gradually, after 1984, with the changes in prison management and policies, prisoners were allowed to choose their own way of living in their rooms or wards—within the restrictions imposed by prison authorities, of course. Politically, certain prisoners and groups did not accept communal living arrangements with certain other groups. At times, this caused serious problems in the quality of life in the cells, rooms, or wards in different prisons. In Room 64 at this time, the prisoners had agreed on a form of communal living. Every other week after the family visit, everyone who had received money would put as much as they wanted or could afford in a communal box. Those who had had no visits and received no money were not expected to contribute. These communal funds were used for public expenses. Everyone in the room had equal access to and equal share of the communal materials and goods. People who were left with extra money in their pockets could spend it on anything they wanted. Usually they would spend it on dental care needs or for eyeglasses (if these things were available). Spending money on food for personal consumption was not considered an ethical practice, though there was some disagreement on this issue. Some saw no objection to buying and consuming extra food personally. Others, though they had funds, too, never used them for this purpose and objected to anyone doing so.

3

Jamshid Sepahvand, the other member of the Fadaiyan Sixteenth of Azar in Room 64, though only twenty-eight years old, was an experienced political prisoner. He had been arrested in an earlier, smaller raid on our organization, in October 1983. In the days leading up to his arrest, security fears had prompted Jamshid and his wife to evacuate their home and temporarily move into the home of an organizational sympathizer. Just two days later, police discovered the sympathizer's address. Jamshid and his wife, together with their hosts, were taken to Evin prison.

The intelligence section of the Revolutionary Guards had discovered the secret *dabirkhaneh* (central secretariat) of our organization and had put everyone associated with it under surveillance. That was how they got to the house where Jamshid was staying, because the owner was a courier in the *dabirkhaneh*. The agents also found the home of one of the leaders of our organization, Behrooz Soleymani, who was in charge of the *dabirkhaneh*. The security agents were very close to completing their surveillance work, which would have enabled them to discover and dismantle our whole organization at that time. But apparently something else was happening independent of and parallel to their activities. In those days, a known *tavvab* prisoner would help the Evin authorities hunt for activists by riding along in a patrol car roaming the streets of Tehran. By pure chance, this *tavvab* prisoner recognized Hebatollah Moini (a.k.a. Homayoun), one of our organizational leaders, getting into his car at an intersection. Homayoun was arrested and taken to Evin prison. This random arrest of Homayoun by the Evin security agents apparently interfered with the master plan of the Revolutionary Guards' intelligence section. It seems that Evin (or rather, Lajavardi) prevailed and took control of Homayoun and the intelligence gathered by the Revolutionary Guards relating to our organization. Security agents from

Evin then attacked the *dabirkhaneh* and all the homes and facilities identified by the Revolutionary Guards' surveillance work. Twelve people, besides Homayoun, got arrested in that sweep, which was minor compared to what could have happened if Homayoun had not been spotted.

When police went to the home of Behrooz Soleymani, he was sitting down with his wife and children, not knowing what was unfolding outside. He lived on the fifth floor of an apartment complex. When there was a knock on the door, he opened it, and as soon as he came face to face with suspicious characters, he turned around, ran, and jumped out of the window onto the street five stories below. He martyred himself because he knew what would happen if he were taken alive. He had seen leaders of other organizations who had been forced to give interviews on public TV, condemning everything and everyone, and implicating themselves and others in a variety of criminal activities, including, but not limited to, spying, having inappropriate sexual relationship, illegal drug use, and even murder. He had decided he was not going to allow himself to be in that situation if he had a chance to prevent it. He also knew very well that because of his involvement in the postrevolution Kordestan conflicts, the authorities would do everything possible to destroy him, and therefore he had decided not to allow them that pleasure.

Apart from Homayoun, the police initially did not succeed in arresting any of the members of our leadership. Behrooz committed suicide and the rest escaped arrest. Despite the loss of two outstanding leaders, the organization survived. The leadership waited for two days and then Mehrdad Pakzad, the man in charge of the security of our organization, decided to go to Homayoun's home to see if his wife needed any help. That was a mistake that cost Mehrdad his life. Homayoun's wife had already left the property as soon as she figured out that Homayoun might have been arrested, but the police were waiting around the house for someone to show up. When Mehrdad arrived, he was arrested and taken to Evin. He was interrogated and tortured brutally in Evin and finally was executed in 1985.

When Jamshid was arrested and brought to Evin prison, he told the interrogators that he was just visiting his friend and knew nothing. But during the interrogations of others arrested in connection with the *dabirkhaneh*, it became clear to the interrogators that he was indeed the person they had been looking for: the internal manager of the *dabirkhaneh*. They put him under severe pressure. They tortured him with the *kubl* (flogging cable) and even brought Homayoun to him on a stretcher with his feet wrapped and bleeding. They took the blindfold off of Jamshid so that he would be able to see Homayoun. Then they told Homayoun to talk to Jamshid. Homayoun, according to Jamshid, stated very painfully but calmly, "Jamshid *jan* (dear Jamshid), there have been some arrests. You should act within the provisions of the organization for these situations, nothing more and nothing less." According to Jamshid, the interrogators threw Homayoun on the ground and started kicking and punching him.

Jamshid was transferred to Amoozeshgah after a year or so. He had been to the Islamic tribunal twice, once when he was in Ward 209 and once more from Room 64. He was awaiting sentence. Everyone liked and respected Jamshid. He was strong, patient, intelligent, athletic, and funny. He was relatively young, but he was a two-regime political prisoner with a great deal of experience.

4

A few days after my arrival in Room 64, two new prisoners entered the room. They were in the same shape as I had been on my arrival day. "Ali," thirty years old, was a really funny, talkative guy with an Esfahani regional accent—he was from Najaf-abad in Esfahan (Isfahan) province. His friend Mohammad-Ali Bigdeli, about thirty-five years old, was from the nomadic tribes in the Kohkilouye and Boyer-Ahmad region and was rather a serious person. Both belonged to our organization and had been arrested in October 1984. As happened with me, their faces were shaved, and gradually they got acquainted with everyone.

There were now five of us from our organization in the room. Next bathroom round, we all got together, joked, and laughed. Jamshid contacted Rooms 62 and 63 to inform them of the new arrivals, and in turn he received information about a few from our group arriving in other rooms as well. Ali, who constantly told funny stories and jokes in his charming accent, told us a story about Mullah Nasreddin, the satirical Sufi mystical figure. We laughed so loud and hard that the guard opened the bathroom door to see what was going on. At night Ali and Bigdeli slept by the door. We laughed for an hour in our beds before falling asleep. Times had really changed for us newcomers, from the miserable loneliness of solitary to the pleasure of being with our comrades. Even in the horrible Islamic Republic prison system, where brutality reigned, life could still be celebrated.

Ali soon told us more about himself. He explained that during his school years in rural Esfahan he had to spend some of his time herding goats and sheep. His skin was rough and tanned from exposure to the central Iranian sun and heat. He had gotten married in Tehran in 1983. A top cadre of the organization had been assigned to live in their home temporarily. The cadre, whom Ali knew only as Samad, got arrested on October 17, 1984, while Ali and his wife were arrested in their home on the eighteenth. His wife was pregnant and gave birth to their son, "Cyrus," in custody. She was released after a few months. Ali said he was in solitary in the Komiteh, lonely and sad, when one day the interrogator brought his newborn son for him to see. He was allowed to keep the baby for a little while. He joked of the baby, "At first sight, I knew he was a *mokh* (had the brains)."

Bigdeli was also married and had a family. He told me that he had joined the organization only a couple of years ago. Apparently, he had been one of the top cadres of a group called Razmandegan (Organization of Fighters for the Freedom of Iranian Working Class). After the group was dissolved in 1981, he joined our organization. He said his political-prisoner experience of the past had helped him to maneuver easily through the interrogations this time around, especially through the early and critical period, when he avoided any serious physical torture. Bigdeli had very high morale, was experienced, and had a very strong character. He was self-disciplined, and he exercised for half an hour in the corner of the room every day. His exercise routine was very light, but sound and balanced, like his personality.

5

One of the most important Islamic holidays, and a rare happy one, Eid-e Fetr signals the end of the hardships of fasting during Ramadan and a return to normalcy. Eating, drinking, and many other activities become normal again. This particular Ramadan, the first for me and many others in prison, finally ended, and we were excited just as if we were kids again, but this time around it was for a different reason. This time, we were happy because we finally could eat during the day without fear of punishment, and especially because we could eat warm food for lunch again.

The day of Eid-e Fetr, we were just enjoying ourselves in the room when an announcement over the prison sound system ordered us all to be ready to go to the *hosseiniye*. Around three o'clock, room by room, the guards took us out. When we entered the *hosseiniye*, we were ordered to take our blindfolds off. The amphitheater was already about three quarters full. Its walls had been decorated for the occasion. *Tavvab* prisoners had already been seated in the front portion, from the stage up to the middle. Women prisoners covered in black *chadors* (shapeless cloaks) were seated on the right-hand side. Prisoners from Salones 1 and 3 were seated in row after row in the back. Behind us, there were some of the most extreme *tavvab* prisoners and some guards standing watch. Overall, there were at least twice as many men prisoners as women prisoners. The seating arrangement was quite calculated. The front portion included people who were going to do the main cheering and chanting. The authorities needed them there for propaganda purposes because the program was going to be filmed and televised. The middle portion included those who were going to cheer and chant, but not enthusiastically or voluntarily. They were the so-called tactical *tavvab* and passive prisoners. The last portion, our group of so-called *sar-e moze'i* (combatant) prisoners, had been brought there to create a larger crowd and to fill the amphitheater for filming. The authorities knew very well that we were going to stay silent. The TV cameras were set up at angles that would make it look like all the prisoners present were participating in the Evin celebration of Eid-e Fetr.

Mansour and Mehran were sitting on my right side and Ali and Jamshid on my left. While we were waiting, I asked Mansour about his experiences of the *hosseiniye* events of the terrible years of 1981 to 1984. He gave a long description.

> Lajavardi himself or a guy named Madjid Ghoddoosi were the masters of ceremony in those days. They organized and conducted the show. They set up coerced confession and recantation interviews almost daily, where prisoners already broken by torture and long solitary would repent and recant their beliefs and actions. Or, they arranged

"discussion groups," which Lajavardi or Ghoddoosi and some prisoners took part in, where the goal was to discredit the opposition and to show how morally corrupt the opposition leaders were, particularly on matters of sex and sexual relationships. These were staged shows aimed at breaking down the morale of the prisoner population. In these gatherings, *tavvab* prisoners abused the non-*tavvab* prisoners verbally and physically, under the protection of the guards.

Lajavardi had a gang of very dangerous hardcore *tavvab* prisoners that he took along with him everywhere. These were people who had become *tavvab*, and then to protect their lives they had decided to go all the way and do anything the regime demanded. Lajavardi had an ideal goal: converting every prisoner into a genuine *tavvab*. He had said on many occasions that Evin was a place where people automatically started entertaining *tobeh* (repentance) as soon as they turned the road entering the compound. He had even named that turn Piche Tobeh (Repentance Turn). He also used to say that becoming a *tavvab* was a long process. Anyone claiming to have become a *tavvab* had to repent first, then show his sincerity by collaborating with other *tavvab* prisoners and prison authorities. The way to prove that one was a true *tavvab* was not only by revealing information and intelligence about his own activities but by spying on non-*tavvab* prisoners and particularly by exposing the tactical *tavvab* and the so-called *monafeghin* (hypocrites), who Lajavardi and other authorities believed were more dangerous to the Islamic system than the non-*tavvab* Mojahedin and Marxist prisoners. That was why *tavvab* prisoners competed in exposing each other, and particularly exposing the newly declared *tavvab* prisoners. On the surface, it was about completing the process of becoming a true *tavvab* as Lajavardi had described, but in reality it was all about gaining the trust of and getting closer to Lajavardi and the system.

These programs were common events in Evin prison in those days. Sometimes they took place every day, and some days for many

> hours. At the end of a session, Lajavardi would issue a verdict indicating if he was satisfied with the repentance of a particular prisoner or not. If he did not accept the repentance, he would advise the prisoner to go back and work harder on his path to "salvation" and return later with a "true repentance." The expression he would use was "you still need to shake yourself more, to rid yourself of the impurities of your soul."

Finally, it was announced that the program was about to start. On this particular day in the *hosseiniye*, the program started with an introduction, and then the MC, who was a *tavvab* prisoner, announced that they had prepared a few songs and poetry recitations for us and then there would be a play called "The Democratic Clinic." The poetry recitations and the group song performances were all about repentance, faith, martyrdom, and praise of Islam and Khomeini's leadership. The play was supposed to be a comedy, in which a variety of animals portrayed different political organizations of the opposition, and they were all supposed to have come together in a democratic clinic. It turned out to be so bad and so not funny that even the authorities and *tavvab* prisoners watching started yawning after a while. We had no choice but to endure it in silence. But afterward, it was a source of jokes and laughter for us for a long while in our rooms.

A Dream

Thought of you
Lighted a red and a white candle
    (one for struggle, one for hope and peace)
Looked at your picture
Turned off the light
And there you were

I was there too
In "prison"
Visiting you
I touched you
And talked to you
About all the things
That have been locked up inside me
In the years of separation

It was so easy
Being there with you
I felt so secure
Talking to you
Although you were behind bars

You hugged your daughter
We hugged each other
And then visiting time was over
The dream was over
But the candles kept on burning.

—Ketty Mobed
Offenbach, West Germany
November 1986

6

The Salone 3 family-visit day was every other Sunday. Prisoners prepared for it by shaving and cleaning themselves up on Saturday. My friends and I, the newcomers, did not have visits yet in Evin. But, still, it was an important and exciting day in the room. Prisoners wore their best clothing and were in a lively mood. People brought news of the outside world or news concerning the prison when they returned from their visits. About 60 to 70 percent of prisoners at any given time would have visits. Some in prison had occasional visits, and there were a few who never had a visit, mostly because either they had no relatives or their relatives were unwilling or unable to come to visit them. But in general, visiting day was the happiest day in prison. Everyone was somehow involved in the activities and the excitement. Of course, it was always tougher for those who had no visits.

In Room 64, we continuously organized different classes. Mostly, these classes were for learning languages; occasionally they were on other subjects of interest. By popular demand, I set up two discussion classes on genetics and evolution. Because prisoners were not allowed books or writing materials, classes were held with difficulty, using very limited resources. At different periods in prison, I taught and discussed genetics and evolution either on a one-to-one basis or in small group sessions with prisoners of different political and organizational affiliations. These classes had to be secret in some periods but could be held openly in others. Teaching evolution in the Islamic prison system was particularly dangerous because it could have been interpreted as engaging in activity contrary to the regime's Islamic beliefs.

We tried to fill our free time with quality activities, within prison limitations, so as not to waste a minute. But the majority of our time was still spent on what we called "walk-and-talk," which took place among prisoners nonstop. In Room 64, I had walk-and-talk regularly with Jamshid and Ali and occasionally with other prisoners. Jamshid and I talked about the political line of our organization, his experiences of the previous regime's prisons, and our family lives. Ali and I were mainly focused on the police raids on our organization in 1984. We wanted to figure out the details of the raids and, if possible, how and where they had started.

7

On July 4, 1985, around eight thirty in the morning, I was called out to the *zir-e hasht* and then loaded on a minibus along with a group of waiting prisoners. I was dropped off in front of the central office building and then taken to the third floor. Around three in the afternoon, a guard led me to the end of the hallway and into a room. He sat me on a chair and took my blindfold off. It took my eyes a couple of minutes to get used to the lighting. We were in a large room. Across from me, a mullah was sitting behind a desk. The mullah wore a white *ammameh* (turban) and had a reddish beard. He was fairly thin and young, maybe in his mid to late thirties. There were folders, files, papers and pens, and a recording device on the desk. I had been told not to turn or look around, but from the noise behind me, I figured there was at least one other person, maybe Haji Mahmood, my lead interrogator, in the back of the room.

The mullah started by reciting some religious texts and then said he was going to read the charges brought against me and I should respond to them at the end. It seemed that this was to be my trial. There were no witnesses, I had no defense lawyer, and there was no jury present. There was only the mullah, who was the judge (*hakem-e shar'*). He read the charges:

"Mr. Yaghoobi, you are charged with . . .

"One: involvement in secretly organized illegal activity to overthrow the Islamic regime.

"Two: membership in the infidel, illegal, and militant organization of Fadaiyan.

"Three: holding the top position of being in charge of the youth branch of the organization.

"Four: holding an editorial position in the youth branch organ, the 'Student Struggle.'

"Five: activity under a pseudonym.

"Six: collecting and contributing financial support and membership dues for the organization.

"Seven: corrupting Muslim youth by subversive ideological and political teachings.

"Eight: activism against the policies of Imam Khomeini regarding the Iraqi-Imposed War against the Islamic Republic and spreading propaganda for the so-called peace policy.

"Nine: withholding intelligence and information, not collaborating, and not repenting."

Then he announced that the maximum punishment had been requested for me for the charges, and he asked if I wanted to respond. I accepted some of the charges, gave clarifications or explanations for a few, and rejected others. He took some notes from my responses. He became very upset over my response to the war-and-peace issue when I told him that we had supported the war as long as it was about defending our nation but that after Iran recaptured most of our Iraqi-invaded lands we should have made a policy change and negotiated a just settlement through the UN. I admitted that I had worked against the regime's war policy because the war had destroyed both countries' infrastructures and the lives of almost a million people. I said I was proud to have worked for peace and against the war. This discussion, an uncommon occurrence in the Islamic tribunals, made the proceedings last about half an hour, four to five times longer than usual. At the end, the mullah gave me a short pep talk advising me to express remorse. Then he asked if I had any requests for the court. I replied that I did not.

My roommates gathered around me upon my return to Room 64, and I described the whole event. I had not yet been sentenced, but in my roommates' various opinions the outlook ranged from my immediate release to my being in serious danger. That was a true reflection of sentencing in the Islamic tribunals, because there seemed to be no logic or rule guiding the decisions. People with very similar charges had been given very different sentences, people with lesser charges being given heavier sentences and vice versa, and many innocent people had been killed over the years in this system. Sentencing depended on the judge, the politics of the day, the interrogators' opinions, the prisoner's behavior during the interrogations and in the court, and many other factors. It was a wry joke among prisoners in Evin that the Islamic judge had a bag full of sentencing balls, and he pulled out one at random for every prisoner, just like a lottery. Of course, that was an exaggeration. The tendency was more toward harsher punishment than leniency.

In "normal" times in the Islamic Republic, the presiding Islamic judge was the prosecutor, judge, and jury. After secret court proceedings (Islamic tribunals) lasting from a few minutes to half an hour, the Islamic judge decided the fate of a prisoner based on the file that the interrogators provided him (all admissions obtained via coercion and torture), plus his own questioning of the prisoner. In many cases, the prisoner sat on a chair facing the judge, while the interrogator stood behind him in case the judge needed his assistance. In times of so-called national security emergency, prisoners who had already been sentenced could get sentenced again to harsher terms and even to death, based on new questioning by the original judge or other judges. There was no guarantee of the sentence you received in your original court proceeding. Normally all prison sentences, except for life imprisonment and the death sentence, were decided by the presiding judge. In those two cases, decisions were sent to the Supreme Council of the Judiciary. The council reviewed those files and either approved the decisions or referred them to another judge for a second opinion. So these cases would take a bit longer to get final approval. But in times of conspiracy to eliminate prisoners (like in 1981), even this limited judicial process was bypassed by a fatwa (religious edict) from the supreme leader, and the presiding judge or a commission decided the fates of prisoners in summary questionings.

From the day that, in the aftermath of the victory of the revolution in 1979, Khomeini set up Dadgah-haye Englab-e Eslami (Islamic Revolution tribunals) to punish the leaders and agents of the old regime, summary justice became the norm. Executions of those "spreading corruption on earth" and corporal punishments like flogging became daily events in those early months. Soon "counterrevolutionaries" were added to the list of those the regime wanted to punish. But everything changed in the prisons in the aftermath of the June 1981 conflicts with the Mojahedin. The reign of terror changed the nature of detentions, interrogations, torture,[10] and trials. Many thousands were tortured and killed by summary execution.

The Islamic Republic prison system was an ideological one where for detainees, from the first moment until the last, there was no break in torture and life-threatening dangers. In contrast to the prison system of the shah's time, where the main interrogation and torture was carried out by SAVAK (secret police) agents during the first few months after arrest, in the Islamic Republic a prisoner might be tortured at any time until he was released or was executed. Prisoners who had served time under both regimes always said that a day in the Islamic prison was like a year or more in the shah's prison.

8

The first visit I was allowed during my time in Room 64 was in the middle of August, about three months after I arrived in Evin, when my younger sister came to visit me. When I got to the *zir-e hasht*, the guards brought my personal belongings they had kept, including a pair of shoes, a belt, and a couple of other things, to deliver to my family. They put these in a plastic bag behind the window ahead of the visit. When my sister walked in and saw a plastic bag in the stall, her face became pale like she had seen a ghost. I quickly got her attention and assured her that there was nothing to worry about. Anyway, she cried a bit and then we laughed, joked, and talked. That was the only time I saw my younger sister while I was in prison, because she would leave later with her family to live in the United States.

Once a month, we were also allowed to write to our families, on an official form. In Evin, this letter-writing form had seven empty lines for writing on one side and seven lines for the reply on the other side. On letter-writing day, we were allowed only two hours for the event. Some people were fast writers and others were very slow. We had to get organized so that everyone could finish his letter within the two hours' time. Some would prepare the content of their letter in their mind or even on a piece of paper, when possible, days ahead of time, but they still had a hard time finalizing their message.

Sometimes, the authorities would accept photos that visitors brought of prisoners' children. Those photos gave a real sense of life to the prison rooms. Our room had prepared a nice board that featured a collage of photos of children of many sorts, except girls older than eight. Girls had to wear *hejab* (veil) when they turned nine, and according to prison rules it was un-Islamic to have their photos posted in public view. This limitation notwithstanding, any prisoner who received a photo might add it to the collage. When I received photos of my daughter later on, I added one to the display. That was the usual practice: if a prisoner had more than one photo of his children, he would leave one for the room. Thus, that collage not only was very lovely and lively but also represented a history of the room. There were photos of children up there whose fathers had been released or transferred, as well as photos of babies whose fathers had been executed.

September brought new prisoners to the Salone and to our room as well. "Dara" and Mohammad-Ali Mohebbi-pour from our organization and "Navid" from the Fadaiyan Majority arrived in our room. Dara had been arrested in October in the sweep that had resulted in my capture as well. He had been connected to Hossein Sadrai in Tehran. They were part of our organization's *grouh-e e'zam* (relocation group), which was responsible for getting the leadership cadres and other members of the organization out of Iran to safety. Mohebbi-pour was a sympathizer of the organization, who had been arrested this February along with some others. When the agents had come to arrest him, he had swallowed a homemade cyanide capsule. They saved him, but his attempted suicide was added to his charges. He was older than the average prisoner and had some disabilities and health problems—he not only suffered from a heart problem but had episodes of unbearable migraine headaches and back and leg pains as well. Nonetheless, he was very strong in his beliefs, and his loyalty to the organization was unshakeable.

Navid, from the Fadaiyan Majority, had been arrested after returning from a trip abroad to meet with his leadership. Before he left, security agents had recorded all of his phone conversations with his leadership. Apparently, the police knew the purpose of his trip and they had decided to let him go, hoping he would return with new and useful intelligence about the organization. He did indeed return and was arrested and tortured for intelligence, particularly about any new contacts that he might have set up abroad. They also wanted ten thousand dollars from him. Apparently, in his phone conversations prior to his travel, he had discussed changing money into US dollars to take abroad, and that was where the money issue came from. Navid had previously served a year and a half in the shah's prisons.

In late September, another new prisoner, Samad Taheri-Eslami, came to our room. Samad and I immediately became very close friends because we were both from Tabriz in Azarbaijan, and spoke Azari. He was a top cadre of the Fadaiyan Majority and apparently had been in charge of their Azarbaijan branch for a while. The organization had transferred him to Tehran because of safety issues following the 1982 arrests of the leadership of the Tudeh Party, their partner in the unification process. In Tehran, he said, he was connected to "Khossro," one of the leaders and central committee members of the Fadaiyan Majority, until his arrest in February 1984. This was part of a strike by the Ministry of Intelligence that resulted in many arrests, including that of Dr. Anooshirvan Lotfi, a central committee member, and Samad Taheri-Eslami, who apparently also was a central committee member. Samad Taheri-Eslami believed that the arrests of different people in this particular strike were not related, but I am not sure he was right. In his interrogation, he had found out that police had even recorded his phone conversations with Khossro, which meant that security agents had reached the top of their organization.

9

After "Hashem," who was in charge of the room, was transferred to Salone 1, Jamshid Sepahvand became room representative (*mass'oul-e otagh*). He, Ali, and I were very close and had a few very good months together in the room, which ended in the middle of September. On a Thursday morning, Jamshid was called out. He had already been to court twice and was waiting for a sentence, which normally was not delivered in the mornings. We were all anxious about why he had been called in the morning. He returned late in the afternoon and described his ordeal.

> They took a group of us to the office of the prosecutor. Soon, they started calling names and taking people one by one inside the office. They were all people I knew from the previous regime's prisons, and all belonged to the larger family of the Fadai organizations, except for one Mojahedin prisoner. Some names that I remember were Dr. Anooshirvan Lotfi, Alireza Akbari, Reza Ghabrai, Razi Taban, Habib Soroosh, and a few others.
>
> Then it was my turn to go in. There was a desk with someone sitting behind it. I was seated on a chair facing him and they removed my blindfold. He said he was Ali Razini, the prosecutor of Tehran. He then looked at my file and asked if I was married or single. I said I was married. He continued by saying that he had been given full authority by the judiciary system to decide my fate. He said he had reviewed my file and the details of both previous court proceedings, and if I did not repent and become a *tavvab*, he would have no choice but to agree with the previous two rulings. Therefore, he said, he wanted to ask me for the last time whether or not I would be willing to participate in a televised interview to denounce my political and ideological views and activities and condemn all antirevolutionary groups and organizations.

I stayed silent for a minute or so and then I said I was not in prison because of my opposition to Islam, but rather I was in prison because I was a political opponent of the regime. I added that I had done nothing to be apologetic about. I said I would not do any interviews and I would not condemn any other person or organization, let alone myself.

He shook his head at my response and asked me to request an in-person visit with my family for Sunday. I said I would never make such a request from the authorities. He said he would do it for me. Then he shook his head again and asked why, if I wanted to take this path, I married and ruined another life as well. I did not honor his comment with any response. At the end, he said that if I walked out without repenting, no one would ask me again. I stayed silent. He sent me out of his office.

We were all stunned. Obviously, they had decided to kill many of the veteran members of the Fadai organizations. From Thursday afternoon till Sunday morning it felt like a lifetime, both for him and for us. Outwardly the mood in the room seemed normal, but every one of us was having an internal struggle. We all tried to pretend that there was still hope and that no one should consider the worst-case scenario. We all tried to give hope to Jamshid. Some even told him that Razini, once in a while, would say stupid things to people and should not be taken seriously. One person held the view that the regime was trying to pressure well-known prisoners, to milk as much as it could out of them, before giving them prison sentences.

This was my first experience in a situation like this. I was very close to Jamshid, and we spent most of what would be the last couple of days of his life together. I was intimately aware of all the emotional and psychological stages that he was going through. The predicament he had been put in was exerting tremendous pressure on him, and I could sense the struggle to reach a resolution and to be at peace with his decision waging inside him. Physically, he was busy doing routine things in the room with us, but mentally, he was tackling this critical life-or-death decision. He lived with this internal conflict for about thirty-six hours after returning to the room. You could see it from his physical appearance and his demeanor. It was early Saturday morning when I found him like his old, normal self: very upbeat, lively, and calm. He had apparently resolved his internal struggle and was at peace again. He really transcended to eternity from that moment on. In the final twenty-four hours, he was very happy, funny, and peaceful and actively enjoying life. He even played soccer with us in the yard. The only thing he asked of us was to arrange another volunteer to be in charge of the room. Samad Taheri-Eslami took that responsibility.

The last hours of Saturday, we pretended that things were normal and acted like nothing bad was going to happen. Therefore we did not arrange any good-bye ceremony. Jamshid got shaved, as we all did, and we prepared for Sunday's family visits. The visits started like always. The first Salone-wide group, including a few from our room, was called, and they went out. Jamshid was called in the second group. Each group would usually take an hour or a little bit longer. Other groups would follow, and previous groups would return later. When noon arrived, Jamshid had not come back yet. The first four groups returned, and their reports indicated that they had seen Jamshid and that his family was among the visiting families. The final news was that Jamshid had been given a private visit with his wife or with all of his family members.

It was lunchtime when our room was sent to *havakhori*. Only "Moharram," who was sick that day, stayed in the room. We were in the yard for twenty minutes, and when we returned we found Moharram in a very disturbed and distressed emotional condition. He explained that two minutes after our departure, some special-unit guards had entered the room, demanding all of Jamshid's belongings. Moharram had said that he was new in the room and did not know where and what Jamshid's stuff was. One of the guards had gone out and had returned with Jamshid. Jamshid had started collecting his stuff, and in the end he took one bag plus his sleeping gear. Moharram said that while they were hugging good-bye, Jamshid had whispered in his ear that if he stayed alive he would send for the other bag that he was leaving behind on purpose, and if he was gone for good, then we should keep it in the room as a reminder of him.

We were all shocked and saddened. We sat around the room and put our heads on our knees. Suddenly "Davar" wept loudly, which caused everyone else to cry and weep as well. For a few short minutes we all lost control of our emotions. I think we were all really upset that we had been deprived of the right to say good-bye to him for the last time. Jamshid never requested his second bag, and we later found out that the following morning, September 20, he had been executed along with some of his comrades from the larger family of the Fadai organizations, plus one Mojahedin prisoner.

There was a time all of us, including Jamshid himself, thought that he might get a maximum of a ten-year sentence, based on what others related to his case had gotten. But that was expecting predictability from the unpredictable judiciary system of the Islamic Republic.

10

After the fall of Lajavardi and his gang from control of the Tehran prisons, a mild change took place in the prison system that had both positive and negative consequences. New officials in charge of the Evin prosecutor's office made new decisions about prison policies and prisoners during 1985. One of these changes was the speedy review of files of prisoners who had been in solitary in Evin and the Komiteh for a long time without a court hearing or sentencing. Some of these prisoners were transferred to public wards; others were executed. On the other end of the spectrum, *tavvab* prisoners had enjoyed the protection of Lajavardi, who had delayed any decision on their fates in exchange for their total collaboration in repressing the combatant prison population. Lajavardi had been like a father to these broken beings. Most of the hardcore *tavvab* prisoners had heavy files, which would have guaranteed their early executions, but Lajavardi had temporarily delayed final judgment on them, keeping them in purgatory to exploit their last drop of vitality. When Lajavardi was sacked, the new rulers activated their files and soon many hardcore *tavvab* prisoners who had loyally served the system were sent to the gallows. That, for all practical purposes, ended the *tavvab* phenomenon in the Tehran prisons. This doesn't mean that the regime did not continue exploiting the remaining *tavvab* prisoners, in Tehran and especially in the provincial prisons, for a while longer, but the back of the *tavvab* movement was permanently broken.

Prison authorities started transferring some of the leadership cadres of different opposition groups from solitary into rooms in Salones 3 and 1. Homayoun was brought to Room 66 in Salone 3. We were able to communicate with him a bit using sign language and lipreading during bathroom rounds.

We also got a new prisoner, named Alireza Tashayyod, in our room. He was thin, pale, and disoriented when he arrived, and his fingers and toes were all deformed. He was a top cadre of Rah-e Kargar. After he rested a bit, we gathered around him and he told us about his prison ordeal.

I was arrested in March 1982 and have been under interrogation, torture, and in solitary since then, for more than three years. I was kept in solitary cells of Ward 209 and Assayeshgah. Because of my religious background and change of ideology in the shah's prison, religious zealots always had and still do have a particular hatred for people like me. Lajavardi himself, who knew me from the shah's prisons, and his gang interrogated and tortured me extensively and brutally. The first half of the year, they interrogated me for organizational intelligence. The second half of the year, they added political interrogations to it. Then, after a year, ideological pressures started as well.

In my first court proceeding, they demanded that I repent, denounce my organization, and announce my return to Islam. Then, they kept me in solitary for another whole year. With ideological discussions they continued exerting more pressure on me. Prolonged solitary and psychological pressures deteriorated my health, first physically then mentally. I thought I was losing my mind. Finally, after two years, they transferred me to a cell with another prisoner. My mental health started improving a bit. I spent another year and a half in different cells, the last year of it in Assayeshgah. I am waiting for a second court proceeding or for a sentence.

With Alireza in the room, things changed a bit for Ali and me. For personal and political reasons, the three of us became very close friends and spent most of our time together. We asked Alireza if he remembered a Rah-e Kargar central committee member who had joined our organization prior to his arrest. When Ali described Samad to Alireza, Alireza said Samad had to be his best friend from the shah's prison era. Samad, one of the three leaders of our organization in Tehran, who had lived with Ali and his family for a while prior to the October arrests, had told Ali that he had joined our organization from Rah-e Kargar. Now Alireza for the first time identified Samad for us. When we revealed that Samad had been arrested, Alireza was truly saddened, because from his own experience he could imagine what his good, old friend was going through in the hands of the torturers. But at the same time he was happy to know that his friend was still alive.

Then "Hamid" arrived in our room. He was one of the nicest people I ever met in prison. He too was with the Rah-e Kargar organization. Both Hamid and his wife were factory workers, and they had been arrested together. After early interrogations in 1982 in Evin, both had been given two-year prison sentences. Hamid was transferred to Ghezelhessar (a.k.a. Ghezel) prison in early 1983 and experienced the Haji Davoud Rahmani[11] oppression period there. As was common in those days, hooded *tavvab* prisoners were sent to the wards by Rahmani to identify combatant prisoners and to report on their activities outside or even inside prison. These *tavvab* prisoners were known as the "KKK" because of their hooded appearance. Hamid was identified by them in early 1984 and was transferred back to Evin for more interrogation. He was given a new eight-year sentence and was transferred back to Ghezelhessar prison in late 1984. In the summer of 1985, he was brought back to Evin for still more interrogation and spent three more months in solitary, and then he was brought to Room 64.

With Hamid in the room, Alireza found the Rah-e Kargar connection and association he really needed. Hamid updated all of us about the situation in Ghezelhessar including its new management, its *tavvab* prisoners, its policy changes, and its problems. While in Evin, he had also been given a visit with his wife and had found out that she might be released soon. They had two children who were being raised by their families. His wife was released while he was in our room, and one time when Hamid went for a family visit, he found his wife on the other side of the glass.

A few days later, a Kurdish member of our organization named

Esmail Hosseini arrived in the room. Esmail was about thirty to thirty-five years old and had been an activist for the Fadai organization in the city of Sanandaj in Kordestan province during the time of the revolution. He had participated in the armed conflicts between the Fadai militia forces and the Revolutionary Guards in the city for control of the region. When the leadership of the Fadaiyan Majority adopted a political line leaning toward peaceful resolution of the conflict with the Islamic regime, he, along with many other known Kurdish members of the Fadaiyan Majority, was transferred to Tehran for security reasons. In the 1981 split, he sided with our organization, the Fadaiyan Sixteenth of Azar, against the policy of unification with the Tudeh Party.

The executive committee of the organization in Tehran in the summer of 1984 apparently reorganized the Grouh-e Vizhe—the secretive "security special unit" of the organization, previously known as "the Special Commission for Security"—and put Samad, a member of the executive committee, in charge of it. It was decided that only a small group of very qualified people would be recruited to the unit. Samad chose Mansoor Noor-Mohammad-zadeh to be its executive manager and Esmail to be the operational team leader. From the recovered documents or the information that the authorities extracted during the interrogations, it had become apparent that the unit had discussed not only robbing banks and the wealthy home of a capitalist but also eliminating an ex-member of the organization in Esfahan, who had apparently become a police collaborator in 1982 or 1983. Whether they had really acted on any of these proposals, as the authorities claimed, was not clear to any of us in prison, and of course the security circumstances in prison did not allow us to inquire about it either.

In addition, Esmail had been involved in preparing safe houses for people and for valuable resources of the organization, including guns, printing machines, and money. When he got arrested in October 1984, besides his involvement in the postrevolution Kordestan conflicts, which in the eyes of the authorities was more than enough to get him ten death sentences, he was also charged with organizing and leading the Grouh-e Vizhe. He was put under intolerable torture at the beginning, torture so unbearable that, he said, he admitted to most of the charges. He thought they were going to kill him at any moment in the Komiteh, and for a while he said he lost control. His morale and his health started improving after he came to Room 64.

With Esmail's arrival among us, and looking open-mindedly at the situation, we wondered why a member like him, or like Behrooz Soleymani, who jumped to his death when he was about to be arrested, should have remained in the country while many of the leaders had left. It was inexcusable that Esmail had fallen into the hands of the interrogators. Our organization had put him in a very compromising situation. We thought that members of this type should have been the first ones to be sent out of the country. But Esmail felt differently. He said that both he and Behrooz had disagreed with the idea of abandoning the struggle just because times were tough.

11

Some prisoners in our room had been to court and were waiting for their sentences, like me, while others remained in prison without a sentence or they had finished their sentences and were waiting to be released. Other rooms were in a similar situation. In contrast to the prison system of any democratic country, in the Islamic Republic a prisoner was not released after serving his full prison sentence unless he satisfied some extra conditions. One of the biggest changes as a result of the recent "reforms" was that the authorities softened the release requirements for these prisoners. Conditions of release varied depending on prosecutors, judges, political conditions, prisoners, and prisons.

In general, though, a prisoner who did not have a sentence because of lack of evidence was asked by the prosecutor or the judge to sign an *enzejar nameh* (self-defamation letter), in which the prisoner would denounce his views and also the views of any group opposing the Islamic regime. A prisoner who did not agree to sign such a form was kept in prison "until further notice" (UFN). Such a prisoner was taken to the prosecutor or the judge periodically and asked again to sign the *enzejar nameh*. Those who accepted the release conditions were freed; those who refused were kept in prison. Sometimes, these prisoners were asked to denounce themselves and others in a videotaped interview or in front of other prisoners.

For prisoners who had finished their sentences, release conditions in general included signing of an *enzejar nameh* or providing a videotaped interview, or both. In some periods, they were forced to interview in front of other prisoners before being released. If prisoners chose not to accept these conditions, they would be kept in prison and were known as the *mellikesh* (serving without sentence) prisoners. To get amnesty or a reduction of their prison term, prisoners had to perform one or more of these self-betrayals. In certain cases, the authorities exploited a prisoner's desire to be released early, forcing him to spy on certain other prisoners in the wards.

Under the Islamic regime, a political prisoner was never really free, even after serving a full prison term—or sometimes more than the full term—and being released. The regime wanted to control former prisoners as if they were still in custody. The guards always joked with us in prison, saying that if ever we got out, we would just walk into a larger prison. If a prisoner was to be released after satisfying all political and security release conditions, his family was required to put up a real-estate title as bail. This way the authorities tied the family to the actions of the released prisoner. Furthermore, they required that a family member sign a document establishing himself as human collateral for the release of his prisoner. In doing so, he was promising he would deliver the prisoner anytime the authorities wanted; if not, he would be held responsible and face consequences. Imagine how difficult it must be for any person to basically sign off his life to the regime, to ensure the release of a son, a daughter, a brother, or a sister. Depending on the political situation in the country and who was in charge in the office of the prosecutor, when a released prisoner did not show up at the request of the regime, in some cases these family members went to prison themselves. In such cases, the real-estate title posted as bail was also lost and the government often took ownership of these properties.

Daftar-e Azadi, Evin's release office, was officially supposed to take care of the administrative requirements for the release of prisoners. But this office had taken upon itself to do more than its official duty. The people in this office would basically interrogate prisoners who were there to be released, and in some cases they would return prisoners to the courtroom or to the prosecutor's office, recommending they be tried again or be kept longer in prison. In 1984 Haji Davoud Rahmani, after being removed from his post as head of Ghezelhessar prison due to pressure by Ayatollah Montazeri,[12] was installed as head of Evin's Daftar-e Azadi. When Ghezelhessar prisoner Heydar Zaghi, after serving close to six years for his original two-year sentence, finally arrived in Daftar-e Azadi to be released, he came face to face with Rahmani, who, upon recognizing him, immediately returned him to court for a new trial. Rahmani attached a note to Heydar's file claiming that while serving time in Ghezelhessar from 1981 to 1983, Heydar had actively advocated Marxism and had organized prisoners there. Heydar got a new, twelve-year sentence and was sent back to Ghezelhessar.

Then, in a sudden shift in late 1985, the authorities reduced the release conditions for prisoners who had served their full sentences to a written oath of political nonactivity or signing an *enzejar nameh*. Many prisoners accepted these new conditions. It became a regular event for prisoners to come to our room from other prisons in Tehran to be released.

For members of the UFN, however, the release conditions stayed tough. The prosecutor held the opinion that these prisoners were "dangerous" people and that they had to keep pressuring them until they retreated. Since the UFN prisoners never accepted the interview requirement, they remained in prison. Then, toward the end of the "reform" period, the authorities were forced to soften their position for members of the UFN, and for *mellikesh* prisoners in general, but most of these prisoners did not even agree to sign an *enzejar nameh* for their release, reasoning that they had never been charged or sentenced in any court and therefore there was no reason to accept any condition for their release from illegal arrest or continued detention.

12

One mid-November afternoon, Ali, Bigdeli, Yashar, Davar, "Omid," and Mehran from our room, and many people from other rooms, were called to the *zir-e hasht*. After an hour or so they returned, having gotten their sentences. It became loud and jubilant in our room. We were happy because some of them, like Mehran and Omid, had "dodged the bullet," and that of course called for celebration. They each had gotten a ten-year sentence. Davar had gotten eight years, Ali and Bigdeli six years each, and Yashar four years. That night, celebrations were organized in most rooms. It seemed ironic that we were in a celebratory mood because people had gotten long sentences for peaceful political activity; but under the Islamic regime, avoiding the death sentence at any stage called for real celebration. Although getting prison sentences did not guarantee the detainees' safety, at least they were off the hook in this round.

The following afternoon, prisoners with a sentence were called to the *zir-e hasht* again and they were told to be packed and ready for transfer the following morning. That night, none of us fell asleep until dawn. This was the first time I experienced separation from my comrades in prison, and I cannot express how sad and depressing it was. Separations in political prisons, particularly under the Islamic regime, were strange and hard. In political prison, where you faced life-threatening danger on a daily basis and where there was no guarantee you would see a friend alive the next day, an especially intense camaraderie was forged between prisoners. Trust, solidarity, camaraderie, and humanity were what the authorities could not take away from us, though they had tried hard during the Lajavardi/Rahmani era to achieve that. Also, your trusted friends were like your family members. The fellowship among us was the primary substitute for most of what we had been cut off from because of our imprisonment. In the morning, we said good-bye to our departing roommates in a very somber atmosphere. Everyone was depressed, whether leaving or staying behind. We were guessing that those leaving were being transferred to Ghezelhessar prison, because other groups in the last few months had all been transferred there. It took about a half hour for them to leave, and within moments a deathly silence took over the whole Salone.

On December 1, many more prisoners, including Dara and me, were called to the *zir-e hasht*. We were then called one by one to a desk in a corner. When I got there, I received a fifteen-year sentence. I signed the form but protested in its comment section. In my heart and mind I felt relieved that I had not gotten a death sentence or the more probable life sentence. But at the same time I knew that sentences did not matter much in this prison system. Uncertainty was the name of the game they played with us. I did not and could not think of times far ahead, such as my projected release. As long as I had survived the death sentence at this juncture I was relieved. I thought I would serve my fifteen years with honor, though I would miss my daughter growing up and I would miss my wife dearly.

As soon as I entered Room 64 and informed people that I had gotten fifteen years, they all jumped up and down in celebration. Dara had gotten six years. On December 2, many of us were called out and were informed that we would be leaving for another prison the next morning. Again, it was time for good-byes. We were leaving, and our friends were staying behind. We packed our bags and got ready. I was happy to think at least I would not be alone; Dara and I would be together in the next prison. I chatted with Esmail and wished him luck. I was hoping he would survive, though in my heart I knew that the regime would not let him live, and therefore I was really saying my last good-bye to him. He was pretty strong and kept his composure. To Mohebbi-pour, I said that I would see him soon after he got his sentence, and I asked him to take care of his health.

When we got to the *zir-e hasht* in the early morning, it was like a madhouse. Prisoners were sitting all around the large waiting area. Amoozeshgah authorities were busy deciding about people's personal belongings. They announced that identification documents like driver's licenses and birth certificates would be delivered to the authorities in the next prison, and other documents would be delivered to prisoners. They also ordered us not to take any prison blankets, plates, spoons, or cups; we paid no attention to this directive because we were not sure we would get any supplies in the prison we were going to. They had brought prisoners from all kinds of wards to form a mixed group. In fact that was the idea for transfers, to mix and match prisoners to form new groups, and to slip in some "antennas" (informants). Therefore, one had to be careful, at least in the early days, until things settled down in the new prison.

Around ten in the morning, they moved us out, and Dara and I got in one of the buses and sat together. We were still blindfolded. The bus driver did not interact with the prisoners at all—he left that to an armed guard from the special transfer unit, who yelled at the prisoners continuously and ordered us to keep our foreheads on the seat in front of us. When the buses began to move, however, we started looking around from under the blindfolds and through the openings in the curtains over the windows. When we exited Evin prison, the guard unexpectedly ordered us to take our blindfolds off and to pull the curtains open. Seeing the streets of Tehran with their normal bustle gave me a strange feeling. Some prisoners were seeing the outside life for the first time in two or three years. During this opportunity, we enjoyed watching the people in the streets and we looked for signs of change and hope. As soon as the buses turned toward the Karaj freeway, we knew that we were most likely heading to Ghezelhessar prison.

Part Three

THE “REFORM” ERA

Chapter Five

QUARANTINE

1

December 1985

After a fairly long drive, we got to Ghezelhessar prison. The guard ordered us to close the curtains and put our blindfolds back on. I noticed some prisoners did not act on this instruction, and the guard did not seem to mind. The prison compound was huge. It was secured behind walls, barbwire, towers, and armed guards. Ghezelhessar prison was composed of three units. Each unit had its own sectional warden, had its own main gate, and in reality operated as an independent prison. There was also a director for the whole prison, who operated from the central office in Unit 3. The buses finally entered this unit and stopped in front of that office. We were led into the lobby and ordered to sit on the floor and wait. The guards allowed us to use the bathrooms a few at a time. Then they gave each of us a piece of *lavash* bread and some feta cheese.

In the afternoon, they had us sit in the long corridor to fill out a form. This was our first written document in Ghezelhessar. Its first section had the usual set of personal questions, which we had named the "ear, nose, and throat" questions. A prisoner was asked these questions hundreds of times from his arrest until his journey ended one way or another. There was also a set of questions about your family members: if they had been arrested, if they had been executed, if they had been politically active, and so forth. The final and main set of questions involved a prisoner's political and ideological views: Do you accept the Islamic Republic? Do you accept your political organization? Are you willing to give a public interview to condemn your views and actions? Have you repented?

Around four in the afternoon they put us back in the buses and drove us to Unit 1. Here, carrying our bags, we were lined up, then we entered into the large waiting area. There was no blindfold requirement in Ghezelhessar prison, and therefore we were asked to hand in our blindfolds. Some gave them up and others kept them as souvenirs. While we were standing in the main *zir-e hasht* (lobby) waiting area, "Ansari," a large, rough man, who was the warden of Unit 1 and the deputy director in charge of prison security, approached with an entourage of maybe ten to fifteen guards. They went to a desk located on the side of the lobby, where they were punishing some prisoners by forcing them to stand on one foot facing the wall.

After the registration process, we were moved into the main corridor of Unit 1. The unit was a one-story structure with a long and wide corridor running down its middle. This corridor was so long that the guards used bicycles for going back and forth along it. On both sides of the corridor, there were doors opening to the wards, the visiting salon, the clinic, the kitchen, and more. We were led to the third or fourth door on the left side, on top of which a sign read, "Ward 5." Soon I would learn that this ward was supposed to be a sort of quarantine, where new arrivals were kept separate from the other prisoners. A guard knocked on the door, it opened from the inside, and we were led into a small *zir-e hasht*, which was separated by a barred metal gate from the ward salon. As we were being taken in charge by a few *tavvab* prisoners, other prisoners in the ward, who had gathered behind the gate, were climbing on each other's backs to be able to see us. These prisoners so interested in our arrival were the ones transferred from Evin just a couple of weeks ahead of us; Ali, Bigdeli, Yashar, and others were among them. I was so excited that we were going to be together again.

Tavvab prisoners led all of us inside a room to the right side of the *zir-e hasht* designated as "the praying room." The prisoner next to me, who was thin and seemed to be in poor health, started talking to me. He was Heydar Zaghi from the Rah-e Kargar organization. I introduced myself and told him my political affiliation. He revealed he had been in Ghezelhessar before for two years during the Haji Davoud Rahmani era and had been sent to Evin for release but was being brought back again with a long sentence. He pointed out that some of the men in charge of the ward were well-known hardcore *tavvab* prisoners. Soon, two at a time, we were taken out of the praying room. When I went out, my bags were searched and then I was sent to the office opposite the praying room. Two *tavvab* prisoners were sitting on the floor in two different locations. When I entered, a prisoner was sitting in front of one of them, so I sat in front of the other one. He gave me a card to fill out my personal information. He asked me about my political affiliation and whether I prayed, to which I replied I did not. He then asked if I was willing to give an interview or to go to the Band-e Jahad (Crusaders' Ward, which was for *tavvab*) to work. I said no to both. He assigned me to Cell 7. I came out, took my bags, and walked through the gate into the ward salon. My friends, Abdi among them, surrounded me. I got to meet all eleven of our comrades who already were in this small ward. Abdi said he was in Cell 9 and took me there for a cup of tea.

The ward consisted of twelve solitary-type cells. Each cell contained a metal bunk bed, leaving only a narrow space in the cell between the bed and one wall. Each cell was separated with a barred gate from the salon. The salon was used during the day for walking and at night for sleeping. There was a small bathroom in the middle of the ward and another room across from it where there were three shower stalls and dishwashing sinks. There was also a door near the praying room in the *zir-e hasht*, which opened to a small yard. The yard was muddy, and its door was closed except for four hours each day under normal conditions. There were sixty prisoners already here, and our arrival brought the count up to about one hundred twenty. Ten or eleven prisoners were assigned to each cell, but only four at the most could sleep there: three on the bunks and one on the floor. The remaining prisoners from each cell, seventy in all, were supposed to sleep in the salon. *Tavvab* prisoners lived in Cells 1 and 2. There were already a few of them in the ward, and more arrived with us and joined them. The *tavvab* in charge of the ward was a Mojahedin prisoner named "Mahmood Taheri." He had been a *tavvab* prisoner of the Rahmani era, involved in all sorts of brutal acts and crimes against other prisoners. Three or four other *tavvab* prisoners helped him run the ward, each being in charge of a duty like food, store, sports, health and hygiene, culture, or cleaning.

After I had had a cup of tea and chatted for a while with Abdi and others in Cell 9, I went to my designated cell, Cell 7. There were eleven assigned to our cell. We all sat down, introduced ourselves, and got acquainted. We also decided to hold a meeting as soon as the first dinner was over. I had already become acquainted with two of my cellmates—I had talked to Heydar a couple of hours ago and I had talked to "Khaled" in the *zir-e hasht* of Unit 1—but I did not know the others. During the introduction process, I found out that the majority in the room (six out of eleven) were from the joint Tudeh Party/ Fadaiyan Majority block. I was with the Fadaiyan Sixteenth of Azar, Heydar was from Rah-e Kargar, Abedin Eftekhari was with the Hormati-pour group, and Khaled and "Farrokh" belonged to the Kurdish Komouleh organization.

In Ghezelhessar, unlike in Evin, it was not *tavvab* prisoners but rather nonpolitical prisoners who were the prison workers. Nonpolitical prisoners did the cooking, distribution of food, and other general and public work. This was possible because Unit 2 belonged to the urban police, where they kept nonpolitical prisoners. For the first few years after the revolution, the whole prison was under the control of the urban police. Assadollah Lajavardi in Evin occasionally would send a few political prisoners to Ghezelhessar to be mixed among the nonpolitical prisoners for punishment. Then, after the 1981 clashes and the arrests of thousands of new political prisoners, he started demanding more space in Ghezelhessar. First, he got Unit 3, and later he managed to get Unit 1 as well.

After dinner and cleanup, people soon started walking and talking in the salon. Maybe a hundred people were walking in pairs in a stadium-shaped circuit. This was my first experience in prison of a public ward. Twelve of us from our organization gathered at the end of the salon and chatted for a while. Around seven thirty, when walking stopped, Mojahedin and other religious prisoners in the ward stood to pray in the front half of the salon. Communal praying was prohibited, so everyone stood individually, but it looked just like communal praying. Some who did not want to be associated with any organized activity prayed individually and separately in other spots. *Tavvab* prisoners prayed individually in front of their own cells. There were a few secular leftists who prayed that first night, and one of them was Khaled from our cell.

In Ghezelhessar, after the fall of Rahmani and the relative improvement of conditions due to "reforms," there was disagreement among different prisoner groups regarding living arrangements. The line was pretty clear regarding *tavvab* prisoners: if there was a choice, non-*tavvab* prisoners never wanted to live with them. Non-*tavvab* prisoners in Ghezelhessar, until the recent "reforms," had either been forced to live a completely individualistic life under the watchful *tavvab* eyes or been allowed to live together in rooms without *tavvab* presence in a form of limited communal life. When and if this latter choice was available, political differences tended to determine the living arrangements. Many prisoners from more radical political trends were not willing to live in a *komon* (commune) with the joint Tudeh Party/ Fadaiyan Majority block prisoners because of their past collaborative political positions and practices outside—and even inside—prison from 1980 to early 1983, when the Tudeh Party leadership was arrested.

Around eight o'clock, I went to our cell for the meeting. After a while, all eleven residents were present and we squeezed ourselves into the little cell. In our cell, there were four from the radical left trends and six from the joint Tudeh Party/ Fadaiyan Majority block. And then there was me, independent of either group but wanting to have a relationship with both trends. The joint Tudeh Party/ Fadaiyan Majority block prisoners knew that any suggestion by them would be turned down by the radical trend, which would have certainly caused a split in the room, resulting in the establishment of two different communes. Personally, I did not see any reason why we should not continue to live in a form of *komon* in the cell. I suggested having the same living system as we had in Room 64 in Evin, and we agreed upon this arrangement. We selected Abedin to be in charge of the "communal funds" and the shopping. Everyone put a voluntary amount in the box, and we emphasized that Abedin should focus on fresh fruits and vegetables and some side dishes like dried figs, dates, and tuna. The meeting ended on a very good note. I thought it was a success, given the circumstances.

2

The authorities had posted the ward rules by the yard door. One rule prohibited visiting other cells, which was impossible to enforce because of the overcrowding. Another prohibited any form of communal living and activity in the ward. And another prohibited any exercise done individually in the yard. We had the yard for four hours every day on alternating mornings and afternoons. The yard was also opened for one hour very early in the morning for exercise, usually from five to six o'clock, or from six to seven o'clock. Prison rules required an appointed *tavvab* prisoner to lead morning activities (jogging and exercises) in the yard. Initially, some prisoners chose to exercise and others stayed away, but gradually this created friction between the *tavvab* prisoners and us. Some prisoners started to create intentional problems and altercations, hoping to force the authorities to retreat from their position regarding the yard issues. Because we were a new group of prisoners in this so-called quarantine ward, had no real ward-wide organization, and had not yet established real trust among ourselves, we did not have a common strategy to deal with this important issue. The authorities kept new prisoners in the quarantine ward for as long as it took to instill the desired norms in us, before dividing and sending us into the main prison wards. They wanted to render obsolete any news and intelligence that we might have brought with us to this prison. They also wanted to collect information on every new prisoner, which was easier in the transitional small Ward 5 with their spies among us, planted from Evin.

At eleven o'clock every night, the TV set, which was mounted on the gate in the salon, was turned off, and the *tavvab* prisoners told us to go to bed. They did their duties at night by standing guard in shifts, so as to watch us all night long. If there were any problems, they would inform the night shift guards or the officer in charge, who would then administer punishment to "troublemakers" during the night hours, and usually it was severe.

In the early mornings, the hot water was turned on for an hour so that religious people in need of a *ghossl* (religious cleansing of body) could shower to be prepared for their daily praying. Once a week, hot water was turned on for everyone to shower. Cells took turns in the shower room. There were three shower stalls in that room, but the whole place was dirty and in terrible shape. The place was also used on a daily basis for dishwashing, because there was no other facility in the ward. The bathroom house across from the shower room had three toilet stalls and two sinks for hand washing.

The ward had been designed to hold twelve to thirty-six prisoners, not our current number of one hundred twenty, or the almost four-to-five hundred kept here in 1982, according to Heydar, who had been in one of these small wards during those days. Heydar explained that at one point thirty to thirty-five prisoners were stuffed into each of these cells. The first time I heard this I could not believe it, but it was true. Heydar emphasized that not only had they kept thirty to thirty-five in each cell but that the cell doors were kept closed as well. They lived and slept standing or sitting. Space was utilized very efficiently. Eight people would sit on each level of the bunk bed, and two more would lie on the floor under the bottom level, while the remaining six to eight people sat or stood in the space between the bed and the wall. They would take turns occupying each position in the cell, except for people with a disability or illness, who were given better spots.

It was during my first or second day in the ward that Ali introduced me to "Morad," and we immediately became friends for life. There are people who lift up your soul, particularly in difficult circumstances; Morad, to me, was such a person. I had not known him before but had heard about him from Ali in Evin. Morad and Ali had been cellmates in the Komiteh for a while. I met many funny people in different wards in my prison experience, but for me personally, Morad had no match. He was a unique character: very funny; highly poetic, with a love of literature and music; and strong in his political knowledge and analysis. But, more important, he was a person who took the gravest situations and found humor in them. People who have experienced situations of high trauma, like war or prison, know very well that you need people like Morad if you wish to survive. He helped us perceive the miserable prison life as tolerable. Wherever he was, he entertained people with his humor and talent for singing.

Morad had grown up in a southwestern Tehran neighborhood where they spoke their own version of street-smart Farsi. His father was originally from Azarbaijan, but Morad was born and raised in Tehran. Morad spoke Azari (the Azarbayjani language), which brought us even closer to each other. Ali could also speak a form of Azari (though he was from central Iran) with a very interesting accent and vocabulary. When Morad and I were alone together, we spoke Azari. When Ali was with us, we preferred Farsi because the "Azari" that Ali spoke was limited, in a complicated dialect, difficult for us to understand.

3

On December 7, around ten in the morning, Ansari, the sectional warden, ordered everyone to sit in the salon. He told twenty people, including Abdi, Bigdeli, and Amir Bagheri from our organization, to leave with all their belongings. Our cell lost three prisoners as well.

Prisoners analyzed every move, change, announcement and news in prison compulsively. Why did they take this number of people? Why did they take that combination of people? What was the common factor for the group? Where did they take them? Analysis of this move continued for a day or two. The common view in the ward was that they were people who had had altercations with the *tavvab* prisoners. Maybe there was some truth to that, but on the other hand, half of them had never had any problems with anyone in the ward.

Then one day, one of them, "Jahangir," returned to the ward. He explained that they had been transferred back to Evin and each sent to his previous room. Again, discussions and analyses started based on this new bit of information. We really did not understand why they would be taken back and put in their original rooms. What was the purpose of this action? Of course, we were not able to figure it out because we had no way of knowing the real purpose behind it, if indeed there was one. Often, the authorities would do things in prison that made no sense at all, but we tried to give all their actions some meaning and purpose. Sometimes they were just messing with our minds, sometimes they were acting purposefully, and at yet other times they disrupted us just for the fun of it, apparently.

When we first arrived in this ward, our feeling was that we would soon be sent to the main wards. But as time passed, we understood the need to prepare ourselves for the possibility of a long stay here. Every cell had some form of internal organization, but we did not have much of an organization ward-wide. We needed to coordinate and organize to be able to deal with the *tavvab* prisoners, and particularly with the authorities. Firstly, we had to find a mechanism through which all non-*tavvab* prisoners could discuss reaching a consensus on any given ward-wide issue without the *tavvab* knowing. A secret council of cell representatives was established. Their discussions were held in pairs on the walk circuit. Issues to tackle urgently were the ward-wide coordination of *senfi* (nonpolitical) matters like turns in dishwashing, bathroom and shower-room cleaning, frequency and length of daily "quiet times," and sports and activities in the yard.

The first potentially major issue was the yard exercise. There were two problems to be dealt with. The first one was accepting or rejecting the leadership of the appointed *tavvab* for the morning exercise. The second issue was about playing sports with the *tavvab* teams in the yard.

A majority believed that we should not exercise behind an appointed *tavvab* leader, nor should we play sports with them. But there was disagreement on how to go about rejecting the appointed *tavvab* leadership. One suggestion was to refuse to participate in the early morning jog and exercise, basically to go on strike. Some were afraid that if we did this, the authorities might close the yard for good, which would work against us because we needed the yard for health reasons.

Initially, about half of the Mojahedin and half of the secular leftist prisoners participated in the morning exercise behind the appointed *tavvab*. Also in the beginning, our teams played soccer or volleyball with the *tavvab* teams, but soon that changed. Gradually an unspoken agreement was established in the yard. The *tavvab* would play a few rounds, mostly volleyball or, rarely, soccer, then would leave the field for us to play. But there were incidents that resulted in altercations. A couple of days later, Ansari came in, talked a bit of nonsense, and then asked what the problem was. Because there was not much coordination in the ward, people said whatever they wanted. Mojahedin followers, who were very coordinated and organized as a unit, insisted on a couple of issues and portrayed them as ward positions. Basically, they said that we did not want to play sports with *tavvab* prisoners and also that we wanted to have our own person in charge of the sports. Ansari responded angrily and rudely that everyone should play with everyone else and that he would choose whomever he wanted to be in charge of the yard activities.

This was the first time many of us newcomers got a taste of how the Mojahedin followers, the largest group in prison, functioned. It was more important for the Mojahedin followers to coordinate and catch up with the tactics of their fellow Mojahedin prisoners in other Ghezelhessar wards than to coordinate with the prisoners with whom they were sharing a ward. As an organizational policy, they believed that they had to lead the way and whoever liked would follow them, which was an absolutely monopolistic view of "cooperation" with other forces. In our particular ward, the Mojahedin made up only about 50 percent of the prisoners. We sent them a clear message that we would not tolerate that behavior anymore. The Mojahedin followers quickly came to their senses, at least in Ward 5, and they agreed to coordinate with us.

A proposition was circulated suggesting the total boycott of the early morning activities in the yard. There were lengthy discussions, but we were not able to reach a consensus by late that night. Most of the Mojahedin followers and some of the secular leftists supported the proposal. The following morning, only ten to fifteen people took part in the morning exercise behind the appointed *tavvab*. This did not look good. Some of us tried to convince the small group of ten to fifteen people to join the majority, which they finally did, and from the following morning non-*tavvab* prisoners did not jog or exercise behind the appointed *tavvab* anymore. We finally had done something as a unified ward. We used the yard in regular hours very efficiently by playing soccer, volleyball, or other games to stay active and healthy but completely boycotted the early morning exercises. After a few days, and as a result of our actions, it was the *tavvab* prisoners who rarely showed up in the yard. They did not even come to play soccer or volleyball.

4

One of the men in our room, "Shahrokh," had lived and worked in French-speaking Belgium for twenty-five years. I approached him and asked him to teach me French. Others also started teaching or learning English or other languages. Gradually, participation in these language classes picked up in the ward, but initially mainly among the open-minded of the secular leftists with only a few of the Mojahedin prisoners joining in. Mojahedin followers and die-hard "radical" leftists did not agree with this practice. They believed that only politically "liberal," "passive," and "soft" people resorted to spending their time in prison learning languages. Political prisoners remaining from the 1981–1982 period, including mostly the Mojahedin and the radical leftists, had created a prison "values system," according to which a strong, resistant, and combative political prisoner was supposed to engage in physical exercise, to discuss politics during walk-and-talk, and to take part in manual labor and chores. Reading or studying in prison, in their view, should be limited to newspapers and some books, if available.

After the removal of Rahmani's oppressive rule and in reaction to the limitations of that era, the Mojahedin and many leftists had turned to an absolute form of communal life. A small percentage of the leftists had swung to the other extreme. They believed that with the availability of books and newspapers, prisoners should spend their time only in reading and studying. Along the way, this latter group had lost their belief and interest in communal and collective activities, and they had become extremely individualistic in their prison living philosophy. This trend had grown out of reactions to the period of 1981–1983 on the one hand and the growing current absolute communal-living trend among prisoners on the other. But overall, the majority of the leftists believed and practiced a form of communal living, though different from that of the Mojahedin.

From 1984 to 1985, prison in the Islamic Republic had changed dramatically in space, resources, and policies. Prisoner demographics had changed as well. A new trend was shaping up among the regime's prisoners, one that generated a more balanced view of life and struggle in prison. When our group of prisoners arrived in prison, we fit in with this trend and therefore we supported and strengthened it. It balanced communal with individual life, serious exercise with fun, and mental with manual work, and its adherents believed in developing a realistic set of tactics for dealing with the authorities and for demanding and protecting our rights as prisoners.

5

It was visiting day for our ward. Prisoners who had arrived here before us were having family visits. The night before, shaving and cleaning took place as usual. We still had to use the manual hair-clippers to shave our faces, which was a torture in itself. As usual on visiting day, the general mood was upbeat. The first group for visit was called out and Ali, "Farzin," Yashar, and Morad from our organization were among them. Later, I talked to our comrades one by one. I asked Ali if he had had a chance to visit with his son. He said that after the regular visit was over, they brought his son back to a small room and he had an in-person visit with him. Ali had an interesting sense of humor. He said, "My son, Cyrus, son of a gun, can not differentiate between a bearded, ugly guard and his handsome father. He looks and laughs with the guard the same way he does with me." Cyrus was only a year old and had been born in prison when his mother was also in custody in the Komiteh detention center.

I also found Morad after his visit. Morad lit a cigarette as we started walking. I was surprised, having assumed that he did not smoke. He said that he was not a smoker but kept a pack of cigarettes, of which he smoked only one after each visit, when he had the blues. On this occasion I was keen to know what had happened to the remainder of our organization after the arrests in October 1984. I asked Morad what they had been doing between October and February, when he was arrested. Morad explained, "When things went fucking crazy and comrades were being arrested right and left, in our section we decided to stay inactive for a while. Later on, assuming that the danger had passed, we resumed our activities. But in retrospect, I think we were naive in thinking that we were safe. A few months later we were all arrested."

After every visiting day, much new information and many rumors floated around. Some came from individual prisoners, others from different political and organizational sources. Especially, the Mojahedin and the Tudeh Party spread their organizational news, which always supported their political agendas. Both groups were masters of manipulating, even creating, news about their organizations, but with different intentions. Tudeh Party members tried to clean up the mess their leadership had created after the arrests. The Mojahedin, on the other hand, tried to establish their organization as the sole serious opposition to the regime, the only organization with the capacity to lead the Iranian people in toppling the regime. Therefore, they would bring either news about the "National Liberation Army," formed by the Mojahedin in Iraq with about seven thousand armed militants plus heavy weaponry gifted by Saddam Hussein, or news about the functions and actions of their organization inside Iran and abroad. In prison, you had to learn how to screen real news from propaganda, which was fed to us continuously by both the regime and the other opposition groups.

After this visit, the guards demanded that one prisoner from each cell clean the visiting salon. Prisoners who had been in this prison during the Rahmani era pointed out that forced labor was common then and prisoners were forced to do all kinds of odd jobs. This practice was discontinued after Rahmani departed, but it looked like the prison administration was trying to bring it back. Apparently, in some wards prisoners had volunteered to clean the visiting room, reasoning that their own families met there and therefore it was all right to do the work involved. In other wards, prisoners had chosen not to take on this task, reasoning that it was forced labor and that therefore they should not do the work unless they were forced to.

In our ward, a variety of opinions immediately formed about the issue. When our cell met to discuss it, we were not able to reach an agreement. Heydar and I came up with a temporary practical formula for our cell, which the whole ward soon adopted. We suggested that for this one time if there was a volunteer in the cell he should go ahead with the work, so that we would have enough time until the next visit in two weeks to decide what position to take. In our cell Khaled volunteered for the task. All the other cells accepted this proposition and produced volunteers, except for Cell 4. In the evening, the guards called visiting-room cleaners out. Volunteers from all cells went out, except from Cell 4. The guards picked a Mojahedin prisoner named Hamzeh Shalalvand, who happened to be particularly opposed to this task, from Cell 4. He insisted on his position and was sent to solitary. The others cleaned the visiting salon. After they returned, the discussions continued in the ward. An absolute majority of prisoners were against accepting any form of forced labor. But there was considerable disagreement over how to go about protesting it. Discussions continued for a couple of more days and then it was mostly forgotten. When Hamzeh returned from solitary and proved that it was possible to individually resist forced labor and receive only small to moderate punishment, it had quite an impact on the general psyche of the ward. But we all knew that the authorities would react very differently if and when we protested the policy collectively.

6

The yard-exercise situation was getting worse daily. The authorities announced that because we did not accept the leadership of the appointed *tavvab*, they would not open the yard in the early mornings. We still had the daily yard time, during which we organized soccer or volleyball games and competitions.

One day, *tavvab* prisoners started moving mostly Mojahedin followers from Cells 3–6 to Cells 7–12. We received two prisoners as well: a very young one named "Kazem" and another older one named "Yavar." Kazem was about twenty years old and had been arrested in 1981, when he must have been sixteen. Yavar was about twenty-seven, which was relatively old for a Mojahedin. Yavar was very conspicuous in the ward because he never took off his winter hat because he said he suffered from sinus problems. He was a well-liked, friendly, and humorous guy. He came from a poor working-class Azari family in Tehran. He belonged to the moderate faction of the Mojahedin and got along well with everyone, even the Tudeh Party prisoners. Although he was a devout follower of the Mojahedin organization, he was also a relatively independent-minded person. For example, as soon as he found out that I was learning French from Shahrokh, he asked to be included in our class. I had already learned some basics of French from Shahrokh, who asked me to work with Yavar to bring him up to my own rudimentary level before class continued.

Yavar and I became buddies. I walked with him and we talked about many things while we practiced our French. During these "practice" walks, I learned a few things about him. First and foremost, I figured out he was one of those people who have little talent for learning foreign languages. I also found out that his views on life and struggle in prison were very similar to mine. This brought us closer and gave me a direct channel of communication with the Mojahedin in the ward. In a walk-and-talk session, Yavar told me about his activities and his arrest.

> In 1980, I opened a store with a couple of friends selling cleaning material. After the 1981 street clashes with the government forces, I was identified by the police through a contact I had. Not being able to go home, some nights a few of us slept in the store. In the spring of 1982, we were arrested in the store and transferred to Evin prison.

> I remember the first time they asked about my organizational affiliation, I replied, "*Havadaram*" (which in Farsi has a double meaning and could mean either "I am a sympathizer" or "I have air"). The interrogators started laughing and then called someone else and told him what I had said. This new guy, who was a giant and had a strong Azari accent, approached and asked, "Yavar khan, *havadari*?" (Which could mean either "Mr. Yavar, are you a sympathizer?" or "Mr. Yavar, do you have air?") I replied, "yes" (admitting being a sympathizer)—to which the interrogator roared, "*Man khoodam havato khali mi kunam*!" ("I will deflate you myself!") Then he took me to a room, beat me senseless, and tortured me to a point when he asked again, "*Havadari*?" ("Are you a sympathizer?") "*Nistam*" ("I am not") was my reply. Then the real interrogations started. I was tied to the bed and flogged with the *kubl* (flogging cable) to the point where I had to give up resisting or prepare to die under torture. I was forced to admit whatever they wanted to be able to survive.

In the postrevolution chaos, initially there was no system for interrogating detainees in the Islamic Republic prisons. Some political prisoners, mostly in connection with the previous regime or people of the Baha'i faith, were questioned ideologically or politically; many of these were killed after very brief trials. Before the street clashes of June 20, 1981, there was only one interrogation branch in Evin for the militant secular leftists, one branch for the nonmilitant secular leftists, one branch for the Mojahedin, and a couple of branches for other political groups like monarchists, nationalists, religious opposition, or arrested current government elements. After June 20, 1981, the branches dealing with the Mojahedin alone increased to many more. Prisoners who survived the executions of 1981 or were arrested later were crammed into inadequate rooms and were kept there for months. For a while, the only food they got was some bread and feta cheese. There was no showering or hygiene, and there was no medical care. There were no family visits for a long time.

On many occasions, Assadollah Lajavardi told prisoners that the only reason they were being kept alive was because he did not yet have specific orders from Khomeini to deal with them. He told prisoners that they were all *monafegh* (hypocrite) and *mortad* (apostate). He told them that they thus deserved to die, and this would happen whenever Khomeini issued a fatwa.

7

The next family visit day arrived. This time, I also had a visit. After we were placed in our stalls, the guards opened the doors in the other side and families rushed in. The interphone system was then turned on. My oldest sister had come to my visit. My first question was about my wife and daughter and their situation abroad. She told me that they were safe and were living in America. Then I inquired about my mother and the other members of the family. My sister asked me if I had received a sentence; I told her I had been given fifteen years. At the end she asked what I needed. I said they were going to accept winter clothing and therefore she should bring my clothes, plus some sugar candy and a tea thermos. She had also given some money for me to the authorities. Then it was time to say good-bye. The families were taken out first and then we were transferred back to the ward.

The ward was not in the best of moods after visiting hours. Most people were depressed; the excitement and joy of the time before and during the visit usually turned into sadness afterward. I started chatting with the usual suspects. First I walked and talked with Ali and Morad. Both had their after-visit cigarettes going. Here I will tell you I was a smoker for more than ten years in the 1960s and '70s, but since quitting in 1977 I had not smoked and had felt no urge to do so either. This was surprising to many, both inside prison and outside, because many non-smokers became smokers in prison.

We exchanged and analyzed the political news we had heard from different sources. Most of the stories were about the Mojahedin organization, the main news being that Massoud Rajavi, its leader, had married Maryam Azdanloo. Maryam was part of the leadership and the former wife of Mehdi Abrishamchi, who was a close friend of Rajavi from their time in prison and was also a member of the leadership of the organization. This story sounded weird and scandalous. But the Mojahedin had declared it an "Ideological Revolution!" Afterward, Maryam had apparently become "equal" to Massoud Rajavi in the organization. The core of the so-called Ideological Revolution was consolidating the position of Massoud and Maryam in the organization at the expense of the collective and democratic leadership. Everyone was talking about the issue, and secular leftists were privately having plenty of fun with the matter. Mojahedin followers, who worshiped Rajavi like God, defended his actions publicly. But we later learned that within their closed community, there was a great deal of turmoil and anxiety about this development. Because the Mojahedin had become a cult-type organization, authoritative figures were very important in keeping the rank and file in check and keeping them motivated. But in prison, there was no one who could provide answers to the followers' questions, and this left them all, but especially the younger and emotional members, adrift.

8

One day a bearded fellow with an entourage entered the ward. He asked his guards and the *tavvab* prisoners to remain in the *zir-e hasht* while he walked along with an assistant to the end part of the ward. Mojahedin prisoners rushed to surround him, knowing who he was: "Meysam," the new, "reformist" warden of Ghezelhessar prison. He gave a short talk about the changes that were currently under way in Ghezelhessar. At the end, he stated that if we lived our lives without organizing and creating political difficulties, he would see to it that we got everything possible within his authority. Then, for about an hour, he allowed a question and answer session.

Mojahedin prisoners collectively tried to raise the issue of *tavvab* prisoners, insisting that we should be in charge of our own ward. Meysam showed sensitivity about the word *tavvab*, especially when the Mojahedin prisoners used it to mean something negative. In turn, he frequently asked the Mojahedin prisoners about their political affiliation, forcing them to declare they were *monafeghin* (hypocrites). The secular leftists in general argued that as political prisoners we had rights. We asked for good food, decent healthcare, time for yard activities, and our right to read and write. Meysam rejected the notion that we had any rights as political prisoners in the Islamic prison system. But he added that it was his Islamic duty to provide us with as much as he possibly could, within his office's limitations. He promised that things would get better.

Prisoners then raised the issue of the yard exercise with him. Meysam said he would talk to the authorities so that people could do sports with whomever they liked. This was important because he was basically retreating from the position that Ansari had insisted on before. Prisoners complained that the main issue was the early morning exercises. He said he would talk to Ansari to find a solution for that problem as well. Then he explained that lack of exercise was good neither for prisoners nor for the prison system, because it would cost both sides more in the long run. It seemed like he was showing some flexibility on the subject.

The overall policy of the authorities in prison at this time was to hand over internal responsibilities in wards to prisoners themselves, and they had started doing this in the main wards. In the quarantine ward, they wanted to show us that we could not demand and obtain rights by struggling, but rather that the authorities could choose to bestow them on us. Before Meysam left, he promised that we would get newspapers and monthly rations of books from the prison library booklist. He also promised to provide schoolbooks for those young prisoners who wished to finish their high school education.

Soon after, Ansari informed us that he would allow us to have early morning exercises on our own if we chose someone as exercise leader acceptable to him and everyone in the ward. Ansari proposed that we select three people and then let him choose one of them to be in charge of the sporting activities. This was certainly a retreat from the position he had taken earlier, and it was clear that Meysam had forced him to it. It was a big victory for us in the ward. As usual, some extremists from both the Mojahedin and the secular leftists suggested that we should not accept the offer and instead demand to select our own single representative to be in charge of the sporting activities. It took a few hours of discussion, but finally the majority of the ward agreed to select three candidates. We decided to present three athletes who were volunteers for the position: "Manouchehr," who was from the Tudeh Party, "Ramin," who was from the Fadaiyan Minority, and "Rahim," from the Mojahedin.

At night, Ansari called out the three candidates. He talked to them individually and discussed with them how they were going to manage the position. The next morning, Ansari called Manouchehr out to tell him that he was chosen to be in charge of the sporting activities and that he would be responsible for the morning exercises and the organized games. He also added that people were free to play with whomever they wished. Manouchehr returned and announced that he had been offered the position and that he had accepted it. There was some opposition at first, but finally everyone agreed, and Manouchehr became the leader of the exercise and sporting activities for the ward. We suggested to him that it would be a good gesture if he could get Ramin and Rahim to assist him. Ramin and Rahim took charge of the morning exercises, while Manouchehr organized the daily sporting games and competitions.

9

With visits becoming regular and so with extra money from families coming in, we could buy vegetables, fruits, and other side dishes to supplement the very poor prison diet. We got plenty of powdered milk and rock candy from the families, and we could buy onions, dates, and figs from the so-called prison store. Regardless of all this, the prison diet was terrible for our health. Prison in Iran creates its own special health problems for prisoners. Enormous stress, terrible diet, confinement in a small cell or room or even in a ward with very little chance of physical activity, and nonexistent medical care is predictably a recipe for disaster. Prisoners would get all kinds of strange diseases and illnesses, mental and physical. One of the common medical conditions that prisoners had to deal with was colitis, inflammation of the large intestine, which in turn caused intolerable pressure and explosive bowel movements. Also, apparently almost 50 percent of prisoners developed some degree of hemorrhoids, which was less serious than colitis but still horribly uncomfortable. But stomach upsets were probably the most common of prisoner problems.

One day, the *tavvab* started calling prisoners to the *zir-e hasht* to deliver the photos of our children that the authorities had accepted from our family members during the last visit. They usually kept the photos for a few days for control and then gave them to us, unless the photo was of a girl older than seven or eight years old, in which case they confiscated it. I got a few photos of my daughter, Bahar, who was only about three years old. These new photos had come from abroad. That was intriguing to the other prisoners, so they gathered around me to see the photos. In one of them Bahar was sitting in a toy vehicle, which was built in the shape of a large shoe. Ali, excited at seeing my daughter in the toy, said she was sitting in a "Shoe-cycle." We all laughed, and that toy from then on was known as a "Shoe-cycle." My cellmates insisted that we put that particular photo up on the wall in our cell. Whenever Ali and I walked in the salon and passed by the cell, he would point to the photo and say, "What a 'Shoe-cycle' rider she has become." Gradually, every cell got a few photos of children. Seeing the photos was a big help in boosting our morale. It gave us a great deal of hope and motivation for survival.

As in Evin, we had a monthly ration of letter writing. As in Evin, we were issued a two-sided form, each side having seven lines. In this prison, a married prisoner was allowed to write two letters a month: one to his wife and children, and another to his parents and siblings. Letters were inspected and censored, and therefore one could write only trivia or, at the most, put in some coded messages. Some prisoners did not write at all; others spent a few days ahead of time to prepare their letters, while some just wrote on the spot. Regulations for writing were tough and limiting. It could not be a "love" letter nor "political"; it could not contain prison "intelligence," nor could it be "agitating" or contain "propaganda." I sent both letters to my mother's address. My sister would then send my wife's letter abroad to her. My wife, in turn, would mail her reply to my sister, who then would send it to me in prison.

There was no way one could share true feelings with loved ones via these letters or even in visits. There was absolutely no way to discuss political and prison issues with outsiders via "legal" means, so we had to use "illegal" means to communicate with the outside world. The best opportunity was during in-person visits. This was a form of visit where a prisoner and his family members were allowed to meet together, face to face, in a room under guard supervision for twenty to thirty minutes. The majority of us non-*tavvab* prisoners never got any in-person visits with adults. The only alternative left for people like us was to exploit our in-person visits with our children, and we did so masterfully and shamelessly. It was the only channel non-*tavvab* prisoners had for a direct but risky contact with the outside world. Prisoners would hide small notes or packages in children's underwear during the in-person visits, and this had to be done somehow under the constantly prying eyes of the guards.

10

"Gholi," a twenty-five or twenty-six-year-old Mojahedin sympathizer from Tabriz, was not praying anymore. That was a bit odd for a religious prisoner. There were Mojahedin prisoners who had joined that organization only for political reasons, but even they pretended to pray in prison, for two reasons: they wanted to stay shoulder to shoulder with their brethren in the organization, and they did not want to provide any more excuses to the regime to harm them on religious grounds. We soon discovered that not only had Gholi rejected Islam and considered himself a secular person, he had rejected the Mojahedin organization politically as well.

Change of ideology and political/organizational affiliation, usually from the Mojahedin or other religious groups to some form of secular leftist trend, though fairly common in prisons of the previous regime, was almost nonexistent in the prisons of the Islamic Republic. The obvious reason was the danger of being labeled by the authorities as rejecting Islam, an apostate, which was punishable by death. Therefore, if someone had a change of belief he had to keep it secret. And though

Gholi was a bit careless in some of his public expressions, officially and formally he would never admit to the change.

On Thursday nights, as usual in any prison in the Islamic Republic, they would broadcast the dreaded "Du'a-ye Komeyl" (Repentance Supplication) program. It was still torturous, though we had learned to ignore it because we were not alone anymore. Some nights in this period, prison TV would broadcast ideological courses, religious lessons, or speeches. But even *tavvab* prisoners did not watch or listen to these programs enthusiastically. Occasionally, an outside speaker, a government official, or a religious leader would come to prison for a visit. The prison authorities would usually set up a controlled visit for this guest with the *tavvab* prisoners, where the guest would give a speech and sometimes would even hold a question and answer session. The visit would be televised, and the public would get the impression the *tavvab* represented all prisoners. These programs were interesting. Though staged, the question and answer parts were very revealing of the situation of the regime and the country. A Friday morning radio program called "Analysis and Interpretation of Foreign Radio Broadcasts" was also interesting, because it provided us with indirect access to the weekly news and political events of Iran and the world.

We spent the first ten days of the Iranian New Year (March 1986) still in this quarantine ward. I think it was on the eleventh day that Ansari and his entourage ordered us to pack up and be ready for transfer. We had spent about five months in that dump and were truly ready for a change, whatever and wherever it might be. The only sad thing was the renewed separations. We had made new connections, developed new friendships, and found a new camaraderie here that now came to an end. Such was the norm in prison.

Ansari first called three names: Heydar Zaghi, Jalil Shahbazi, and Sa'dollah Zare'. They went to the *zir-e hasht* with all their belongings. All three of them were among the most veteran political prisoners in this regime, having been arrested at the end of 1979 or at the beginning of 1980. It was obvious that the warden had decided to separate them from the rest of the prison population. Later we found out that they had been taken to Ward 6 in Unit 3. Ansari then called a few lists of twenty prisoners each. Our group of twenty basically included secular leftists, with a few Mojahedin prisoners. From our organization Morad, "Dariush," Asghar, "Habib," and I were in this group, as was Yavar from the Mojahedin. We were all taken to Ward 2 of Unit 1. Other groups went to different wards in Units 1 and 3.

Chapter Six

GROUP OF 93

1

March 1986

Our group of twenty prisoners was taken out in a single line into the main corridor and to Ward 2, which was located just across from Ward 5. We entered into a fairly large *zir-e hasht* (lobby). Behind the barred gate separating the *zir-e hasht* from the ward corridor, prisoners were waiting to welcome us. *Tavvab* prisoners, who received us, quickly directed all of us without our bags into what was called the ward mosque or *hosseiniye*, located to the right of the *zir-e hasht*. After we sat down, a *tavvab* took down our names while another one explained the rules of the ward to us. They finally assigned us to rooms. Morad, Dariush, and I were sent to Room 22, while Habib and Asghar went to Room 20. Others in the group were sent to a variety of other rooms. Every one of us who entered the ward corridor was greeted by a group of ward prisoners who helped us carry our belongings to our assigned rooms.

Room 22 was on the right side, close to the end of the ward, where there were already thirty or more prisoners. The first thing that caught my attention was the overall youth of the room members. The *mass'oul-e otagh* (room representative) greeted us and then asked if we wanted to sleep on the floor or on a bunk, and what level of the bunk we preferred.

There were more people in the room than bed space. Morad said he preferred a bed, but Dariush and I declared we had no preference. Some prisoners started asking us typical questions such as what were our organizational and political affiliations? How long were our sentences? I was assigned to the second level of a bunk bed, the first level of which was occupied by a Tudeh Party member, Mehdi Hassani-pak. So he helped me set up my bed.

This was basically a Mojahedin room. Except for Mehdi and a Fadaiyan Minority prisoner, who was the *mass'oul-e senfi* (food service representative) in the room, everyone else was from the Mojahedin. After dinner, two daily workers collected the dishes and cleaned up the *sofreh* (dinner cloth). Meanwhile the majority of the ward prisoners poured out into the corridor for the after-meal walk. I found Mamad, who, you might recall, had served with me on the youth section leadership committee of our organization and was arrested shortly after me, and we started walking and talking as well. We had known each other in the organization for three years, and most of that time we had worked together. We had a lot to discuss. Mamad provided his analysis of the ward news and politics. He said that out of about 550 or more prisoners in the ward, 450 were from the Mojahedin and the rest were secular leftists. He added that the Mojahedin, as a complete majority, dictated the lifestyle and day-to-day living policies of the ward. Mamad then pointed to Cells 1 and 2, where twenty-five *tavvab* prisoners lived, but he mentioned that only five were hardcore; they were in charge of the ward and openly cooperated with the guards, while the rest were just tactical or passive *tavvab* prisoners who helped them.

In the old days, before our imprisonment, Mamad had a famous habit of locking onto an issue and not letting go. It seemed he had not changed in this regard. He talked so much about an incident among the Tudeh Party prisoners in the ward that we ran out of time that night before we could discuss other issues. The ward's daily workers were getting ready to clean the corridor and prisoners had to be in their rooms, where they would have tea or fruit at this hour. Mamad and I set up our next walk-and-talk appointment, and each of us went to his own room.

2

After having tea, I went out, and this time I hooked up with "Anoosh" for a walk-and-talk. At this time of the night, it was not as busy as before, but there were still many people walking and talking in the corridor. I knew Anoosh from outside as well. Anoosh gave me more insight about the ward. He said that secular leftist prisoners had tried to reach an agreement with the Mojahedin in the rooms, so that the minority views would be incorporated in the running of the rooms and the ward, but everything was still basically run according to the lifestyle philosophy of the Mojahedin. Consequently, he added, in some rooms the relationship between the Mojahedin and some secular leftists was confrontational. Apparently, in a few rooms, some prisoners had separated their living from the Mojahedin. In one room, the majority was with the secular leftists belonging to many different groups, but they had gone to the other extreme by choosing to live individually, and there was no order or discipline in that room. Anoosh explained that the *hosseiniye* was basically a TV-watching salon, besides being the praying room for the religious prisoners. During "quiet hours," people also used it for reading or studying. On Fridays, it was used for the *kar-e melli* (communal work).

This ward was one of the oldest Mojahedin wards in this prison, and some prisoners had been here since 1982 and experienced the Haji Davoud Rahmani era. This was the ward where Behzad Nezami, a tall, heavy, twenty-year-old *tavvab* prisoner from the Mojahedin, along with a gang of other *tavvab* prisoners, then ruled with absolute power given to him by Rahmani himself. He had control over the lives of eight hundred to nine hundred prisoners in this ward. He kept them in closed-door rooms and forced them to live strictly segregated lives, forbidding them even to have eye contact with each other. He punished the violators severely by flogging or sending them to solitary. He and his gang had total control of the ward at night. They used that authority and power to torture and even rape underage prisoners. At least two prisoners in that period hanged themselves in the ward bathrooms.

The ward had sixteen small and eight large rooms. In those days, every large room held sixty to sixty-five and every small room thirty to thirty-five prisoners. When Rahmani first started his brutal reign in 1982, there were only a few *tavvab* prisoners who had been brought from Evin. Most prisoners in the ward were Mojahedin, who pretended to have repented and were forced to refer to themselves as *Monafeghin* (hypocrites), plus some secular leftists who also had to declare they were politically passive. Rahmani, knowing well that most were *sar-e moze'i* (combatant) prisoners, gradually increased the pressure on the ward: room gates were closed, the amount and quality of food decreased, there was no yard privilege, beatings were administered for any excuse, and solitary confinement became a norm. The resistance of the ward started to crack after a few months. Once in a while, a few prisoners would announce they had had a "change of heart" and would like to join the *tavvab* brothers. The numbers in the *tavvab* camp grew quickly, while the other side shrank daily. But the conversion rate was not satisfactory to Rahmani. He decided to keep the newly converted *tavvab* prisoners mixed with non-*tavvab* ones, requiring and forcing *tavvab* prisoners to put more pressure on those who were still considered combatant. This created a large network of *tavvab* prisoners, who now were living in rooms mixed with other prisoners, basically controlling every movement of the non-*tavvab* prisoners. Yesterday's comrades had become today's oppressors. That *tavvab* network, which gradually became more sophisticated in their control methods, made life miserable for the non-*tavvab* prisoners, who were under tremendous stress and were shrinking in number daily. But their resistance continued.

Then Rahmani asked his *tavvab* network, which he referred to as the "*Monafegh*-finder," to identify the most resistant non-*tavvab* prisoners. In 1983, Rahmani put these prisoners in a pressure-and-torture system he had invented to break down resistant prisoners. Rahmani called this system the *dastgah* (apparatus); prisoners had other names for it, including *ghabr* (grave), *jahannam* (hell), *taboot* (coffin), *ghiamat* (resurrection), or *ghafass* (cage). These *ghabrs* or whatever they were called were actually boxes made out of plywood, which opened only at the back. Prisoners were seated in these boxes and *tavvab* guarded them 24/7. They were built in a large room in the *zir-e hasht* of Unit 1 to create the sense of absolute isolation and of being buried alive. Inside it was cramped, dark, and damp. An eerie silence was maintained, and rations consisted of only a very little bread and water. Resistant prisoners, men and women, were kept there as long as it took to break them down.

Under this inhumane pressure, prisoners fell one by one. Then those prisoners, who had been broken not only politically and ideologically but also in many cases psychologically, were brought back to the wards to teach a lesson to others. After this, resisting prisoners gradually retreated from their positions and pretended to become—or even became—*tavvab*. There were exceptional cases where prisoners endured months of Rahmani's special treatment and still resisted, but in general, prisoners had to retreat to a position acceptable by Rahmani's standards.

But Rahmani did not even stop there, because the level of repentance was still not acceptable to him. He started public recantation and self-defamation ceremonies in Ghezelhessar prison. A given prisoner who had broken down would be required to participate in a public demonstration of repentance, in which he would condemn all political and ideological opposition organizations and would try to show that he or she had genuinely repented and was a true *tavvab*. That became a recurring event for months, so that all prisoners were forced to sit for hours daily to witness these repentances. Later, Rahmani used the closed-circuit prison TV network to bring these repentance ceremonies to all the wards in the prison. Prisoners would confess by telling outrageous stories about their deviant habits, mostly sexual in nature, to show that they had truly repented. They would offer more information than even Rahmani wanted, to show that they were sincere. They would become more religious than even Rahmani himself.

According to prisoners who had suffered through this period, it haunted them even today. They compared every new experience to their experiences under Rahmani. Some of them did not trust the recent changes and reforms, believing they were all part of a conspiracy by Haji Davoud Rahmani. They thought he might return and start his repression all over again. Others knew that Rahmani was gone for good and those days would not return, but still they were haunted. They could not let go. The "Rahmani prisoners" were a group in themselves, regardless of whatever political background they had begun with. It would take a long time and a very drastic change of conditions to bring them to normalcy, if that was ever even possible.

3

As newcomers, we spent most of our first day enjoying the yard. There were three table-tennis tables in the yard, which had been purchased by the prisoners themselves. We played table tennis, walked and talked with other prisoners, and made contacts with the next-door ward prisoners whose windows looked into our yard. Back in our room, Morad and I signed up to play soccer with room prisoners. Real shoes were not allowed in this prison, but prisoners would fashion "athletic shoes" out of closed-toe sandals: they sewed a piece of strong fabric around the back of each sandal to create a heel, and they reinforced the soles by sticking on other soles from extra sandals, using a "hot and cold" pressing process.

One day, Yavar asked if I would be willing to talk to a Mojahedin friend of his, named "Pedram." I met him and we walked and talked. He was from a neighborhood in south-central Tehran. He had heard that I was a geneticist and a close friend of Yavar and had decided to talk to me about an inherited condition in his family and his chances of being a carrier of the gene. I agreed to explain to him the basic principles of the science of inheritance and discuss his chances of being a carrier. During those few sessions, we also talked about prison and his experiences of the last five years. He told me about his arrest:

> In early spring of 1981, there were many meetings held in preparation for the big confrontation. It was within that climate that in early June 1981 on a Friday, about three hundred of us had gathered in the main neighborhood sports complex on an invitation from the neighborhood sympathizing cultural organization. The gathering was about to get under way when suddenly Revolutionary Guards, Committee[13] Guards, and Basij militia, with support from the plainclothes *chomaghdaran* (club-wielding vigilantes), poured in from doors and windows.
>
> The regime knew that the Mojahedin were in the process of a major political shift and therefore had prepared to start clashing with us at a time deemed appropriate. I think they had decided that this would be a good place to start since there were three hundred of us gathered in one location. This was still before the June 20, 1981 conflicts.

group of 93

Anyhow, after all the dust settled, ninety-three of us were arrested and brought to Evin prison. The Mojahedin organization, on the following day, demanded that the regime release us because we had done nothing illegal. We became known in the official Mojahedin publications as "the Group of 93," and that is what we are still known as in prison. Although we had been arrested in a peaceful gathering and before June 20, Assadollah Lajavardi and the gang put us in the front line of the torture and persecution. Fifteen of us were executed, fifteen of us got life sentences, thirty of us got fifteen to twenty-year sentences, and the other thirty-three got five to ten-year sentences. Then, those of us with prison terms were transferred to Ghezelhessar prison in 1982, where we went through hell during Rahmani's rule.

Chapter Seven

UNITY AGAINST ALL ODDS

1

April 1986

It was early April when we found out that some prisoners of Wards 1, 3, and 4 had been pulled out with all their belongings. The authorities were about to empty Unit 1 to give it back to the urban police to house nonpolitical prisoners. This made it clear why a couple of weeks earlier some prisoners had been transferred to Gohardasht. Because Gohardasht could not handle all the political prisoners at this time, we were being transferred to Unit 3 for now. We did not generally care where we were, but in fact Ghezelhessar at this time had the best conditions among the Tehran prisons. The following day, our ward was divided into two halves; one half went to Ward 1 and the other half to Ward 2 in Unit 3.

I was in the group assigned to Ward 1 in Unit 3. As soon as we entered, we faced a totally new phenomenon in the Islamic Republic prison system. The authorities had told the four hundred prisoners in the ward who had arrived from different locations during the last week to select their own rooms and to organize their own lives as they wished. This was unheard of in the prison system's history. There were only a few *tavvab* left in the office in the *zir-e hasht* (lobby), who had been ordered not to intervene with the prisoners' internal ward affairs. A prisoner named Darvish had been put in charge of the ward; he greeted the ward prisoners every morning via the sound system and tried to be as accommodating as possible. He had apparently been an adviser to Abolhassan Banisadr, the ex-president of the Islamic Republic, and had been in prison since 1981. He was middle-aged and well-educated.

The general policy of the authorities at this time seemed to be the relaxing of conditions, apparently to prepare prisoners for a new round of questioning and classification. They were hoping to be able to break down the non-*tavvab* prisoner community into three groups: one to be released with minimal conditions, another to receive sentence reduction and be released later, and the last group to be transferred to Gohardasht or Evin and to be dealt with in the future. In general, their approach this time seemed to be less religious and more political, and mainly aimed at reducing the number of political prisoners.

In these new, "liberal" conditions, everyone's inclination was to live with their own comrades and other like-minded people. Mojahedin prisoners counted for about half of the ward prisoners, and the other half consisted of all shades of secular leftists. In their first-ever freedom of choice in living arrangements, Mojahedin and "radical" leftist prisoners exercised their long-suppressed wish to boycott living with the joint Tudeh Party/ Fadaiyan Majority block prisoners, who had organized themselves in a few rooms. The Mojahedin settled in a few large and some small rooms. The rest of the secular leftists, other than the joint Tudeh Party/ Fadaiyan Majority block prisoners, were grouped mainly based on political and lifestyle preferences.

There were seven of us (Habib, Dariush, Morad, Asghar, Yashar, Farzin, and me) from our group in this ward plus "Rasoul," who had indicated he wanted to stay with us. Under the circumstances already prevailing in the ward, we knew we should not live in a Tudeh Party room. To do so would have signaled our deliberate siding with the Tudeh Party in the eyes of the rest of the prisoners. That would have been a disastrous beginning for our group in that ward. Among the large rooms, we tended toward Room 22. It was a non-Tudeh leftist room with a moderate lifestyle, in contrast to the other large rooms. The so-called passive and individualistic secular leftists, who basically had adopted an anarchic "liberal" lifestyle, occupied Room 21. Room 23 had hard-line "radical" secular leftists from a variety of groups, who tended to prefer a less intellectual life. The rest of the secular leftists were organized in a few small rooms in a variety of combinations. But whatever our inclination, there was also a practical consideration. There were only fifteen people in Room 23, while there were more than twenty people in each of Rooms 21 and 22. So Room 23 considered accepting us—on one condition, as "Hooman," their representative, informed us: "There should not be anyone from the joint Tudeh Party/ Fadaiyan Majority block among you!" We replied that as a group we did not believe in that criterion but that we did not have anyone from that block among us. Hooman returned in half an hour and announced that Room 23 had no problem with us joining them. Therefore, we went to Room 23.

Room 24 was a large room across from Room 23, which the authorities had reserved for use as the "cultural room." In reality, there was nothing in it but some junk. We decided to approach Darvish, the prisoner in charge. The next day he informed us that we could take Room 24 to live in. There were no bunk beds in the room, but we were promised that they would arrive soon. We announced in the ward that anyone except *tavvab* prisoners were welcome to join us. Some people indicated their interest. Farzin and Rasoul plus two prisoners named "Assad" and Mehran from the Fadaiyan Minority organization, Gholi (the nonpraying Mojahedin), and a Fadaiyan Majority doctor named "Abdol" decided to join us. And then, from a small Tudeh Party room, a

Fadaiyan Majority prisoner named "Rajab" also joined our room. When we formed the room, we were thirteen people. A few from other rooms also indicated their potential interest in joining us. Asghar nominated Rajab to be *mass'oul-e otagh* (room representative), which was accepted unanimously. Then, we discussed room policies. As a general policy, it was decided that our room would be open to all except *tavvab*. Admission of new people was to be by nomination of an existing member, followed by a room vote. Decision making in general was to be by consensus. If consensus could not be reached, then the majority vote would be accepted as the room policy, while other opinions would be declared as minority views.

2

A few weeks had passed since the formation of this new ward, and prisoners were still in the process of breaking bunk beds, tearing down walls, and constructing shelves and storage. Times had changed so much that prisoners were openly destroying prison property. It was unbelievable that prisoners were being allowed to carry on with this level of freedom in this prison. A year before, you could lose your life for doing only a one-hundredth of what was going on now. Within three to four weeks after the establishment of the ward, all rooms were decorated the way prisoners wanted. You could not believe how nice some of them looked. All beds had colorful sheets and blankets on them. Shelves were built and covered with clean fabric and then the whole unit was covered with a clean curtain. All extra bags were stored in storage places built under or between beds or on wide shelves built around the room close to the ceiling.

Once the ward was relatively established, discussions began about the organization and responsibilities in the ward. It was the first time ever that prisoners were "free" to choose their own way of living in a large ward holding about half Mojahedin and half secular leftist prisoners. It was a situation where neither side could dictate their way of life to the other. This was especially true for the Mojahedin, who had pushed their value system and lifestyle on others whenever and wherever they were in the majority. The authorities, on purpose, had put an almost equal number of Mojahedin and secular leftists in this ward, both as an experiment and to exploit differences between the opposition groups.

These were the issues under discussion: What should the decision-making mechanism be in the ward? How should the ward be run? How should we select people to be in charge of duties, and for what length of time? Opinions ran the gamut from a militaristic, regimented way of life (which was more the Mojahedin way) to an absolutely individualistic way of life (which fit the lifestyle of a small group of the secular leftists). It was a difficult task to bring all these trends into a consensus. The situation seemed very disheartening.

A secular leftist prisoner along with a more moderate Mojahedin friend of his took the lead and distributed a proposal to all rooms. It was written on a piece of paper in a few simple phrases: "Decisions should be made in a democratic way by a majority vote. People in charge should be selected for three months. Accepting and following agreed-upon provisions should be voluntary." This became a basis for further discussion.

Soon serious opposition to the proposal emerged from a variety of corners. Leftists in general, and correctly so, objected to the idea of the rule of simple majority. With simple majority rule, the Mojahedin, who were the majority in the ward, would have selected their own people to all the positions and would have dictated their way of life to the ward, as they had done before. In the end, there were four main responses: one from Room 24 (our room), one from Room 22, one from the Tudeh Party rooms, and one from the Mojahedin rooms. It became a very complicated situation, which probably was the goal of the warden in this experiment. But the positive side of it was that for the first time, we prisoners were in the process of getting organized, and not only about life in the ward but also about defending our rights as political prisoners.

After the four viewpoints were circulated, the first reactions were sectarian, factional, and undemocratic. The Mojahedin suddenly declared that the *mass'oul-e band* (ward representative) had to be from them. As for the other ward positions, they announced that they would prefer to hold them for one term and to let the secular leftists hold them for the next term. Basically, because they could not dominate in this new arrangement, they did not even want to be part of a governing body with others. Furthermore, they still pressed the idea of simple majority rule, trying to impose their way of life on others. From the radical leftists came the objection that they did not want to share anything with the joint Tudeh Party/ Fadaiyan Majority block. Some of the Mojahedin also supported this notion, but to exploit the differences within the secular leftist camp they did not voice their support at this time.

In reality, an absolute majority wanted the ward prisoners to stand united against the regime. They also wanted to have a democratic system, where all sides shared responsibilities and where decisions were made by consensus or at least by a large majority. The discussions continued for many days and nights. Many suggestions and propositions were analyzed and discussed. Finally, reason and necessity prevailed, and the following basics were agreed upon:

First, decisions in the ward should be reached based on a consensus. After a serious attempt, if consensus were not achievable, then a 75 percent majority would be required to establish a given policy. Second, for each position two people would be appointed, one from the Mojahedin and one from the secular leftists. These two would have equal and shared responsibility for the position, and together they would decide how to run their department. The term of all positions would be three months. Third, because currently the authorities did not recognize our *mass'oul-e band*, the appointees to this position would act as the coordinators of the ward's governing body and would also work as liaisons between us and the authorities or their representatives in the ward. They would have no decision-making power; they would only act as the contact persons for the ward. Fourth, contact between those in charge of duties and room members would be via room representatives. The combined council of room representatives and those in charge of duties would constitute the ward's governing body. Fifth, any prisoner, with the exception of the *tavvab* prisoners, could be a candidate for any position.

With pressure from a large majority in the ward who really believed in a democratic system, the extremists from all sides finally backed down and these new rules were adopted as the "constitution" of the ward. After the adoption of the constitution, the Mojahedin and secular leftists were supposed to introduce their candidates for each position. But nothing is that simple in practice. The main problem arose when we were discussing the *mass'oul-e band* position. The Mojahedin had indicated at the beginning of the discussions that they would not want to share that position and would like to have sole right to it. That was of course not acceptable to the secular leftists, who labeled this demand as authoritarian. The Mojahedin in reality were planning for the future, hoping that the authorities would remove the appointed person-in-charge someday, and then they would be ready to take over. They were proposing that the position should be filled only with persons belonging to the so-called revolutionary trend, people who had passed the test of hard times in prison. In short, they believed that the Mojahedin—and only those Mojahedin who were known to be combatant—should fill this position.

The discussions about the *mass'oul-e band* position continued for a while. "Saied" from the Mojahedin, who had become the de facto person in charge, continued holding that position informally. On the other hand, to be fair, there was no agreement among the secular leftists on this issue. Some of the leftists had similar views as the Mojahedin on this subject and openly declared that the *tavvab* and the joint Tudeh Party/ Fadaiyan Majority block should not be eligible for this position. The Mojahedin then suggested that we could not and should not have parallel people for this position at all; rather, only one person at a time should hold it. The leftists agreed with the general basis of that argument, and in return they suggested that the selection for this position should alternate between the two blocks. To encourage the Mojahedin to accept, the leftists declared their agreement that the Mojahedin should take the first term. The Mojahedin accepted the offer and the compromise. The position was a formality at this time anyway, and its responsibilities were designed in a way that the person would have no extra powers or rights except to be a contact person. Saied assumed that position for the first term.

Finally, after a month or so of discussions and arguments, we had a complete governing body, a constitution, rules and regulations, and a bill of rights for living in the ward. It created a more relaxed, open, and creative time for us afterward, one of the best times during this period of our prison experience. And, most important, we had shown the prison authorities that despite our differences, we could cooperate in all aspects of our prison life. We had shown them that we could present a unified front and so could not be defeated.

3

This was by far one of the quietest periods since June 1981, particularly in Ghezelhessar prison. There were more than five hundred people in our ward, over which a "religious-liberal" *tavvab* was nominally in charge, but he did little more than wish us "good morning" and "good night" over the sound system; there were also a few more depressed *tavvab* prisoners in Rooms 1 and 2, but they were starting to feel the heat of their shame. We were basically ruling the ward internally, and this resulted in the most liberal conditions that anyone could remember in prison, at least since June 20, 1981.

It was also the most productive era for most prisoners as well. Three phenomena characterized this period: the variety and extent of classes organized on different subjects and topics; the level of sporting and exercise activities; and the amount of TV watching.

For the first time ever, most people in the ward got involved in some type of studying, whether it was in the form of individual or group reading, writing, or art. Even the most hardcore Mojahedin and secular leftist prisoners were getting involved in these activities. The majority of these classes involved learning a foreign language; English was the most popular, followed, in descending order, by French, German, Spanish, Italian, and Russian. There were also other classes teaching Iranian minority languages like Azari (Azarbaijani) and Kordi (Kurdish) to interested people.

"Ezzat" in this ward taught German exclusively. He was a very likable guy who had studied and lived in West Germany for many years. He belonged to the Ranjbaran Party. Prisoners really liked his teaching style. He held many classes on a daily basis. After breakfast, he would go to the yard, where his first class would have already spread a blanket in a corner of the yard to be ready for him. He would get there with a thermos of hot tea in one hand and his notes and book in the other hand. Because of a hearing impediment, the volume of his voice during teaching would gradually rise. The way he taught German was fascinating because of his hand gestures. It was a funny scene, and there were always some who stood by just to watch him teach.

Reading was critical for political prisoners. The authorities, aware of this desire, always used it as a pressure or bargaining tool, particularly in solitary. But general reading material was available in the public rooms and wards in some form or another. Before June 20, 1981, the authorities had allowed all kinds of books to be delivered to or purchased by the prisoners in Evin. When conditions deteriorated after 1981 and the authorities confiscated everything, including reading materials, prisoners hid some books in their original printed forms or in hand-copied editions. These were saved and transferred from prisoner to prisoner until the present time. For example, we had in the ward a hand-copied version of *The Origin of Life* by A. I. Oparin (published in 1924 in Moscow). Books also had been purchased in book exhibitions organized by the authorities during the past year in the prisons or had been brought in by those who had previously either been *tavvab* or lived in a *tavvab* ward. Plus, the prison library periodically would lend books to prisoners.

Here in this ward, every room had a small library, partly public and partly clandestine. Under the supervision of the person in charge of cultural matters in the ward, a list of all books was prepared and a copy of it was provided to each room so that we all knew what was available. Also, the authorities provided a long list of books from the prison library. We could each borrow up to three books per month. Therefore, we had a wealth of reading material at this time, and book reading had become a main pastime for most people.

As might be expected in a facility for political prisoners, there were few books to be had on politics, philosophy, or economics. But there were many works of literature and history. Many poetry books, short stories and novels, and classical writings (by writers as diverse as Leo Tolstoy, Fyodor Dostoyevsky, Jack London, Victor Hugo, Charles Dickens, and Mark Twain) were available. There were large volumes on all kinds of history: the history of Iran, world history, the history of science, the history of the arts, and, in particular, many books that negatively portrayed the Soviet Union and communism. Of course, the majority of the books in prison were related to religion, written by a variety of religious scholars and "intellectuals."

It was about a month after the arrival of some newcomers to our room that the guards notified us we had to evacuate Room 24 because it was going to be turned into the ward kitchen facility. Prior to this, a little room in the *zir-e hasht* of the ward was used as the kitchen. The guards said they were going to use that room as the office for the newly installed ward guard. They were going to empty Room 2 for some of us. Fifteen of us moved to Room 2, and the rest were dispersed among many other rooms. Room 24 was indeed converted into the ward kitchen facility. The burners and the tea equipment, plus the stored ward food items, were moved there.

As soon as we arrived in the new room, the person in charge of the ward library list informed us that it was our turn to read *Don Quixote*. When we got the book, room members signed up for time slots for all day and night to read it. Both the book itself and the reading of it by different people were fascinating. Whoever had the turn would get the book and jump on the top level of one of the bunk beds and start reading it quietly. I would watch the different people and their facial expressions while they read. It was an incredible experience. Then at lunch or dinnertime we would talk about the stories and the characters in the book.

Morad and Hooman were the room's leaders in playing practical jokes, in telling jokes, and in the room's fun hour (*carevan-e shadi*). Some nights, Morad would sing for us. If it was safe, we would have him imitate the clerical and civilian leaders of the country. There were some who had mastered this mimicry, and Morad was the one who did Ayatollah Gilani and Ayatollah Ardabili imitations really well. Many people could do Khomeini and Montazeri, because they were so easy to mimic, but this was dangerous if you were caught.

As well as the huge increase in opportunities for studying, we were given far more opportunities for sports and exercise. The yard was opened at daylight and closed at sunset. This meant ten to twelve hours of yard time in spring and summer. The yard was clean, neat, and large. There was a small pond in the middle, which the prisoners maintained. Surrounding the pond, there were four large gardening lots with walkways between them. Along three sides of the yard were sidewalks about six to nine feet wide. The fourth sidewalk was about thirty to forty feet wide; this was where volleyball and small-goal soccer fields, table-tennis tables, and other exercise equipment, like for bodybuilding, were located. Every morning, early risers were ready even before the yard opened. The number of participants in morning exercises fluctuated between one hundred fifty and three hundred depending on the weather conditions. The maximum number was about four hundred people. Exercise in these wards had to be communal. The authorities now prohibited individual exercise, which was amazing compared to the restrictions that had prevailed in the Rahmani era.

We were also allowed far more access to TV. During the summer of 1986 we enjoyed watching and following the World Cup soccer matches. The ward mosque, where the TV set was located, was usually packed for these games. There was also a lot of betting happening on the side for the World Cup.

I spent my daily free time reading newspapers and books, exercising, and playing sports. Plus, I walked and talked with as many prisoners from different backgrounds as I could. Among them, I kept up my friendship and contact with Yavar, and we regularly exchanged information and opinions.

4

The prison sound system, under "normal" conditions, relayed the 2:00 PM national and international news program of the "Voice of the Islamic Republic of Iran." There were two very important news items we heard on one of those early summer days. The first was the arrest of Mehdi Hashemi and his followers. Mehdi Hashemi, one of the founders of the Revolutionary Guards and head of its liberation movements unit, was also the brother of Ayatollah Montazeri's son-in-law. Montazeri, the heir-designate of Khomeini at the time, was a very important figure in the Islamic regime. Apparently Mehdi Hashemi had exposed the secret travel of Robert C. MacFarlane, the special envoy of US president Ronald Reagan, who apparently had led a secret delegation to Tehran with a symbolic gift package of "bible and cake" to meet and negotiate with Akbar Hashemi Rafsanjani and other Khomeini appointees. Khomeini was forced to order the arrest of Mehdi Hashemi and his followers and the investigation of some others in the office of Montazeri. This was the beginning of the end of the longstanding close and trusting relationship between the two ayatollahs. Mehdi Hashemi was executed later, despite all attempts by Montazeri to save him.

The second piece of news related to the arrests of a group called Ayyaran. This was a group that belonged to a Sufi dervish order from western Iran. Part of their leadership lived in a small town near Karaj called Sorkhe Hessar. The news item claimed they had killed some of their own members and had been involved in corruption, drugs, indecent activities, and the like. As soon as I heard the news, I realized that it related to one of my friends and coworkers, Dr. Sadrollah Siah-Mansouri. I had met him in the Ministry of Agriculture in early 1984, when I took a position as a consultant on a project with which he was also involved. He was one of the noblest human beings I ever met. The official Islamic news releases always attached the same kind of criminal charges—inappropriate sexual relationship, corruption, alcohol consumption, prostitution, gun possession, drug trafficking, money laundering, and murder—to any group or person arrested from the opposition. It had become so ridiculous that even many followers of the regime did not believe or trust these accusations anymore, but the regime persisted with its claims and methods.

In Ghezelhessar prison we had three methods of contact with our fellow prisoners in Evin. The first was through prisoners who were taken to Evin for a variety of reasons and were brought back later; the second was through new prisoners who were transferred to Ghezelhessar from Evin; and the third was through families who had members in both prisons. About this time, we received news from Evin that some of the leaders of different groups had been taken from Evin to the Komiteh detention center. The authorities wanted to pressure them and extract new interviews or other types of cooperation. Apparently, a few had given in to the new pressures, accepting some form of interview or collaboration, but many others had not.

In the Islamic Republic, obtaining public confessions and recantations from political opponents became an integral part of the regime's judiciary and prison systems. Pressure to obtain an interview in which the prisoner would condemn his own beliefs and activities and those of all other opponents to the regime, admit to all kind of crimes whether political or sexual in nature, admit to spying for all kinds of foreign interests, and finally acknowledge his past mistakes and declare his repentance and loyalty to the supreme leader and the Islamic regime became the norm in the prison system of the Islamic Republic. This chronic pressure is very different from the acute pressure brought upon a prisoner for obtaining intelligence. The pressure for intelligence is severe, focused, and short-lived, but the pressure for obtaining an interview from a prisoner, though mild, could last as long as necessary and it could come at different periods of his prison experience. Although there was pressure for such interviews on almost all prisoners in the Islamic Republic prisons, it was certainly heavier on leaders, cadres, and well-known members of the opposition.

In general, different types of interviews for different purposes were demanded. There were interviews obtained for widespread public use through mass media, mainly television. There were interviews obtained for use only within prison. And then there were interviews demanded as a condition of the release of a prisoner. Each type served a purpose as far as the regime was concerned. The first type aimed at discrediting individuals or opposition groups in the eyes of the masses and also aimed to display the power of the regime to destroy any kind of opposition. It was designed to create fear and increase the regime's control over people in general. The second type aimed at breaking down the resistance of prisoners and preventing any notion of solidarity and struggle within the prisons by bringing down the morale of the prison population. The third type, which was an invention of the Islamic regime, forced prisoners who had served their full sentences, and often even longer, to provide an interview in front of the prison population or record one on videotape prior to their release. The purpose of this was to have a document in hand to control the prisoner even when he was freed, to force him into self-censorship even outside in freedom.

5

For the first time since 1981, there was an atmosphere in prison where prisoners could relatively freely discuss issues concerning prison life. From all these discussions, three main views had developed. The pessimists believed that the changes in prison were part of a game plan of the regime. They prepared for the bygone days of the Lajavardi/Rahmani era to return soon. The consequences of this view were more distrust, more secrecy, and increasingly close-knit organizations and relations. The optimists thought that the changes had produced a level of liberality that could never return to anything remotely close to the oppression of the past. The consequences of this view were passivity and a tendency to be apolitical and even accommodating to the authorities. The realists felt that though the changes were tactical and temporary in nature, the Lajavardi/Rahmani era was not coming back anytime soon. They thought that conditions could change to something worse than that era, but it was not going to be the same thing. They thought prisoners should be smart and remain alert, adjusting their tactics according to the changes that were taking place in the prison system. They believed in struggling to exploit the new conditions and to extract more concessions from the regime, but they also believed in being prepared to face the worst in the future.

In the middle of the summer of 1986, we started noticing some new changes in the prison system. Gradually, the *tavvab* prisoners were taken away until their numbers decreased to only a few in the ward. The *tavvab* phenomenon at this time not only did not help the regime's cause anymore, it had become a liability for their new prison policies. Soon, the authorities decided to move all the *tavvab* out of the combatant prisoners' wards. Some were freed, and others were kept separately, out of sight. The authorities even pulled out large groups of prisoners from other wards, and Meysam or intelligence authorities talked to them in the unit corridor. The bottom line of these talks was that as far as the regime was concerned, it was the last chance for those who wished to be freed. The regime basically declared that it was the end of the road for both sides. They announced that, with the permission of Khomeini, they were going to separate those who had changed and could be released from those on whom the prison experience had had no effect at all.

The main discussion in our ward was whether the regime was retreating because of weakness or was just engaging in another tactical offense on prison resistance. What was the goal of the regime with this aggressive tactic? What should prisoners do under these circumstances? A majority of the prisoners in the combatant wards were still steadfast in their rejection of any offer. Though prisoners differed in their analyses, when faced with practical matters they took very similar positions. They agreed that we should not accept any conditions put forward for term reduction involving parole or amnesty that the regime could exploit politically and socially. Overall, non-*tavvab* prisoners did not agree to sign an *enzejar nameh* (self-defamation letter) and they did not participate in interviews for parole or reduction of prison terms. Only a few individuals in our wards accepted any offer.

The case was different, though, for conditions for release at the end of a sentence. Even before these recent events, we had disagreed about accepting these conditions. Traditionally, the authorities had demanded, at the least, the signing of an *enzejar nameh* but more usually a videotaped interview. The Mojahedin as an organizational policy agreed to the videotaped interview. They wanted to be released so that they could join their organization and its National Liberation Army (NLA) based in Iraq. The leftists, historically, were opposed to accepting any condition for release at the end of a prison term. At the most, they agreed that signing an *enzejar nameh* would be acceptable. Some had recently proposed that it would be all right to agree to a videotaped interview if it was for a sizable reduction of the prison term, but not for release after serving the whole term.

The leftists thought that the Mojahedin policy was contradictory. On the one hand, the Mojahedin were promoting resistance and offensive moves in prisons and therefore they opposed accepting any conditions for sentence reduction at this juncture. But on the other hand, they recommended that their followers agree to self-defamation and condemnation interviews to obtain release at the end of their prison terms. The leftists saw a double standard here, but the Mojahedin did not see any contradiction in their policies or in their actions. To be fair, you could see that from their point of view their policies in both cases made sense. On the one hand, they wanted to strengthen their NLA, and therefore they encouraged their followers to get released at the end of their sentences and join the NLA. On the other hand, they believed that the final conflict would arrive soon, and therefore they opposed their followers accepting any prison-term reductions or retreating from their positions against the regime, wanting them instead to raise the level of their resistance and struggle in prison.

The authorities were busy these days trying to convince as many prisoners as they could to accept conditions for parole, term reduction, or amnesty. Some Mojahedin and a few leftists—some of the combative, resistant veteran prisoners who had previously experienced harder times—accepted the offers and were moved out. Seeing such strong opponents of the regime give in had a negative psychological effect, at least on the more passive elements in our ward.

It was also during this period that Mansoor Davaran, a Fadaiyan Majority prisoner, was being released at the end of his sentence. He was from Tabriz, my hometown, and we had become friends in the ward during these past few months. He came and talked to me before being transferred to Evin for release. He asked if I needed anything to be done in Tabriz. I asked him to visit my mother and to give her support and strength from me. We said good-bye and he was taken to Evin to be released.

6

One day, a propaganda display was erected in the *zir-e hasht* of the ward by the prison cultural office. It contained articles and photos indicating that an armed conflict had taken place within the ranks of the Fadaiyan Minority organization forces in the mountainous area of the Kordestan border. It also indicated that Mojahedin forces had joined with one side in the conflict against the other. This had a profound effect on the prisoners in general, and on the relationship of the two groups in particular. The Mojahedin and the Fadaiyan Minority had had a close relationship in prison since 1981. This recent incident and the purposeful spread of the news about it in prison by the authorities were about to end that united tactical front. Moreover, the news created a crisis within the ranks of the Fadaiyan Minority prisoners, reflecting their support for the two opposing sides in this conflict.

This was also when we found out that in Evin the authorities had opened room doors in Salones 1 and 3 of Amoozeshgah, turning them into public wards where the prisoners could choose their own rooms and organize their lives as we did here in our ward. Making Salones 1 and 3 public wards was one of the most drastic changes in Evin prison since 1981. In these Salones, most of the veteran prisoners who had been in solitary or in closed-door rooms for years were now living together with other prisoners.

But the move did not go as the authorities had hoped, since it increased rather than decreased the prisoners' combativeness. The first successful strike, the boycotting of prison food and store items, was organized by the Salone 3 prisoners. After a month, the authorities were forced to accept the demands of the prisoners to temporarily ease the situation. This set the tone for the upcoming struggle in Tehran's prisons. The news from Gohardasht prison was also encouraging, indicating that the new wards formed there were run by the prisoners themselves without any *tavvab* presence, and also that the family visits there were weekly while in Ghezelhessar they were biweekly.

It was during the summer of 1986 that the news of massive arrests of members of the Fadaiyan Majority organization was publicized. The last major opposition organization had been destroyed inside Iran. It was a sad day for all of us, whether or not we agreed with the politics of that organization. With this blow, the security forces of the regime had completely wiped out all major organized opposition inside Iran, starting in 1980 and finishing in 1986. This included organizations attempting to overthrow the regime, organizations supporting the regime, those that had resorted to armed struggle, and those that were against the use of violence. This turn of events had a generally demoralizing effect on us political prisoners, who needed a grain of hope to be able to serve our long sentences and endure the hardship and torture while resisting and struggling. The regime, at least in the short run, had ended the danger of being overthrown by an opposition group from inside Iran, forcing the insignificant remainder of its opponents out of the country. The leaders of Iran knew well that uprooting these organizations and forcing them into exile or into prisons would marginalize them. Even Iranian Kurdish organizations, which had a sizable base of support in Iranian Kordestan, had been forced into the remote mountainous regions of the border or even into exile.

7

Quite a bit of activity had recently started in Ghezelhessar prison. It was obvious the authorities were preparing to move us out of the unit and maybe out of the prison itself. Recent news indicated that the *tavvab* prisoners had all been evacuated. One day, groups of people were called out with all of their belongings from both Wards 1 and 2. The normal living routine in the wards was again disrupted. People started packing their personal belongings. Some of us were going to be separated from each other again. Sadness took over the whole ward in a matter of minutes. You would think that after so many years and so much experience in prison, one would get used to these sudden changes, particularly the separations, but that was not the case. Separations were the saddest of events in prison. We tried to find out where we were going, but the guards would not leak any information. Finally, we got some indirect indication that we were not going to Evin. This meant that we were going to Gohardasht prison, which in turn meant that we would probably be divided into three wards, at least.

We remained in this limbo for a couple of days. Every day, the guards called a list from our ward and one from Ward 2 as well, until about two hundred of us were left in each ward. One night, we were told that the following morning we were all leaving as well. We gathered in our rooms for a last meal, while everything was packed.

In the morning, they first called the remaining two hundred people from Ward 2. After breakfast, they called us out around ten o'clock. Each of us had to carry our sleeping gear and our other bags in addition to some communal stuff. It was a good thing that no blindfold was required in this prison. A group of about thirty to forty prisoners was brought out of Ward 5, and they joined us as well. We had heard that one of our organizational comrades named "Nasser" was among them, but we did not know him yet. We tried to stay together, so that in case they divided us randomly we would end up in the same group. But Ansari showed up with lists in hand. That disappointed us because we knew we would probably be separated. This time around, the list was alphabetical.

They called about half of the prisoners, put them in the buses, and took them away. In the half left behind, only Asghar and I were from our organization, plus Nasser, whom we still had not met. Our roommates were all gone. Asghar and I were sitting down, sad and lonely, when Nasser found us. We hugged and greeted each other. Nasser told us how happy he was to have found us because his lonely days were over now. Life has such strange and funny sides to it. We were sad because we had been separated from our friends and roommates, while he was so happy to have finally found at least two of his comrades. He explained that after transfer to Ghezelhessar prison he had developed a severe back problem, landing him in Ward 5 of Unit 3, the ward containing mostly sick and disabled prisoners.

They finally boarded us on the buses. There were about one hundred twenty to one hundred thirty of us left, and we were going together to the same ward. In total, the ratio of Mojahedin to secular leftist prisoners was about two to one in this group. It was 4:00 PM when finally we got on the buses with two trucks full of our belongings following us. In each bus, there were two or three plainclothes guards plus the driver. They told us to have our blindfolds ready to wear when ordered. From Ghezelhessar prison to the Gohardasht area was not too far, and we took mostly side roads to get there. Along the way we could see only farms, orchards, and some residential neighborhoods.

An Anniversary

It's an anniversary
But nothing to celebrate about
I tried to be happy today
Although there was no reason to be
It was only because you wanted us to.

Two years ago
(It's so painful to remember)
I expected you to come home
It was a cold October day
Unusually cold

The baby was dressed up and ready to go
(We had an appointment, you know)
But the door didn't open
You didn't come
And I got angry, scared, and sad

I knew what had happened
But tried to be optimistic
I made excuses for you
And looked to the door
It never opened

The baby fell asleep in the chair
I saw a war movie
And felt so empty inside
Now I was alone, all by myself
What to do?

It's an anniversary
Two years have passed
We're alive, but not living
I try to be happy (pretending is so hard)
It's only because you want us to be.

—Ketty Mobed
Offenbach, West Germany
October 1986

Part Four

ISLAMIC INQUISITION

Chapter Eight

WELCOME TO HELL!

1

November 1986

As we neared our destination, I could see that our new prison, located on a hillside near the town of Gohardasht (a.k.a. Rajaishahr), was a huge compound surrounded by tall concrete walls and security towers. When we were almost there, the guards ordered us to put our blindfolds on. They also pulled the curtains over the windows. While we traveled in darkness, prisoners who had served months or years in solitary in Gohardasht during 1981 to 1984 explained to the rest of us what they knew of this prison.

The shah's regime had begun construction on this prison with the help of the Israelis, but it was not yet completed when the 1979 revolution occurred. The Islamic regime completed it by 1981. The original idea for this prison was to have prisoners kept in cells round the clock, except for meals and yard time. There was a "dining salon" at the end of each ward, where meals were supposed to be served, and each ward had access to a small yard.

In 1982 the first group of one hundred twenty prisoners from Evin arrived at Gohardasht and were set up in a public ward. Then, gradually, Assadollah Lajavardi in Evin and Davoud Rahmani in Ghezelhessar sent "problem" prisoners to Gohardasht for solitary confinement. Soon there were many "solitary" wards with hundreds of prisoners. It was only around 1984 that new public wards were formed to accommodate more prisoners brought from Evin and Ghezelhessar, in addition to those coming out of solitary in Gohardasht.

The main prison structure was a three-story complex. On each floor, the main corridor connected wards and other facilities on both sides. Between any two consecutive buildings, there was a small yard. There were only three public wards—wards with large rooms—in this prison. These were Wards 1, 2, and 3. Most other wards had twenty-four "solitary" cells with metal doors opening to a narrow hallway. Attached to each ward, there was a small side unit called *far'i* (minor) with two rooms and a bathroom and shower service, which was mainly used for prisoner isolation and punishment.

In general, ground-floor wards were not used for housing prisoners because the cell windows had a direct view of the yards. At one end of the ground floor's main corridor, there was a large building attached to the prison complex. It was originally meant to be an amphitheater, but it was now designated as the main mosque or *hosseiniye* of the prison.

Once we were inside the outer gate, the buses continued driving for a while before they finally stopped. Guards poured into the buses, yelling about our blindfolds and other nonsense. The warden was a mullah named "Haji Naseri," who had taken delivery of us in Ghezelhessar and also greeted us when we got out of the buses in Gohardasht. A head guard gave a pep talk about the regulations of this prison. Finally, they directed us out of the buses and lined us up blindfolded. Each of us had only a small bag because the rest of our belongings were in the two trucks. The guards started moving us while barking and yelling nonstop.

We entered through a gate into a wide driveway, which we later learned was located under the kitchen building. Club-wielding guards were shouting that we were not in Ghezelhessar prison anymore and that we had better get used to the new situation. Asghar, Nasser, and I tried hard to stay together. They directed us through a stairway up a floor and then we entered the main corridor. After passing through a door and a *zir-e hasht* (lobby), we entered into a ward hallway. They walked us through and we ended up in a place where they told us to remove our blindfolds.

We found ourselves in a very strange large salon. There were thirty to forty bunk beds, with some space left open in the middle. The guards locked the only entrance to the salon and left. There were windows all around the salon, but they were covered from the outside with metal shades in such a way that you could see only the sky. The floor was covered with thin, dirty, wall-to-wall carpeting. In the west side of the salon, there was a nook that looked like a kitchen or food service station. There were no bathrooms in the salon.

The pressure started to build up among the prisoners. It was late afternoon, and the crowd was getting really angry. More than twenty people at any given time were knocking on and kicking the door, but it seemed as though there was no one in the vicinity to even hear us. It was early evening when finally a guard opened the door and asked what we wanted. People were shouting and arguing chaotically. The guard listened for a while, then closed the door without saying a word.

Around seven o'clock the door opened again and someone entered with two guards by his side. He introduced himself as "Haji Mahmoud" and said he had come to answer our questions. It became extremely chaotic again. People were yelling and demanding to know why we had been locked in there that long, why we had not been given our daily rations yet, demanding to go to the bathroom. Haji Mahmoud replied that in Gohardasht there were no wards with rooms like we had in Ghezelhessar, and he indicated that we had to live in the salon as a group. About rations, he said they had not included us for the daily ration, but he would try to get us some bread and cheese for the night. About our belongings, he replied that it was going to take a couple of days before they could deliver them to us. He promised to get us some prison blankets. Finally, someone asked about bathroom access. He replied that the guards were going to take us three times a day to use the bathroom facility in the yard.

This was unacceptable, especially following the so-called reform era of Ghezelhessar prison. We started protesting and shouting at him. Suddenly, his mood changed: "The fun time is over. No more vacationing in prison. This is Gohardasht, not a hotel. You are prisoners, and we will treat you like it. Some of you, whose faces are familiar to me, can tell others where this place is." He then turned around and left without answering any more questions.

Around nine o'clock, the guard threw in some blankets and some bread and feta cheese. As usual, some prisoners took charge and divided the bread and cheese and distributed the blankets. At 10:00 PM, the guards took all of us to a yard to use the bathroom facility. We went to bed at 11:00 PM, not knowing what surprises would be waiting for us in the morning. Within a matter of a day, our lives had turned upside down.

In the morning, there was no sign of the guards. We needed to use the bathroom very badly. Anger was building up again. Some prisoners were behind the door knocking and kicking constantly. Finally a guard opened the door, listened to the crowd for a while, then closed the door and left. This was the strangest of behaviors, something none of us had experienced before. Historically, guards were very talkative, interactive, and aggressive. But suddenly, they had become mute and deaf.

It was, of course, all part of a game plan. The authorities wanted to establish a new norm after the "excesses" of the past two years in Ghezelhessar prison. They believed they had given us every chance to accept a deal offered by the regime and we had rejected it. Now, they had decided to change the game plan for those of us who had chosen to resist.

Later, the guards returned with some bread and cheese again, but there was no sign of a tea ration. They also took people, a few at a time, to use the bathroom. After breakfast, the door kicking and knocking continued, but no response was heard. We finally got a bit organized and conducted some discussions. There was a consensus that we might be stuck there for a while, and therefore we needed to get our act together to be able to have a strong voice.

Haji Mahmoud entered the ward again and gave the same kind of speech as before about the vacation being over, but finally he said, "I will allow a few people to go check the pile of stuff downstairs and separate whatever belongs to you." That was ridiculous. We all wanted to go get our own belongings, but he would not agree to that. Haji Mahmoud threatened that if we did not accept his offer, he was going to leave. We had to accept it. So five or six people went with the guards and returned after an hour or so. They had been taken to the ground level where a large pile of prisoners' things was in the hallway, but apparently nothing in it belonged to us.

Concluding that we might be kept there for a while, we rearranged the bunk beds all around the salon, leaving a larger space open in the middle. This space was used for meetings, eating meals, and other activities. We decided to get tougher in demanding our rights.

One day, we knocked and kicked the door so much that Haji Mahmoud showed up again. After his usual speech, he finally promised that he would have the door kept open so that we could access the ward hallway and the bathrooms there, emphasizing that the cells in the ward would be kept closed for now. Though this was not acceptable, it was much better than our present situation, where we had no direct access to any toilet or bathing facilities; it made life easier, especially for the sick and the elderly with bladder issues. We could also use the ward hallway for walking. Although the conditions were not comparable at all to Ghezelhessar prison, things were changing slowly for the better.

Basically, the authorities wanted to force us to live with limited resources and under constant pressure, hoping that maybe some or most of us would give up resisting and accept their conditions for release. But we were in no mood to retreat or to accept any deals. Instead, the combative prison population believed that our resistance struggle in the prisons had grown stronger during the last couple of years and therefore we were in a position to get more and more concessions from the regime. Whether we were right or wrong was yet to be seen.

2

After almost a month, the guards finally took us a few at a time to claim our belongings from piles in vacant wards and storage areas. Gradually, we pulled out our own blankets and sheets, and life was "normalized" in the ward. We spread *sofreh* (dinner cloth) in the middle of the salon for meals, where we all ate together as one large *komon* (commune). This was unheard of in Ghezelhessar prison, where at the most you ate in your room as a small group. We had not yet been given any yard time and had not even seen the upper-ward prisoners in the yard either. One day, finally, they came into our yard. We could see them through the small dents on the edges of the metal shades covering the windows, which had been made by previous prisoners kept here. People recognized some among the yard prisoners from the past years. The following day, we were allowed to go to the yard as well.

We had many people in our ward who were in need of continuous medical attention. There was a Mojahedin who had had heart surgery;

Fereydoon Tafreshi from the Tudeh Party had been tortured so severely that the nerves in the soles of his feet were exposed and he could not stand or walk without assistance; and Javad Arteshiar, the oldest Tudeh Party cadre in our ward, needed constant care. Because of the needs of these men and many others, there were always a few of us behind the ward door demanding medical attention for someone.

A few more times Haji Mahmoud came to respond to our demands, but not much resulted of it. Constant pressure from us forced him to bring one of his superiors, Haji Davoud Lashgari (a.k.a. Lashgari), who was in charge of prison security. Lashgari had been a regular guard here in 1982 when many prisoners served time in solitary. Apparently, because of his brutality he had climbed the power ladder fairly quickly to become the deputy warden in charge of prison security by 1985. He was a large man, probably in his late thirties. He came in, talked to us, then held a question-and-answer session.

In his talk, he basically repeated what Haji Mahmoud had frequently stressed before, namely that we were not in Ghezelhessar prison anymore and that things were different in this prison. Then he added that if we followed the regulations, we would be left to live our lives. But if we did not follow the regulations and tried to engage in political activity, they would teach us a lesson we would never forget, if we were lucky enough to survive. After these threats, he let us ask him questions or express our concerns. Different demands, questions, and requests were presented, to which he gave very short responses. Basically, he gave no definitive answer to anything. He then left, while truthfully nothing had been resolved, although we had been warned that the authorities in Gohardasht seriously intended to break us.

One day, prisoners from Ward 1 on the south side of our building finally came into their yard. We could see them from our windows, through the small dents in the metal shades. Asghar had already found out that one of our comrades, "Rostam," was in that ward. We soon established contact by dropping a small note and then took turns to talk to Rostam via lipreading, Morse code, or exchanging notes. We would drop a line of thread through the window into their yard and exchange notes by attaching them to the line. Rostam informed us that three people from our organization—himself, "Naghi," and "Saman"—were in that ward. We told him about us three as well. Asghar managed to get a good Webster's dictionary and a couple of short-story books in English from Ward 1. This made him very happy. To exchange larger material, a rope attached to a small bag was dropped to their yard through a window with a completely bent or broken metal shade.

One distinctive aspect of prison policy toward our ward was that they would never tell us the schedule for anything. We had to figure out for ourselves if there was any order at all. The general policy they pursued regarding us was that they would not inform us or give us anything unless we requested it. They wanted to force us to have a continuous dialogue and negotiation with them.

3

Because of the pressure we were putting on the shift guards, and particularly on Haji Mahmoud, he was forced to bring the top man himself to talk to us. One night after dinner, he ordered all of us to be present in the ward hallway at 8:00 PM to meet a top prison authority who, he claimed, could answer our questions and resolve our problems. We were forced to sit on the floor in the hallway, waiting. Then Mullah Naseri entered with his entourage. They set out a chair for him, and a guard stood by, while Haji Mahmoud stood at the side.

The mullah said he was in charge of the prison. His speech was basically the same as those of others before him: that we were not in Ghezel-hessar anymore. He said he had a different system for two main reasons: first, because the physical structure (the building, ward and room space, and yard facilities) of the prison was limited; second, because visits were weekly here and prisoners were in charge of their own wards. He said that we had to take the good and the bad together.

Generally speaking, his talk was not threatening like Lashgari's. He tried to convince us that he could deliver more if we accepted some limitations, and particularly if we stayed away from the path of political activities. He finally permitted prisoners to ask questions or raise their concerns. There had been no preparation or coordination on our part for this. But still, some questions were asked, points were raised, and a few requests were made. The meeting ended around ten o'clock without any clear resolutions.

A few people gave prepared lists of requests and demands to Naseri, which he promised to take a look at personally. The demands were very basic: a regular yard schedule, open cell doors, letter-writing and visitation rights to be established, legal rations of food and other items to be provided, and the right to medical attention. But the authorities wanted to use these so-called privileges as bargaining chips in getting us to follow prison regulations. When Naseri left, he promised that he would look into correcting all these issues. And gradually things did get a bit better in some areas.

One morning, we found all the cell doors open. A ward council, which had taken shape during the previous weeks, soon arranged cell assignments. Three of us got a cell in the middle of the ward on the north side looking out to our own yard. As soon as cells had been assigned, prisoners started to bend the metal window shades using metal bars taken off the beds. This way, we could have a better view of the yards. Then we moved our belongings from the salon into our cells.

Blankets were spread, and prisoners started decorating to make their cells more livable.

Prior to this, the guards would come every night and ask us for a head count. The first night in the cells, around nine o'clock, the guards asked us to go to our cells for a roll call. We did, and they made a head count. They did not say a word about the dents made in the window shades or about anything else. Assuming that they had no objection to our decorating actions, the following day we started constructing shelves and compartments in the cells using broken pieces of some of the bunk beds. There was digging, banging, and bending all over the ward. The thick heating pipe in each cell was used as base, and a shelf or shelves were built over it. Decorations were built to cover the shelves as well.

I think it was Asghar who suggested we bring a bunk bed inside our cell. We succeeded, with much difficulty. Pretty soon, many other prisoners put a bunk bed in their cells as well. Maybe only ten beds were left in the salon. A few had been broken up, and more than twenty had been squeezed into cells.

When the guards came that night for the roll call and noticed what had happened, they went crazy. Soon, they returned with Haji Mahmoud. He said we had no right to do what we had done with the beds and the cells. Then he threatened that if we did not return the beds to their original locations the following day, he would order all cells to be closed again. Discussions among us continued late into the night. No one wanted to return the beds to the salon. We were wondering what the authorities would really do in response.

The following day, Haji Mahmoud himself came to see if we had obeyed his orders, then he ordered the guards to put all of us back in the salon. They locked the salon door and left us there. We spent that night there without anything. In the morning, the guards opened the salon door and let us into the ward hallway. All the beds had been removed from the cells and taken away by the guards the night before. All of our belongings in the cells had been searched and thrown in the middle of the hallway or on the cell floors. They had confiscated all metal, wood, cardboard, and everything else used in shelf construction. We organized our cells with whatever we had left.

This was our first collective action in this prison, and we were actually happy with the way it had gone. Though we had lost some physical possessions and comforts, we had gained solidarity, camaraderie, and strength in our shared resistance. After another incident, they closed the salon completely, and we were left with the cells and the ward hallway. We did not retreat from our positions and were proud of our resistance, solidarity, and unity.

This was the beginning of 1987 and about three years since the start of the "reforms" following the removal of the Lajavardi and Rahmani gangs from control of the Tehran prisons. These prisons had witnessed the culmination of the reform era a while back and currently were seeing a rise in the level of resistance and struggle. The news was indicative of this shift in the Tehran prisons, both Evin and Gohardasht. The authorities had not yet been able to regain the control they had had before the reforms. In Gohardasht prison, the authorities had started a campaign to take back all that the prisoners had gained during the reform era, but the prisoners, resisting collectively, were not allowing their hard-won gains to be lost so easily.

4

Ward 11, where we had been kept for about four months, turned out to be a temporary station for us. One day, we were told to gather in the hallway, and afterward Lashgari called a group of names and ordered those prisoners to prepare to leave. About half of the ward was on that list, mostly Mojahedin with only a few leftists. Later we learned they had been taken to Ward 2, which was similar to Ward 3 in that they both had large rooms instead of small cells and the majority of prisoners were Mojahedin. A few hours later, we were told to get ready to leave as well. We were taken to Ward 3 upstairs. It held about one hundred ninety Mojahedin, ten Tudeh Party, and a few other leftist prisoners. Our group contained twenty-five more Tudeh Party, seven or eight other leftists, and ten more Mojahedin prisoners.

We entered the ward, put our belongings in the entrance area, and were greeted by the other prisoners. Everything looked and felt different from Ward 11. Instead of solitary cells, there were rooms with regular doors. Near the entrance of the ward were a shower room on the right and a bathroom on the left. Then Rooms 1 and 2, opposite each other, were the kitchen and storage room, respectively. The rest of the rooms, 3 to 16, were dedicated to prisoners' quarters. Only four non-Tudeh leftist prisoners occupied Room 3, while ten Tudeh Party prisoners lived in Room 4. Rooms 5 to 16 had Mojahedin prisoners, about fifteen to sixteen per room. The salon at the end of the ward was used as a multipurpose room. At night, about a hundred prisoners slept in it. Religious prisoners used it for prayer. During the winter, when table-tennis tables were moved back up from the yard, it was used as a game room. Fridays, it was used for *kar-e melli* (communal work). But it was mainly used for daily communal meal services, for studying and holding classes during quiet hours, and for TV watching.

"Kamran," Ezzat, and "Mostafa" went to Room 3. There were too many Tudeh Party prisoners now for one room, and therefore the Mojahedin evacuated Room 6 for them as well. The Tudeh Party prisoners now had Rooms 4 and 6, with sixteen to seventeen people per room. The Mojahedin prisoners who had come with us were quickly divided among the different Mojahedin rooms. Only three of us were left without a room, our bags sitting by the entrance door. We faced a dilemma again. It was unfortunate that rooms were assigned based on political and organizational lines, but that was the reality here and we had to adjust to it. Because there were only three of us, we could not expect a room of our own in this crowded ward, so we had to make a political decision very quickly. Not wanting to go to a Tudeh Party room, we ended up in Room 3 with the other leftists. There were ten of us now: four from the Fadaiyan Minority, three from the Fadaiyan Sixteenth of Azar, two from the Peykar organization, and one from the Ranjbaran Party.

This ward offered us the most interesting communal-life experience we would have in this prison. The authorities had tolerated a large *komon* in this ward where prisoners contributed to a public-funds box and used these funds to buy food, which they prepared, ate, and shared collectively. This was unheard of in any other prison, especially for such a large number of prisoners. The base unit in the ward was still the room. The room representatives operated as a council, channeling all discussions to all rooms. Additionally, there were elected representatives in the ward to implement and administer the policies. They were in charge of different duties including *mass'oul-e band* (ward representative), *mass'oul-e senfi* (food service representative), cleaning, *kar-e melli*, health, sports, and cultural activities. The *mass'oul-e band* represented the interests of the ward with the authorities, though they never officially acknowledged this position.

Other representatives also dealt with the authorities regarding their own area of work. The *mass'oul-e senfi* and the *mass'oul-e band* were in charge of the public funds. They prepared the weekly shopping list based on prisoners' agreements and used it to order items from the prison store. The representatives were also in charge of receiving prison rations from the guards and the Afghani prisoners helping them.

Afghani prisoners were regular criminal prisoners who were kept in a separate ward in Gohardasht prison. At this time Iran had an Afghani refugee population of about two million. These Afghanis had fled to Iran after the Soviet invasion of Afghanistan in 1979. The Afghani prisoners in Gohardasht had been arrested for a variety of criminal and illegal activities.

While we were settling in Room 3, everyone was called to the salon for communal dinner. Many long *sofreh* (dinner cloth) had been spread for over two hundred people to share the meal together. Each pair of prisoners sitting across from each other shared a plate of food. There was no seating assignment, except for the ill—in particular the chronic *me'dei* (prisoners with any kind of digestive-system related illnesses). They sat at the top section of one of the long *sofreh* to receive specially prepared food, because the prison *aash* (thick soup) for that night was full of beans and not suitable for their digestive conditions.

Generally, a considerable portion of our time, money, and attention was devoted to taking care of digestive-related issues in prison. Because the authorities, regardless of the recommendations of the prison-clinic doctor, did not provide *me'dei* prisoners with their prescribed dietary needs, prisoners took it upon themselves to support their sick comrades by purchasing extra food items supplemented with what they could separate from the daily food ration. The ward's daily workers distributed plates or bowls of prison food and the supporting side dishes, then cleaned up after dinner, when everyone else left for walk-and-talk in the corridor. The whole process was well organized and impressive.

In fact, the ward was over-organized, as the Mojahedin rooms had typically been in Ghezelhessar. The Mojahedin put more emphasis on the communal values of living and did not pay so much attention to individuality and personal needs and rights. This difference was most pronounced in the Mojahedin rooms, but even at the ward level, the Mojahedin tried to organize and control every aspect of everyone's lives as much as possible. The people in charge of the ward, who were all from the Mojahedin, administered everything on a daily basis. However, each room had its own internal organization. In our room, there was only one person in charge and a pair of daily room workers who kept the room tidy and clean and helped in the distribution of food or shopping items to our room. The Mojahedin rooms had a more complicated arrangement, and Tudeh Party rooms were somewhere in between.

Our first Friday, we found out that *kar-e melli* was a very extensive and serious business in this ward. For the whole day, the salon was dedicated to these activities. From early morning, all kinds of shops were set up around the salon. The day before, the person in charge of *kar-e melli* assigned prisoners to different stations. After breakfast on Friday, people set to work on all kinds of chores: repairing sandals or converting them into athletic shoes, breaking sugar cubes into smaller pieces, cleaning dates and figs, sewing, weaving, and woodwork. We had seen *kar-e melli* in Ghezelhessar prison, but not to this extent.

Reactions from the secular leftists to this extreme practice varied. We generally thought we should participate conditionally, meaning that we would participate only in those activities that we recognized as necessary for the community, but we would stay away from those that did not have much to do with our normal lives, such as activities the Mojahedin created just to keep their young forces occupied.

We had electric shavers in this ward. The shavers belonged to various prisoners who had obtained them when they were in wards or prisons that allowed them. In this ward, the owners had agreed to supply them for communal use. The person in charge of the cleaning and hygiene of the ward had control of the electric shavers. As part of the Friday community work, he would have the shavers cleaned and lubricated every week. Some people even had razor blades, an illegal item. Because they were illegal, prisoners who had them kept them secret and were responsible for the blades themselves. Smuggling razor blades in was mostly done through family members during in-person visits or through Afghani or other nonpolitical prisoners working in prison. Haji Mahmoud often emphasized that Muslim youth should not shave with a razor blade. His point of emphasis was, of course, on the Mojahedin prisoners because they were an Islamic opposition group. He picked on them continuously. No one admitted to having used razor blades, but it was obvious from their faces which prisoners had used regular blades. This was always a source of friction between guards and prisoners in this ward.

About a month after entering this ward, we finally got our first family visits. We learned we could expect only biweekly visits, not weekly as we had hoped and been led to believe, because of the current overcrowding. The day before these visits, people shaved and cleaned up.

The next morning, a group of us were called for visiting. Blindfolded, we were taken to the main corridor of the third floor. The visiting salon was located across from the kitchen building, about halfway along the corridor. My sister had come to my visit. I learned that my wife and daughter were now living in West Germany after their initial stay in the United States. My wife, who had been born and raised in West Germany before emigrating to the United States with her family when she was seventeen, was now volunteering as a translator to help Iranian refugees in West Germany.

5

There was a Mojahedin prisoner named Ali Taherjouyan who suffered from some form of depression. He would sleep until noon in a corner of the salon and mostly would stay up at night. He did not bother anyone and was very quiet. Everyone tried to accommodate him, especially those Mojahedin prisoners who were his close friends and took care of him. He seemed normal at times, but at other times he would be very depressed. When depressed, he did not want to eat or do any activity, even play with a ball in the yard, which he usually loved to do. When he felt well, and if the yard were open, he would get up and go in the yard. He would play with the ball the whole four hours that the yard stayed open. But if the guards did not open the yard, for whatever reason, then he would very quickly fall into a depressed mood.

This was true for every prisoner, to some degree. Having the privilege of freely walking to the yard and back gave us a sense of freedom. But besides that, it provided a major change in the daily prison routine, especially for those with mental disorders. It was critical for prisoners' health to have the yard open regularly. When we first came to this ward, the yard opened every day for four hours, either in the morning or in the afternoon. As in other prisons, yard time was highly organized in the ward, so that everyone would be able to use it in the most efficient way possible. Jogging and exercise, soccer, or volleyball were daily activities, and a portion of the time at the end of the period was dedicated for walking only, because some people did not or could not participate in the more rigorous forms of sport and exercise.

Life had become relatively calm after the stressful months since our arrival in this prison. The food ration was not as good as in Ghezel-hessar, but in this ward the supplemental food, which the prisoners themselves prepared, complemented the prison food both in quality and in quantity. In the kitchen, there were a few kerosene burners, which prisoners took care of and used in cooking. Prison did not provide or sell loose tea so that we could make our own extra tea. Tea was provided only as a ration already prepared in large steel containers. These containers were filled with boiled water, and a large, long net or bag full of tea leaves was hung inside the hot water. The guards gave us three of these containers, three times a day. As soon as they were sent in, the *mass'oul-e senfi* and the daily workers pulled the tea-net out to reuse the tea leaves to make more tea with boiled water prepared in the kitchen. Then they provided extra tea in thermoses to each room. During breakfast, lunch, and dinner, each room could receive many thermoses of tea.

The *mass'oul-e senfi* did wonders in preparing the supplemental food for us. He took the top layer of fat off the hot lunch pots as soon as they were delivered. He kept that fat to reuse in his cooking of the dinner supplements. He would buy canned tuna fish or sardines, tomatoes, potatoes, onions, lettuce, and herbs, when available. Fruit was bought weekly and hung in a specially designed net in the storage room of the ward. It was examined daily to make sure it did not spoil. I would say that most of us felt that during our time in Gohardasht prison, we ate best in Ward 3.

One day, the guards posted a declaration of new policies on the inside of our ward door. It particularly dealt with rules concerning our yard activities; it threatened that violation of these new regulations would result in the yard privileges being taken away. It was a move by the prison authorities to try to impose a more restrictive lifestyle on us. The declaration marked the start of an aggressive assault on the minimal privileges and rights that we still had.

One of the new rules declared, "Collective jogging and exercise in prison yards is prohibited. Prisoners must do it individually. Violators will be severely punished." The yards in Gohardasht prison were very small. It was ridiculous to suggest that two hundred or more prisoners could all exercise at the same time yet do so individually. This arbitrary rule was the exact opposite of the yard policy in the main Ghezelhessar wards. This was clearly designed to provoke us. The authorities wanted to pressure—and, as it turned out, beat and torture—us into submission. Their main goal was to crush our resistance and the high morale of the combative prisoner population.

Meetings were held in all rooms, and discussions started as soon as the posting appeared on the ward door. Should we follow the new rules or should we ignore them? Naturally, in the short time available before the following morning, the ward was not able to reach a decision. Next day when the yard opened and we were no doubt being watched, we behaved defiantly and did our collective jog and exercise as usual. Toward the end of the exercise routine, the guards poured into the yard, forced everyone back inside the ward, and closed the yard door. They had decided to punish us by taking away our most valuable privilege. Although it was hard on us to lose it, this gave us the time we needed to discuss and review our situation and response.

A minority in the ward thought that exercise was important for our health and struggle, and therefore being able to do it was more important than the form in which it was carried out. They believed we should follow the new rules and not allow the authorities to deprive us of this very important privilege. The majority, on the other hand, believed that if we retreated on this issue and accepted the new rules without a fight, the authorities would not rest until they had broken our backs and forced us into complete submission; we had to take a stand on this issue, even if the authorities succeeded in crushing us in the end.

After long discussions, the ward agreed to the following course of action: we should continue our collective jog and exercise, but at any stage those who felt they did not want to continue should pull out and support the campaign in other ways. We would also use all the means at our disposal, like family visits, to expose the oppressive policies of the warden. Meanwhile we would keep putting pressure on the authorities, demanding that the warden come and discuss these issues with us here in the ward.

The yard stayed closed for a week or two, during which time we informed our families on visiting day about the issue, our decisions, and the possible consequences. We knocked on the door of the ward continually, demanding that the authorities come tell us why our yard was closed. Finally, after about two weeks, Haji Mahmoud walked into the ward without saying a word. It was obvious that he had come to see what we had to say. After a few people started asking him questions, he said, "You need to follow the new regulations. If you don't, we are going to keep the yard closed and you are the ones who will suffer. We do not care if it stays closed forever." Before leaving, he said he would talk to the authorities to see if they would allow the yard to be opened.

That same day or the day after, the yard reopened. Again a large number of prisoners went to the yard and started jogging collectively, and again guards poured into the yard, but this time they beat everyone with *kubl* (flogging cable) and clubs, forcing and pushing us back inside the ward. The yard stayed closed this time for almost a month.

Losing the yard had a negative effect on all of us, especially on prisoners with psychological difficulties. Two people in particular were adversely affected: Taherjouyan and Kamran. Taherjouyan stayed in his bed all day and night. He was certainly showing advanced degrees of depression and despair. Kamran, too, started showing signs of stress and anxiety. His mental state declined daily as conditions worsened in the ward. It was midsummer 1987, and the conflict over yard issues had gotten serious.

One day, Lashgari and his guards entered the ward. He called a few names from a list and told those prisoners to leave with all of their belongings. Kamran was among them. All had sentences of more than fifteen years. This had happened in other wards as well. It seemed likely that they wanted to gather these prisoners in one ward and in one prison (possibly Evin). Kamran was collecting his possessions, and many fellows from the ward had gathered in front of our room to say good-bye to him. He seemed both excited and anxious. For days after he left, I wondered what was going to happen to his mental health in prison.

The conflict over the yard exercise issues continued. From the time it started in mid-spring, it had consumed our minds and lives. Every night we were anxious about what was going to happen the following morning. Every morning something new happened relating directly or indirectly to that issue. The Tehran prison authorities had made yard privileges the cornerstone of their strategy in control and suppression of prisoners. The conflict had gone on for a while in Evin prison and still was not completely resolved, but it was now under control as far as the authorities were concerned. In Gohardasht prison, on the other hand, things were starting to heat up. The cat-and-mouse game between the guards and us was continuing. When they opened the yard in midsummer, after a month of closure, many again jogged collectively. Again they were beaten and forced into the ward, and again the yard was closed for weeks.

Discussions about the effectiveness of our strategy continued as well. Personally, I felt that the authorities had made a decision to enforce the new guidelines and were going to succeed one way or another. But I agreed that we had to take a stand and resist the pressure to a certain degree and then end it on our own terms. Day by day, the reaction of the guards and authorities to our collective exercise got rougher. Accordingly, the longer it continued, the number of people participating in the collective exercise declined. The summer season put more pressure on us, because it was hot inside the ward and not having the yard open made life unbearable. Taherjouyan had been really suffering since the start of the summer; his depression was getting worse daily. Many times, prisoners pressured the guards, demanding that they take him to the prison clinic so that he could get the necessary treatment.

On one occasion, when the yard opened and we exercised collectively again, the guards attacked us and were able to surround a group of people. They took us to the ground level of the prison. After some beating and abuse, Lashgari and "Naserian" (whose real name was

Mohammad Maghisei), who was an assistant prosecutor and apparently had recently been put in charge of this prison, talked to us. They gave us a last warning and declared that they were not going to tolerate this "cat and mouse" game any longer. They told us to let everyone in the ward know about the final warning.

We returned to the ward and described what had happened. This caused a serious discussion among us. By night, a suggestion was circulated, which I thought made a great deal of sense. Someone or a group of prisoners suggested the following course of action: we temporarily change our tactic so that we would go out in the yard when it opened next, and we would use it just for walking and getting fresh air and sunshine, which we desperately needed, but as a protest we would not engage in any other activities. This would give us a chance to improve our health and strength, and it probably would relax and soften the authorities' position and behavior. We would then restart our collective exercise at another time of our own choosing. I thought at that particular point it was the best tack we could take. This suggestion won some supporters, even from among the Mojahedin, but in the end a majority did not agree with it, and therefore our previous tactic of total rebellion against the new yard rule continued.

It was the end of summer, and the yard had stayed closed for a while. After lunch one day, I was walking and talking with Nasser. There was, as usual, a long chain of people in rows of two walking in the hallway. Nasser and I were walking in the direction of the ward door. As we got closer to our room, which was next to the kitchen, I noticed from the corner of my eye that Taherjouyan came out of the storage room and went inside the kitchen. At that moment, only a couple of daily workers were in the kitchen, heating up water to wash the dishes.

We were only a few yards away from our room when we heard a loud scream and then a ball of fire rolled out of the kitchen into the hallway.

Taherjouyan, ablaze like a fireball, was running and hitting the walls and doors. I will never forget his cries and screams as long as I live. People were chasing him with blankets and buckets of water but could not catch him. Finally, a few prisoners threw water and blankets over him and pushed him into a shower stall, where they were able to put out the fire. It was the most horrifying scene to witness. It really broke our hearts. His severely burned body was lain on the floor.

Meanwhile, prisoners knocked on the ward door and informed the guards. They came in pretty quickly and immediately ordered everyone out of the shower room and then asked a few prisoners to help put Taherjouyan on a cart, which they pushed to the prison clinic. The prisoners soon returned and told us Taherjouyan was still alive but so severely burned that the doctor did not think he would survive. Initially, silence and sorrow took over the ward, but soon it turned to anger. We were certain we had to do something in protest. We had to show that Taherjouyan's suicide was a direct result of the prolonged yard closure and make it the central theme of the conflict. We had to demand that the authorities accept responsibility for the fact that their inhumane policies had caused his suicide.

That same evening, Lashgari and his guards entered the ward and ordered everybody to their rooms, then confiscated all the kerosene burners from the kitchen. Apparently, because Taherjouyan had used a kerosene burner to set himself ablaze, they had decided to collect burners from all wards in the prison. We learned later that Taherjouyan had died in the clinic from very severe burns all over his head and body. Following these events, it did not take very long for the ward to reach a unanimous decision to stage a serious protest.

We decided to write a letter to the warden putting the responsibility of Taherjouyan's death on him and demanding that he personally come to our ward to explain the situation and to answer our concerns regarding the issues. We also declared in the letter that in protest we were not going to accept any prison food. We knocked on the door and delivered the letter to the guards. We then contacted Wards 1 and 11 using Morse code and informed them of the issues and our decisions. Ward 1 staged a few days of hunger strike to protest the confiscation of burners and the closure of their yard. They could not do anything regarding Taherjouyan's death because officially they could not have been aware of the incident yet. The ward above us, Ward 11, which now had new prisoners, informed us that they would support our campaign in any way they could.

We were staging an open-ended but limited hunger strike. We were not going to accept or buy any food or food items from the prison. We were going to ration whatever we had, or could get our hands on, to last us for a while. We were hoping to keep going until our next visit, so that we could inform and recruit our families to increase pressure on the authorities. Meetings were held and preparations were made. The ward leadership committee informed us that with rationing of what we had in the ward, we could support ourselves (two hundred or more people) for a week or so. We really had no plans for after that and, under the circumstances and with emotions running so high, we did not care about the future anyway. We just wanted to do something in protest at that moment of frustration and anger. We had made a decision not based on logic and reason but on the basis of what we felt we should and needed to do.

The first day of our strike, when they delivered our lunch, we sent it back. The guards took it back without saying a word. From then on we returned all rations, prison food, and food items. We were getting used to eating minimal portions of leftover bread and other stored food items.

After a day or two, Haji Mahmoud came to our ward and also to Ward 1. He said that prison authorities were saddened by Ali Taherjouyan's death but that they could have done nothing to prevent it. He also blamed Taherjouyan himself and us for what had happened. He said the removal of the burners had nothing to do with the incident because they had been going to confiscate them anyway. Finally, he warned us that Islam does not allow one to starve oneself and we should think about the consequences of what we were doing.

Our protest continued. We realized after a couple of days that we could survive with very little or no food for a while, but the absence of tea was having a negative effect on most of us. Our addiction to tea was stronger than our need for food. And the smokers faced a real challenge. They rationed their smokes to only half a cigarette three times per day, so their supplies would last longer. Four days passed, and the authorities did not show any sign of softening or retreating. Our visiting day was a few more days away, and we knew we had to last until then if we wanted to increase the pressure on the authorities.

After a few days, Ward 1 ended their strike. Lashgari went to their ward and explained to them that taking the burners away was a decision made at higher levels and that it would have happened anyway. That same day, Lashgari came to our ward as well. After threats and shouting, finally he declared that Taherjouyan's death was the result of his own act and the responsibility of prisoners who had insisted on collective activities and had forced the closure of the yard. Basically, he blamed us. He also said that taking the burners was a decision already made, except that Taherjouyan's action provided an excuse to do it at that time. In the end, he threatened that the hunger strike was against Islam and said that they would not tolerate it any longer. In return, we put the blame on them and repeated our demands that the prison warden himself had to face us to respond to our questions.

Ward 1's visiting day was a couple of days before ours, and they informed their families about what was happening and asked them to spread the word to other families through their connections. A week had passed, and we were on our last bits of food. The following day was our visiting day. We were very excited and hopeful. In the morning, we were ready as usual for our visits, but nothing happened. No lists were called, and no visits took place. When lunchtime passed and nobody had been called yet, we knew that the worst that could have happened had indeed happened. The authorities had canceled or delayed our ward's visits. This was bad for us, because it meant that they would have enough time during the next two weeks to deal with us without having to face our families.

Later, we learned that on that day the authorities had posted signs outside the prison indicating that because of repairs on the visiting structure, visits were canceled for one time. This was a very smart move because one round of cancellation was not too much for the families and would give the authorities enough time to take care of the situation in prison. They had made a decision to deal with us once and for all and to have us ready for our visits in two weeks' time. In any case, not having the visits we had been looking forward to and were counting on was a big blow to our morale.

The only things left for our consumption in the ward after the ninth day of the strike were a few bread crumbs. Smokers were in trouble, having run out of cigarettes. We had not had tea for a while and were feeling the withdrawal symptoms. After the tenth day, serious discussions finally arose about what our long-term plans were. We were surviving on bread crumbs and some limited items that Wards 11 and 1 were able to smuggle to us. But that was in no way enough for more than two hundred people. We now knew that we couldn't hold out much longer. The decision to declare an open-ended strike had been emotional and unrealistic. We realized that we should have called for a limited—maybe a week-long—strike to protest Taherjouyan's death and the other issues, then we should have continued our protest using other tactics.

I think it was the fourteenth day of the strike when the guards opened the yard door for us. It seemed odd that they would do this in the middle of our strike, but we were happy and excited anyway to have the yard finally open. We needed sunshine and fresh air, and because most people in the ward were weak as a result of the strike, they just relaxed and enjoyed the yard. There were, however, sixty or so hardcore prisoners who started their collective jog in the yard as usual. This yard opening turned out to be a trap. Guards poured in from doors and windows and surrounded those sixty prisoners. They led them through the yard door into the ground floor. The rest of us were sent back inside the ward, and they closed the yard again. It was about eleven in the morning when this happened, and we thought these prisoners would be abused for a couple of hours and would then be sent back in, as on previous occasions.

It was very late in the afternoon when the ward door finally opened and guards threw in a tortured, bloody body. It was one of those sixty from our ward. He seemed to have lost five pounds in those few hours that he had been out; he looked exhausted, weak, and broken. Because of the lashes and beatings he had received, his shirt was torn, and blood and bruises covered his entire back. Prisoners took him into one of the rooms and started tending to him. Minutes later, the door opened again and they threw another tortured body in. It continued like this until at around seven o'clock all sixty tortured prisoners had been returned. One prisoner had a damaged eye, and others had broken bones and other injuries.

While we were caring for those of our roommates who had been tortured, they described their ordeal.

> On the ground floor, the guards had formed two lines, like the walls of a long tunnel, extending to the entrance of a room down there. They directed us blindfolded into that tunnel and beat us down the line with sticks, clubs, *kubl*, and metal rods until we got to that room, where they pushed our bloody, beaten bodies through the door and

> closed it tight. We could barely stand in the room, which had no windows, no light, and no ventilation. There was only a bit of air coming in from under the door. It got humid and hot in there very quickly. Breathing soon became difficult, especially for a few who suffered from illnesses. We pushed those few to the front and opened some space for them, so that they could take turns to get some air.
>
> They kept us in that room for about an hour, then the door opened and we were led into the tunnel of the guards again. Our exhausted and soaked bodies were beaten up again until we reached the front of a desk, where Lashgari was sitting. He asked us, one by one, if we were ready to eat prison food to break our strike. We all gave negative replies. Then he read a ruling from a prison judge, ordering the strikers to be flogged frequently until they agreed to break their strike by eating prison food. Afterward, each of us was lashed and sent into the ward. We have been told that in a short while they are going to ask us again, and we will be lashed until we accept the verdict.

The tactic the authorities used was a smart one because they had put these prisoners at risk of being tortured continuously, and at the same time they had put the rest of us in a dilemma as well. We could not sit back and watch our fellow prisoners be repeatedly tortured. The sixty prisoners, of course, did not want to be the ones who would be responsible for breaking the strike, and the rest of us did not want them to bear the whole burden of punishment. Peer pressure and pride were preventing each of us from speaking up to stop the madness and admit that we had made a tactical mistake when we emotionally declared an open-ended strike. But something had to be done quickly, before they came back for these poor souls. A few people bravely ignored the peer pressure and proposed that if these prisoners were taken out again we should require them to eat prison food to break their strikes. After a short discussion in the rooms, the majority of the ward agreed.

Shortly, around eight o'clock, those sixty prisoners were called out. They all returned after about half an hour or so, after having accepted the verdict and forcing themselves to eat a few spoonfuls of prison food. A few minutes later, our dinner ration pots were sent in as well. We set up our dinner while the guards came to supervise, and a couple of prison authorities, including Lashgari, who was armed with a handgun inside the ward for the first time in prison history, came and ate with us. The strike officially was over.

We later learned that during our strike the authorities had beaten and abused prisoners from other wards over the yard and burner issues and had forced all the wards to accept the new regulations for yard activities. In our ward, the crackdown was used for both purposes: breaking the hunger strike and forcing the acceptance of the rules regarding the yard activities. After these events, there was no more collective jog or exercise in Gohardasht prison.

It was time for us to analyze our actions of the past few months. But the authorities were smart enough not to give us any breathing room after they had just broken our morale. In our ward, they kept the pressure up by making excuses to punish a few of us every other day. We kept our cool and tried to adjust to the new situation. Although temporarily broken, our resistance was by no means completely worn down.

There was a consensus among us that we should still continue resisting the new rules regarding yard activities, but this time around we thought we ought to approach it differently. We decided that we would not jog or exercise individually in the yard at all; instead, we would use the yard only for getting fresh air, walking, and playing collective sports like soccer and volleyball. It was obvious to the authorities that the majority of the prisoners were still following a coordinated collective approach to the yard issue. The authorities had decided that they would keep the general pressure on everyone and would not allow a return of the previous situation, where prisoners refused to follow regulations.

Letter to Prison

Where are you now my darling?
What are you thinking now?
Your love penetrates the prison walls and reaches us
The burden of the world lies on your shoulders
And you are willing to carry it.
Have they left you any humanity?
Have they left you your soul?
Your daughter is growing
But no one here to share her blossoming and beauty
She's a real spring

How are we going to meet?
How am I going to take it?
Will I have changed?
Will you have changed?
Will we be able to understand each other's pain?
We will have to get to know each other from anew
All the happy memories we share
All the sad times we spent apart
Will we be able to bridge our emotions?
You suffered a lot
Will I understand all the inhumanity you have experienced?
Will you be able to tell me about your experiences?

Your hands are tied
My hands are wide open
You cannot choose
I have the whole world to choose from
Or so you think
But each choice ties me down
For each choice I make is a commitment
To our daughter and to ourselves.

—Ketty Mobed

Offenbach, West Germany — February 1987

Chapter Nine
NEW CLASSIFICATIONS

1

December 1987

One night we were ordered to prepare to move out. The next morning, they moved a large group, including Asghar, Nasser, and me, to Ward 2. This ward already had about one hundred fifty prisoners, and with us it became a ward of about two hundred fifty. Every room now had seventeen to twenty people. Ward 2 was a large ward like Ward 1 and was located across from it. We three went to Room 1, which had all non-Tudeh leftists. There were three or four rooms of Tudeh Party prisoners, and the rest of the rooms held Mojahedin prisoners.

The ward lifestyle was not similar to what we experienced in Ward 3. There was no ward-wide *komon* (commune), no storage or kitchen rooms here. Most of the storage and food work was done in the salon at the end of the ward. Apart from communal work, which was organized at the ward level, everything here was room-based, just as in the Ghezel-hessar wards. Apparently, Wards 1 and 2 had been organized like this from their formation. The authorities had experimented with a variety of different policies.

We found out through contacts during clinic visits and other means that a new group of prisoners had been brought to Ward 3, where we used to be kept. They were the remaining prisoners of Salone 3 of Amoozeshgah in Evin. The authorities had transferred them to Gohardasht apparently "to teach them a lesson." They had been beaten into submission after arriving here. They became known as the Evin ward.

2

Toward the end of 1987, two political trends were growing stronger and heading for a clash in the prisons. The Mojahedin prisoners had decided to raise their resistance to a qualitatively higher level. The change in strategy for them was inspired by the fact that the Mojahedin organization forces based in Iraq were preparing to stage a military campaign against the Islamic Republic of Iran in the near future. Some Mojahedin prisoners had decided to prepare politically and mentally for the final clash with the regime and to fulfill their duty as sympathizers of the organization. Therefore, they started to make certain changes in their political declarations and in their interactions with the prison authorities.

They started taking certain positions that for them had been taboo in prison since June 20, 1981, because in the past these positions had resulted in the torture and execution of many hundreds of them. Though they had abstained from taking these positions in front of any authorities since then, a group of them thought that conditions were ripe for a major shift. Radical Mojahedin prisoners in particular, as leaders, took up this challenge to help raise the level of resistance and morale.

The main issue for them was the choice to use *Monafeghin* ("hypocrites") versus Mojahedin ("Islamic warriors/crusaders") when they referred to their organizational affiliation in front of the authorities. After the mini–civil war of the Mojahedin organization with Khomeini's forces in 1981, captured Mojahedin followers were forced to declare themselves as *Monafeghin*. This was a condition of their survival; otherwise, they were killed. Now this leading radical group of Mojahedin prisoners thought that the time had come for them to take back their true title of Mojahedin, even if they died for doing so.

The other political trend was brewing within the regime's ranks, including even some members of Khomeini's inner circle, like his son Ahmad Khomeini, but particularly within the security, judicial, and prison services. They believed that the political prisoners remaining were hardcore and dangerous for the very existence of the regime and should be dealt with accordingly. Especially knowing what they knew about the military preparations by the Mojahedin forces in Iraq, the regime had drawn up a contingency plan to take care of the prisoners at an opportune time. The prison authorities, magnifying the gradual changes in the positions of some of the Mojahedin prisoners, had convinced leading members of the regime, like Ahmad Khomeini, that dealing with the remaining political prisoners was a necessity.

These two extremist trends were growing stronger daily, and their paths were about to cross in prison. Secular leftists did not in general support the analysis, strategy, or tactics of the Mojahedin, whether outside or inside of prison. Even those leftists who had had a love affair with the Mojahedin in the past had recently distanced themselves from them. But the fire, if and when ignited, could potentially burn every one of us in prison. Leftists were stuck in the middle of a growing potential clash of extremism from both sides, just as had happened to them in 1981 in the mini–civil war.

When, for any reason, radical Mojahedin prisoners were called out and questioned about their organizational affiliation these days, they would reply, "Mojahedin" instead of *Monafeghin*. They were usually abused mildly by the authorities but were sent back to their wards. To the authorities, this indicated a measure of the political pulse of the

Mojahedin forces in prison. For the Mojahedin prisoners, this meant that resistance and change of position was indeed possible.

The authorities questioned Mojahedin prisoners more often than usual, on purpose, to provide them with many more opportunities to declare their true intentions and positions. In fact, this was part of a net they were spreading for the Mojahedin forces.

3

In early January 1988, we were all taken out and questioned one by one by Lashgari and some unknown official sitting behind a desk. This time around, the questioning was different, in the sense that they specifically asked us about religious practices. The questions were as follows:

> What is your organizational affiliation and sentence?
> Do you still support and defend your organization?
> Are you willing to give an interview in front of the prison population to condemn your activities and your organization?
> Do you accept Imam Khomeini and his leadership?
> Do you pray?

The fact that these questions were being asked of all prisoners indicated a coordinated and planned effort by the system. This by itself should have alarmed us, but we interpreted the questioning to be related to a normal reclassification and reorganization of the prison, like many in the past. But in reality, the questions and their order had been designed carefully and purposefully to obtain prisoners' true positions and intentions. The first three were for "political screening" of all prisoners, while the last two were for "religious screening."

After these questionings, there were a few strange and calm days without any confrontation in prison, during which we found out that, for some odd reason, the *mellikesh* (serving without sentence) prisoners, who had always been kept in Evin, had been transferred to Gohardasht. A few days later, news indicated that the whole prison was indeed being reorganized. Soon we too were told to pack up and prepare to move again. After lunch, Lashgari came in, gave a short talk, then started reading out the names of the first group, and soon they were gone. The second and then the third group were taken away as well. These were all religious prisoners, which meant that the authorities had decided to separate them from nonreligious prisoners. Other factors involved in the new classification were length of sentence and the prisoners' political positions. The majority in our ward were religious prisoners. After they were gone, seventy to eighty secular leftist prisoners were left, who were called out in different groupings as well. Two groups were called who had less than ten-year sentences. Then a group of prisoners with sentences of ten years or more was called, and I was in this group. The remaining prisoners were a mixture, with different sentences but with, in general, a neutral or a passive position toward the regime.

So, in this recent classification they had firstly separated "believers" from "nonbelievers." Secondly, they had grouped people into wards based on the length of their sentence and their current political position.

The three of us from our organization were finally split up, and each went to a different ward. Asghar, because of his neutral political position, went to new Ward 5, the so-called passive ward for secular leftists. Because of his less than ten-year sentence, Nasser was put in Ward 7, and I was sent to Ward 6 because of my fifteen-year sentence.

There were already about twenty or so prisoners in Ward 6, and with our group it became about thirty to thirty-five; all of us were secular leftist prisoners with sentences of more than ten years, gathered there from different previous wards. As soon as I entered, my comrade Farzin greeted me. We had been together in Ward 5 of Unit 1 of Ghezelhessar prison for about five months. Once in a while, individual prisoners were still being sent in, but the main core of the ward was already there. Gradually, we started to settle in the cells in groups of two or three. Farzin and I took our gear into one of the cells.

A new prisoner sent in very late that day was a young man named Mohammad-Reza Tababati. He was carrying only a small bag and stood behind the ward door, which he continuously knocked on to argue his case with the guards. It turned out that some of his belongings had been left behind in his previous ward. He looked very unhappy and disoriented. A prisoner named "Farhad" talked to him by the ward door, then informed Farzin and me that Tababati was one of our organizational members. Neither of us knew him. We went and introduced ourselves to him. Immediately, his demeanor changed and he became lively and upbeat. We took him to our cell.

We soon found out that they were installing a metal gate on each floor in the middle of the main corridor to divide the main prison structure literally in half. It was clear that they were preparing for a time when they might want to separate the religious and nonreligious sections from each other completely. Why? No one could explain. After that, they started fortifying the ward doors by installing a metal gate behind each door. Why, for the first time in the regime's history, did they seem to be in a vulnerable, defensive mode in prison? Was the regime about to fall, as the Mojahedin believed? Or were there other reasons beyond our knowledge and understanding? Naturally, the Mojahedin saw all these developments as supporting their analysis: the Mojahedin forces were about to attack and overthrow the regime, and therefore these were indeed defensive measures taken by the prison authorities because of the imminent dangers they faced. The leftists, in general, did not agree with that analysis but had no sound explanation for the extreme measures being taken by the authorities.

After a few weeks, we had gathered enough information to know exactly what the reorganized prison looked like. There was the religious southern half and the secular northern half. The ground-floor wards housed no prisoners. Overall, we estimated that at this time Gohardasht prison held about eight hundred Mojahedin prisoners, about six hundred secular leftists, about two hundred prisoners brought from other locations, and about two hundred prisoners in Band-e Jahad (Crusaders' Ward)—a total of around eighteen hundred to two thousand prisoners.

4

In the early days in Ward 6, life was very chaotic and hectic. It was a new experience, with its own unique problems. The absence of Mojahedin prisoners changed the living dynamics. There were prisoners here from ten different leftist groups with historical and political rivalries and animosity, even hatred, toward each other. We had to put aside our political and petty organizational differences to find common grounds to live in harmony. This was a real test for all of us to create a more democratic system in our ward. Most leftist prisoners felt like living according to their own free-spirited inclinations, being sick of the Mojahedin totalitarian lifestyle and control system in the previous wards.

But soon we faced some common issues that needed to be tackled collectively. A couple of prisoners led the discussions. After some initial attempts in forging a communal living arrangement, it became obvious that a ward-wide *komon* was out of the question because some groups would not want to be in a *komon* with certain other groups. But a majority of the ward agreed on a limited communal living arrangement, where shopping for the ward would be done from a common-funds box, and then the purchases would be divided equally among all prisoners. The idea was that any person or group of people would control their own particular extra spending. A few extremists, on the left and right, declared that they would not be part of any communal scheme and that they were going to be on their own. Other than those few, the rest participated in this limited form of the communal life. We selected people at the ward level to take charge of responsibilities like food, cleaning, sports, and health.

Gradually, some sort of an order was established, but it certainly looked and felt nothing like a ward ruled by the Mojahedin. There was no *dahi* (organized snack serving at 10:00 AM), *panji* (organized snack serving at 5:00 PM), or extensive *kar-e melli* (communal work). Every person, cell, and subcommune lived their lives as they wished, and they participated in the general ward life as individuals or independent entities with equal rights. Life started to look pretty good, and for a short while we actually had a comparatively relaxed time here.

There were twenty small cells on both sides of the hallway, with bathrooms and showers at the end of the hall. Then there was the salon at the end of the ward, but the authorities had locked it and would not allow us to use it. After a while, and after some pressure from us, they permitted us to store our extra bags there. The guard would open it once a week for us to put in or take our things from there, and then he would lock it up. We watched TV in the hallway, where the set was kept on a rolling cart.

One day, the authorities sent in twenty new prisoners. From the moment they walked in, we could tell from their age—they were much older than most other prisoners—and from their timid and reserved behavior that they were not "typical" political prisoners. They were Baha'is. We rearranged ourselves to free up seven or eight cells for them.

We also decided to put more pressure on the authorities to have the salon opened, since we were about sixty prisoners now in the ward. The Baha'i prisoners informed us that though they would support our demand about the salon, they could not participate in any action. They also announced that they would have to stay independent on everything, political or nonpolitical. We understood their situation. We knocked on the door and informed the guards about our demand. They returned after a while and informed us that the salon could not be opened and that some of us could sleep in the hallway at nights.

The ward now held about forty secular leftists and twenty Baha'i prisoners. Our average age was above the general average for political prisoners. The Fadaiyan Minority prisoners were the youngest group in our ward. Most of the prisoners in the ward had been arrested in 1981 or 1982 and were considered veterans. Most of the Baha'i prisoners were middle-aged or elderly. In general, they were educated and well-traveled people. There were a couple of younger Baha'i prisoners who represented their group in its contacts with us; "Siavoush" and Ibrahim Najjaran, a Rah-e Kargar prisoner who had recently joined our ward, knew the younger Baha'i prisoners and served as our contacts with them. The Baha'i prisoners basically lived as an independent group in our ward. When rations were delivered, the *mass'oul-e senfi* (food service representative) would separate out their share and give it to them. They would also prepare their own shopping list. In general, our relationship with them was very respectful and friendly.

5

Nowruz (Iranian New Year, on the first day of spring) of 1988 was upon us. The majority of the ward was in agreement that we should exploit this Nowruz as a unifying occasion to express our opposition to the religious Islamists, who were trying to destroy our national identity and heritage. Prior to Nowruz, the authorities announced that any kind of public celebration in the ward was prohibited. After some discussion, we decided to celebrate the first half hour after the arrival of the New Year in our separate cells and then at a predetermined time come out and move in a very orderly fashion to congratulate prisoners from the other cells. The guards were caught by surprise when we put the second part of our plan into action. They basically chose not to do anything, or they had been told by the higher-ups not to get involved.

The month of Ramadan that year began a week after Nowruz. Ramadan is the ninth month in the Islamic lunar calendar. Beginning of this calendar shifts about eleven days each year in comparison to the Iranian solar calendar, which begins with Nowruz. The Baha'i prisoners indicated that they had to observe fasting for political and religious reasons. We thought we should demand to have hot lunches this year, though we were sure we were not going to get them. The Islamic regime's prisons had never provided lunch to prisoners during Ramadan. We coordinated with other leftist wards, and all of us presented this demand to the guards a day or two before Ramadan.

On the first day of fasting, surprisingly there was no typical Ramadan early morning meal provided. Was this a sign that we had gained our desire? It was uncertain until the noon hour, when the ward door opened and a hot meal was sent in just like on a regular day. This was a strange but historic event. We were all jubilant. In our minds, even the very suspicious ones, we had achieved something impossible in the Islamic prison system. Or so we thought.

But this particular event had negative consequences. It had such a delusional impact on the leftist prisoners that some even leaned toward the Mojahedin analysis that the regime might indeed be in a vulnerable, defensive position. Others thought it a result of our long struggle, which was finally yielding some fruit. In fact, the authorities had succeeded in setting a trap for the leftists, as they were similarly doing with the Mojahedin concerning their political/organizational identity issue.

The move, as we would learn later, was part of a devious plan to influence prisoner behavior toward radicalization. The authorities knew that prisoners who were feeling in control and powerful would generally reveal their positions honestly and freely. Under such circumstances, it was less likely that prisoners would resort to tactical positions and retreats when questioned by the authorities about their political or ideological beliefs. And this was exactly the kind of attitude the authorities wanted and were planning to create.

In any case, during Ramadan the behavior of the authorities was very strange, to say the least. The whole month of fasting we were provided with hot lunches and dinners, which we openly and publicly ate in the wards. After the reorganization of the prison, the authorities generally seemed softer. It seemed strange, and we could not make any sense of it at all. I think the majority of us had no clear understanding of what was really happening. Nobody could think strategically and with enough foresight to predict what the regime was conspiring to do.

6

The yards now were primarily used for walking and for playing soccer and volleyball. The authorities had clearly shown they had no tolerance for breaking of the rules by us in this particular arena. News from other wards indicated that any move by prisoners to resort to any kind of collective exercise was severely suppressed. We could not explain the contradiction. On the one hand, they were feeding us hot lunches during

Ramadan, something that had never been done in prison and was considered a sinful act by religious standards. But on the other hand, they would not allow any collective exercise in the yards.

We had to let go of the yard conflict. Some of us thought, for the sake of our own health, we should exercise individually, while others felt we should totally boycott the exercise in the yard. "Iraj" was in charge of the sporting activities of the ward, and he organized soccer and volleyball competitions, which we were all involved in. In the yard, there were two strips of dirt intended for gardening. A couple of people took the initiative to cultivate the dirt and plant some herbs and flowers.

The two-story prison kitchen-workshop building was located to the south of our yard. To the east, a tall wall with a very large gate separated the yard from the prison grounds. There was also a large bathroom unit attached to this wall on the southeast corner of the yard. Our building was located to the north of the yard, and to the west the yard connected through a door with the main corridor of the ground level. The *far'i* (minor) wards attached to Wards 5 and 6 had windows looking out on our yard. We communicated with those prisoners when we were in the yard and found out they were Mojahedin kept isolated from the other religious prisoners.

At first, the building to the north of us was empty, and therefore we could not contact Wards 7 and 8, which were located in the northeast corner of the main prison structure. Soon some prisoners were brought to that middle building. When they came into their yard, we noticed they were few in number and we were not sure who they were. As we watched them from our cell windows, I recognized Dr. Sadrollah Siah-Mansouri and figured out they must be the group called Ayyaran, which had been arrested in 1986. There were about twenty of them in that ward. We tried to contact them, but because they could not recognize us they were cautious and did not respond at all. It was fruitless. I could watch my friend Siah-Mansouri in that yard but could not establish contact with him.

A few days later, this problem was resolved when a large group of prisoners was brought to that same ward. We quickly found out that they were the so-called Evin ward, transferred to Gohardasht a while back and housed in the other half of the prison until now. This was incredible for three reasons: we could see our old comrades; we would get some firsthand information about Evin prison; and, most important, their arrival meant that contact between Wards 7 and 8 and our wards could finally be established.

We quickly established contact with the Evin prisoners in their yard. Sometimes, three or four contacts were happening simultaneously from different cells in our ward. Some people even exchanged hand-copied texts and other dangerous material. Most of my group's contact was with Abdi, who was with a few of our comrades in that ward. We learned from them about the events of Salone 3 in Amoozeshgah and gave them an analysis of what had happened during the past year in Gohardasht. Every political group had contacts with their own trusted comrades, but there was an unspoken agreement among most groups to share their news with others.

It was after the arrival of the Evin prisoners in Ward 14 that I finally was able, with the help of Abdi, to establish contact with Dr. Siah-Mansouri. He informed me that at my wife's request, he had gone to my house with another friend the night of my arrest to take care of some of the items I had in the house, destroying them immediately. I thanked him for his help to my wife and his courage under those circumstances. A couple of weeks later, the leadership of Ayyaran, including Dr. Sadrollah Siah-Mansouri, were taken out of that ward, and they did not return. We read in the newspaper a few days later that some of them had been executed; eventually many of the rest were also executed.

A few days after the Evin prisoners had been brought to Ward 14, another group of prisoners was brought to Ward 13 above them. They were the *mellikesh* prisoners, transferred to Gohardasht a while back and kept initially in the other half of the prison. The transfer of the *mellikesh* prisoners to Gohardasht made no logical sense to any of us. They had always been kept in Evin, where the courts and the release office of the prison system in Tehran were located. There were about one hundred of them, all secular leftist prisoners. They believed the only logical reason for their transfer here was to enable the authorities to put extra pressure on them to force them to accept some conditions for release. Therefore, their transfer here carried a kind of a positive tone.

Our analysis was that the regime wanted to end the war and therefore had to prepare to deal with the prisoner issue because of the domestic and international pressures, in particular the demands of its European economic partners. We thought that the regime would release the *mellikesh* prisoners following the acceptance of a cease-fire to end the war with Iraq soon and then would use that release as a propaganda tool in covering up its larger political-prisoner issue. It made sense. A prisoner release was a good move for public and foreign relations, and the *mellikesh* would be the least dangerous and the least costly group to choose for this.

Unfortunately, this notion created more optimism among prisoners. The logical extension of this line of thinking was that if such a day came, meaning the end of the war and the release of the *mellikesh* prisoners, then prison conditions would have to improve because the government would have to prepare the prisons for potential international observers and visitors. Some prisoners would go even further by proposing that the separation of the Mojahedin from the secular leftists was also in line with this policy, because the regime would claim that those prisoners belonged to an organization waging war against the Islamic Republic and therefore deserved to be kept under stiffer control, while they would improve the conditions in our part of prison to show that the regime was treating the political prisoners better.

After Ramadan, there was a quiet period in prison. It was an eerie sort of calm. We were out of control in our "illegal" activities, especially in our contacts and exchange of material between wards. In retrospect, this situation certainly raised our morale and demands to an unrealistic level. In short, by the end of the spring of 1988, a relaxed and optimistic atmosphere had overcome all of us, the direct result of the regime's tactics and our own misinterpretations of the situation.

7

The guards here were a very heterogeneous group of people, whose commonality was their religious belief and loyalty to the regime, especially to Khomeini. But in terms of character, they were very diverse. Most were nasty, like the guard called "Ne'mati," while a few were a bit kind and compassionate. The majority of the guards in this prison had historically been rough and tough, but these days they generally showed a softer and kinder side, which seemed very strange. After Ramadan and the hot-lunch service, they did not argue with or threaten us that much anymore. They were very accommodating, calm, and quiet, and some even tried to be "philosophical" with us.

There was an old guard in charge of the daily bread, which he would distribute to the wards with the help of an Afghani prisoner. This old guard was the only one who did not change much in his attitude. His Afghani helper knew Ibrahim Najjaran in our ward since they had served time together in another ward a while back. Ibrahim would use his daily-worker excuse to make contact with the Afghani prisoner to get extra bread and "illegal" items like razor blades.

Elections for the Majles (Parliament) happened during the month of June 1988. As always in election times, the guards took all of us ward by ward to give us a chance to vote. No one in any of the secular leftist wards, except the prisoners in Ward 5 (the so-called passive ward), took part in voting. Though we declared we did not want to vote, surprisingly the reactions from the authorities again were very mild. They even joked with us, saying, "If you don't vote and don't get your birth certificate stamped, you are not going to get any coupons!"

The month of July arrived and with it the summer heat. All the plants and flowers were doing well in the yard, but we needed to water them daily. Life was quiet and as normal as it could ever be in the Islamic prison system. On July 16, 1988, while we were watching the evening news, as we did every day, the acceptance by Iran of UN Security Council Resolution 598 on a cease-fire to end the Iran-Iraq War surprised and shocked us all. We knew the war needed to end; this had been obvious for a while to everyone. But we were shocked that the Iranian regime had finally agreed to a cease-fire. This must have been even a bigger shock to the Mojahedin, who had always emphasized in their analyses that "the end of the war will be the end for the Khomeini regime." The regime used the war to organize and energize its support base, and therefore most in opposition had believed that the regime would not agree to end the war. Now that it had happened, we were all in disbelief.

Ending the war was going to be problematic for the regime ideologically, politically, and logistically. Khomeini himself, on so many occasions over the years, had declared that the war was "God's will" or "a gift from God." He also had declared that we would not stop "until we slap Saddam Hussein in the face." Many of the ruling clerics had emphasized that they would not end the war until they reached Karbala, a Shiite holy city in Iraq. After hundreds of thousands of casualties, billions of dollars' worth of damage to the infrastructure of the country, and all Iranians feeling the socioeconomic effects of the war, it was very hard for the regime to justify ending the war in a state of impasse. But the news was very clear. Iran had accepted UN Resolution 598 with the blessings of Khomeini, and there was going to be an official signing of a cease-fire with Iraq soon.

After the initial shock and surprise, this news started to have a negative impact on us, in the sense that it strengthened our mistakenly positive outlook toward the improvements in prison conditions. Logically, one would expect any government to relax its control under similar circumstances. In any society, after a prolonged war, during which a government has put justified or unjustified restrictions on people's lives, the government would logically introduce all kinds of reforms to bring normalcy back to society. This was what we thought would start happening after the war, in the country at large and consequently in the prison system as well. But we were wrong, at least about the prison system.

During the final year of the war, when both sides started using mid to long-range missiles, the goverment pragmatists perceived the serious threat of war to the existence and future of the Islamic regime; they understood that it was no longer safe to extend and exploit the war for internal political reasons. These new developments forced some major figures and factions of the regime, in particular Rafsanjani and others, to reach the conclusion that the war must be ended. Apparently it was they, particularly Rafsanjani, who convinced Khomeini that they had to end the war to save the Islamic Revolution and the Islamic Republic. This was why Khomeini, against his personal beliefs and wishes, approved the acceptance of UN Resolution 598 to negotiate a cease-fire with Iraq.

Some might not appreciate how difficult the acceptance of the cease-fire must have been for Khomeini. In his televised speech to the nation after the acceptance of the resolution, he admitted that he did not like accepting it but that he had to do it to save the Islamic Revolution. He said he was forced to "drink the chalice of poison" (apparently making a reference to Socrates) in accepting the UN resolution.

The so-called war faction of the regime mobilized their flock in the streets of Tehran and other major cities to demonstrate against the acceptance of the resolution, because they claimed Khomeini had been forced to accept it. We saw news clips on TV of clashes between government factions in the streets of Tehran in the days following the acceptance. Khomeini was forced to appear on TV again to declare those demonstrations provocative in nature; he denounced those moves as treasonous and demanded they stop immediately. Rafsanjani and his circle were victorious; Iran accepted UN Resolution 598 and signed a cease-fire with Iraq. Conditions in the country subsequently seemed a bit unstable, but soon the situation calmed down and everyone in the regime accepted the final decision made by Khomeini.

In This Dead-end

They smell your breath.
You better not have said, "I love you."
They smell your heart.
These are strange times, darling...
And they flog
Love
At the roadblock.
We had better hide love in the closet...
In this crooked dead end and twisting chill,
They feed the fire
With the kindling of song and poetry.
Do not risk a thought.
These are strange times, darling...
He who knocks on the door at midnight
Has come to kill the light.
We had better hide light in the closet...
Those are butchers
Stationed at the crossroads
With bloody clubs and cleavers.
These are strange times, darling...
And they excise smiles from lips
And songs from mouths.
We had better hide joy in the closet...
Canaries barbecued
On a fire of lilies and jasmine,
These are strange times, darling...
Satan drunk with victory
Sits at our funeral feast.
We had better hide God in the closet.

—Ahmad Shamlou (1925–2000)

Chapter Ten
LET US WATER THE FLOWERS

1

July 1988

Conditions seemed to be improving in prison, or at least that was what we thought at the time, until our world suddenly turned upside down. On July 19, the evening TV news reported an attack by Iraqi-based Mojahedin forces on the west of the country. For the Mojahedin, there was no other way out. They had preached for years that "the end of the war will be the end for the Khomeini regime." It was indeed their best chance, and maybe their only chance, to prove to themselves, to their followers, and to the Iranian people that they had been right all along.

We knew this event was bad news for all of us in prison. Obviously, the military attack was going to put the Mojahedin prisoners in grave danger, and we were afraid that collaterally more pressure and danger might await us as well. That was how we interpreted the situation, and that was the extent of the repercussions we anticipated from this event. Of course, it shattered the high hopes that many prisoners had developed after the regime's acceptance of UN Resolution 598.

The following day, guards entered, went to the TV set, and removed it from the ward. We argued with them, demanding an explanation. At first we thought it was a punishment for our ward alone, but later we learned it had happened in the other leftist wards as well. Even the TV set in Ward 5 (the so-called passive ward) had been taken away. The exchange of news, information, and analyses between wards via Morse code continued until late that night. We thought the authorities did not want us to know what was going on in the country, notably about the Mojahedin attacks and the infighting in the regime over the ending of the war. It made sense. They probably did not want the Mojahedin prisoners, in particular, to resort to aggressive behavior and action in prison. We understood why they would try to isolate us, at least for a while.

The following day, there was no regular prison radio broadcast and no newspaper delivery. The yards did not get opened either, and this did not make any sense unless the authorities wanted to prevent the neighboring wards from contacting each other. But then they knew we could and would make contact through Morse code and in a variety of other ways. So why not open the yards? We knocked on the ward doors, demanding answers, all day long. The guards systematically provided coordinated replies. Very calmly, they said that it was out of their control and that these things had been decided by the authorities in higher positions.

In our ward, later that day, the nasty guard Ne'mati opened the door and, in reaction to our continuous protests and demands, calmly and "philosophically" (which did not suit him) stated, "If I were you, I would not think about these petty things. I would rather make good use of my time to review my positions, my life, and my future."

The following couple of days, we put coordinated pressure on the shift guards, demanding that conditions return to where they had been a few days ago. We were told again and again, calmly, and with an eerie kindness, that it was out of their control. As the guards got calmer and quieter, some prisoners got louder and more aggressive. The guards even stopped taking ill people to the prison clinic, something that had always been done weekly and in emergency cases. The situation had to be more serious than we had originally thought. They wanted to prevent any flow of information in or out of prison, or even between wards. The prison was in an absolute lockdown. Why? What was going on?

In reaction to this situation, two views were forming among us. One view was that it was all preventive in nature, meaning that the regime wanted to isolate us from hearing the news of the Mojahedin attacks and the infighting of the regime, to prevent us from radicalization and aggressive action in prison. The alternative view was that something more serious must have happened or might still be going on in the country (e.g., Khomeini had died or was on his deathbed). No one at this time thought that horrible events necessitating the complete lockdown might be happening inside the prison itself.

After a few days and the cancellation of the visitation rights in a couple of wards, even the most optimistic people felt that the whole situation made no sense anymore. Whichever way you looked at it, you were forced to conclude that something horrible must have happened or was about to happen. Everything else could be explained and even justified, but canceling regular family visits without any explanation meant that the regime was taking risks, knowing very well that news of the lockdown would spread quickly throughout the country and abroad. In our ward, we decided to resort to a hunger strike to protest the situation. But this time around, we acted realistically by declaring that we would not accept prison food for a limited period of three days. We returned our prison rations, and the guards took them back without showing any reaction and went about their business.

The prison had fallen into a weird mood. The level of communication between wards had decreased substantially, because the bulk of contacts between adjacent wards normally happened through the exchange of notes and items in the yards; now we had to communicate via long-distance Morse code, using a light source and mainly at night. The wards were still in constant contact, though. We knew that the authorities were able to pick up our Morse-code communications, but we had no other choice. It was essential, however, that the identity of the prisoner or prisoners making the contacts be concealed from the authorities. We knew that these communication channels would be critical if a life-threatening situation arose.

Less than a week after the start of the complete lockdown, the situation started to change drastically. During one particular day, many strange events were reported from different wards. In our ward, I woke up that morning to whispers and commotion among the prisoners. Farzin and Tababati, both early risers, informed me that the authorities had brought a group of blindfolded prisoners into our yard. This was the first sign of any serious activity in our section of the prison since the start of the lockdown.

Farzin, Tababati, and I ran to the toilet and shower room at the end of the ward; it was already packed with prisoners who were quietly observing the yard through the metal window shades. People took turns to watch the yard and to report their observations quietly for the others behind. The rotation finally got to the three of us.

The large gate in the yard had been left cracked open, and there was a pile of sandals behind it. Inside the yard, there were ten to fifteen unfamiliar guards in control. Between the yard gate and our building, fifteen to twenty blindfolded prisoners, in their street clothing but wearing sandals, were sitting and leaning against the wall. Guards were taking them, one by one, to the yard bathroom. Some prisoners seemed to be smiling, while others were calm and serious. We could not recognize any of the prisoners. We knew only Lashgari among the authorities in the yard. After a while, the prisoners in the yard were ordered to stand up and were taken out of the yard. The gate was closed and locked.

Most of us returned to the hallway and started walking and analyzing. A few people remained in the bathroom and shower room, watching the empty yard, wondering if other groups of prisoners would be brought in.

Who were those prisoners? Some believed they were the regime's own followers, who had been arrested for opposing the ending of the war. Others thought they had been arrested in the recent Mojahedin military operations in the west of the country. A third group believed they were opposition sympathizers and activists who had been arrested or rearrested because of the current political turmoil in the country. No one thought that they might be prisoners from the other half of our own prison. Taking them one by one to the bathroom gave us the impression that they were newly arrested prisoners. The only suspicious feature we could not explain was the pile of sandals behind the gate.

Another group of prisoners was brought to our yard in the afternoon. They went through the same routine and then were taken away. At night, news of these events was relayed to other wards, and we were informed in return that the same thing had happened in the yard of Wards 7 and 8. Furthermore, Wards 7 and 8 indicated that some activity was going on behind their building, which mainly looked like sewage repair work. But they also indicated that they had observed two suspicious things close to the prison amphitheater, which they had a view of from their northern cells.

First, they had seen many strange-looking shaven-headed guards in butcher outfits apparently working in or outside of the amphitheater, sometimes spraying a liquid around the amphitheater using pumps and with masks on and at other times resting and smoking out there. Second, they had seen refrigerated trucks at night loading up a cargo and then driving out of view. On occasion, they had also seen open flatbed trucks loaded with a covered cargo, which had looked to them like dead bodies. These observations, though circumstantial, were horrifying. They kept knocking on their ward doors, demanding an explanation.

One day, Lashgari unexpectedly showed up and provided some explanations about the situation. He told them that the lockdown was by the orders of the higher authorities and he could do nothing about it. When asked about the activities behind their wards, he replied:

> Although watching activities out there through the windows is illegal, I am going to explain what you might have seen. We are repairing and cleaning up the sewage and plumbing systems of the prison. Because of this repair work, trucks carrying meat and other essentials can't enter the prison building through the normal entrances, so they have to deliver their cargo through the amphitheater door. The guards with masks that you might have seen are spraying the open sewage to prevent the stench and control mosquito reproduction in the summer heat.

Initially, the prisoners were convinced by his explanation, because their own suspicions seemed so far-fetched or unbelievable that they were subconsciously looking for some logical explanation to put their minds at ease. Lashgari succeeded both in calming them down and in misleading them. After he left, discussions started among these prisoners regarding his behavior. Some thought that his explanations seemed convincing, but his behavior was not typical of the Lashgari that they had known over the years. Never had he felt obligated to provide explanations and justifications to prisoners for their observations made through an "illegal" channel in the first place! So they questioned: why would he feel obligated to come into their wards to explain and justify what was happening out there? After some analysis, they reached a frightening conclusion: the cargo on the open trucks, or in the refrigerated ones, must indeed have been corpses, and that was the main reason why Lashgari had felt it was necessary to mislead them.

For us in the other wards, it sounded surreal but frightening. It was unbelievable that they were busy killing people during the day, storing the bodies and keeping them from spoiling in the summer heat by continuous spraying, then sneaking them out at night to bury them in some unknown mass grave. This narrative still seemed so far-fetched that we naturally tended to return to the "logical" explanation given by Lashgari, thinking that we were just being paranoid because of the lockdown and were being influenced by some circumstantial observations.

2

If dangerous events were unfolding in the country, and especially in the prisons, we needed to find direct evidence of them soon, before it was too late for us. A few of us reviewed possible means of getting any kind of reliable intelligence. The fastest and easiest option was the Afghani prisoner who helped deliver our bread ration. We decided to accompany Ibrahim Najjaran to obtain some information from this prisoner when Ibrahim picked up the bread ration.

One day, when the bread cart was pushed inside the ward, a few of us surrounded the old guard and started talking to him about his favorite subject—the quality and quantity of the bread ration—plus we asked him to advise us on how to approach the authorities on easing the lockdown. During those few valuable minutes, Ibrahim was receiving our bread ration from the Afghani prisoner. Normally the old guard would watch the Afghani prisoner when he had any contact with us political prisoners, and he had a watchful eye on him this time as well, except for short moments when we blocked his view or were able to distract him. Ibrahim and the Afghani prisoner were both kneeling during the bread delivery, facing each other. In one of those rare safe moments, Ibrahim asked the Afghani prisoner, "What is going on in prison?"

Without saying a word, the Afghani prisoner made a gesture with his right hand. He carefully and quickly moved his hand around his head, and then repeated it a couple more times. The old guard ordered him to finish up, and soon they were out of the ward.

The ten or twelve of us who had gone out for the bread ration returned to our cell, and Ibrahim explained what had happened. Ibrahim and a few of us who had observed the hand gesture of the Afghani prisoner interpreted it to mean a turban. We thought he was trying to tell us something about turbans and mullahs. But what did that mean? Maybe it meant that Khomeini either had died or was on his deathbed. Or it might have meant that an important mullah was in our prison. Both were possible and could relate to the lockdown, but they still did not explain the events happening in the prison.

We also wanted to establish contact with the *far'i* (minor) wards attached to Wards 5 and 6. We knew from our previous contacts that they held Mojahedin prisoners. We had to find a way to contact them. The only location inside our ward where it was possible to get a closer view of those *far'i* wards was through the window of Cell 1. A couple of guys who knew prisoners in those *far'i* wards entered Cell 1 and for ten to fifteen minutes tried to establish contact with them, but there was no reply. We were pretty sure there were still prisoners living in those wards, but it looked like they were not willing to make any contact.

We tried again on another occasion. This time, there was a response. It went something like this:

> Warning! Warning! Mass execution might be under way in prison! Last night, some of us were taken to the *far'i* ward above us and ordered to pack up and put out the belongings of the prisoners who used to live there but were all gone now. When we asked whether we should put their names on their belongings, the guards told us that it

was not necessary. Be very careful; we think a grave danger is threatening the lives of all prisoners.

The statement shocked and horrified us. Put together with the observations of the prisoners in Wards 7 and 8, and our own observations of the prisoners brought into our yard, plus the hand gesture of the Afghani prisoner, we had to take the situation seriously, as was stressed in the statement. We decided to make another contact with that *far'i* ward to confirm what they had said before spreading the warning to other wards. The following night, when our side attempted to make contact, there was no reply from the other side, and no one seemed to be living there anymore. They were all gone. We decided to immediately transfer their warning to all other wards. Taking away prisoners without their belongings was nothing new, but the fact that the guards did not care about labeling prisoners' belongings was a very dangerous sign.

Arguments with the guards continued in our ward, and we even resorted to a few short-term hunger strikes, but the reaction from the authorities and the guards stayed mostly the same: eerily calm, cold, and silent.

In the third and fourth week after the lockdown, the guards clearly looked tired and depressed. We had never seen them in this condition before. One more change we noticed was that the older guards were kept more in the shift-rotation for the wards, while younger ones were moved out of the rotation.

One of our main arguments with the guards these days was about watering the flowers and plants in our yard. We insisted that they allow us to water the flowers that were dying of drought in summer heat. The answer from them generally was that they did not have permission to let us do that. I remember when we asked Ne'mati about it, he pondered for a few seconds and then replied, "If I were you, I would pay more attention to my own safety and future rather than the plants in the yard."

Those who had put time and sweat into caring for those flowers and plants were insistent on finding a way to water them.

One night, some prisoners finally decided to use a short hose we had in the ward. They connected it to the faucet in the bathroom and put its tip out of the window. They let the water run out of the building and into the yard overnight, watering the plants and flowers.

Early next morning, we were still asleep when the guards stormed in, went directly to the bathroom, took the hose, turned the water off, and left without saying a word. In the past, this act would have brought the wrath of the warden on us, and the parties involved—or the whole ward—would have been punished severely for it. But now they behaved as though nothing had happened. This encouraged some prisoners to be more adventurous, aggressive, and radical in their thoughts and deeds.

In mid-August, in the heat of our daily arguments with the shift guards, suddenly Ne'mati closed the door and left. He soon returned and called three people out: Tababati (from our organization), Mohammad-Ali Pezhman (a.k.a. Kaku, from the Peykar organization), and Hossein Haji-Mohsen (from the Rah-e Kargar organization). These three had been very aggressive and outspoken recently with the guards. They left and never returned to the ward. We thought that they had been sent to solitary for punishment, as would have been a normal practice.

The Baha'i prisoners were also worried about the lockdown and the potentially dangerous situation. They were kept informed by Siavoush about everything that we found out. Though they were never involved in any activities in prison—they felt they would be safer this way—through experience they knew that no one was ever safe at any time in the prison system of the Islamic Republic.

The Islamic regime had a very strange system of justice, which seemed without rules, without principles. Rather, it was like an organized chaos—with a dose of pragmatism, and a generous dose of brutality—and its strength derived from its unpredictability. In a sense, this applied to the whole regime and was not limited to the judiciary or the prison system. When you thought they were weak, they came out swinging aggressively. When you thought that conditions should get better, they resorted to actions that made things much worse. When you thought they could not end the war because that would mean the end for the regime, they accepted a cease-fire. You could never know just what you were up against.

3

These days, Siavoush, "Parham," Farzin, and I often hung out, eating together and pondering the situation and what could possibly be done. One day Siavoush or Parham asked if there was any possibility of making a crude radio receiver to listen to the news to find out what was going on in the country. We thought we might learn if Khomeini were dead or on his deathbed, and we could also find out what the outcome of the Mojahedin military campaign had been.

A couple of days later, without revealing who or how, Siavoush indicated that someone had put together such a device and was ready to test it, but this person needed our help to do so. I guessed someone had "borrowed" the hearing aid of one of the old Baha'i prisoners and had devised a mechanism to allow it to receive radio waves. The most important bits of news we found out from this source were that Khomeini was still alive; the Mojahedin military campaign had ended in a disastrous defeat; and Khomeini, in a letter to Ayatollah Mousavi Ardabili, the head of the judiciary, had ordered him to deal aggressively and mercilessly with the *monafeghin* (hypocrites), the *mortaddin* (apostates), the *moharebin* (those warring against God), and drug traffickers. Though this did not directly explain our situation in prison, we interpreted it to mean the following: Khomeini was still alive and active, and therefore the hand gesture of the Afghani prisoner did not mean anything relating to him. Consequently, we concluded that he might have been trying to tell us either that a mullah was in prison or, more probably, that prisoners were being hanged. If Khomeini was still alive, if the Mojahedin had been defeated in their military campaign, and if there was no sign of unrest or revolt in the country at large, then why were we still being kept in a complete lockdown? It seemed more and more possible that a mass killing of prisoners was under way.

The next few days of the lockdown for us felt like the proverbial calm before the storm. On August 24, a few people from our ward including Siavoush, Farzin, and Ibrahim Najjaran were called out. My two comrades and cellmates, and also my best buddies, were all gone now. Contacts with other wards indicated that a few people from each, except Ward 5, had also been taken out. They did not return. Had they perished, or would we see them alive someday? After Siavoush and Farzin left, I hung out mostly with Parham. He was an anxious type, who worried constantly and was as slim as a thread.

The morning of August 25, I woke up because of noise and commotion in the ward. I was sitting in my bed, sleepy, when Parham walked in and told me that everyone in Wards 7 and 8 had been pulled out. Apparently, as soon as the guards had poured into their wards like hyenas, some brave prisoners had made sure to inform Wards 13 and 14 of what was happening. Those wards, in turn, had immediately informed our ward. The building housing Wards 7 and 8 was the most northern part of the main prison structure. There were about two hundred prisoners in those two wards.

I think this was the first time when doubts of any kind left the minds of even the most optimistic leftist prisoners. All of us finally felt that there was something serious and dangerous going down in prison. It was obvious that whatever had been going on during the first month of the lockdown in the other half of the prison had now reached our half. From this moment on, everything dramatically changed for us. None of us in Wards 13, 14, 6, and even 5, could remain calm from then on.

Our ward guards went about their normal business, giving us our food and other rations as though nothing unusual was going on. Only their demeanor was different: they continued to behave, as they had recently, in a very melancholic, mysterious way. They looked depressed and tired, and they did not converse with us much at all.

Late that afternoon, Wards 13 and 14 indicated that some prisoners had finally returned to Wards 7 and 8. It was late at night when those prisoners reported the following: unfamiliar, shaven-headed guards had poured in in the early morning and demanded that everyone get out quickly. On each floor, blindfolded prisoners were pushed into the *zir-e hasht* (lobby) and the stairways. After a while, in an atmosphere of absolute terror, the prisoners were lined up in the corridors. One by one, they were taken in front of a desk, behind which Lashgari, Naserian, or an unknown authority was sitting. Each prisoner was asked a few questions and then assigned to the right or the left side of the corridor. The questions were as follows:

Are you a Muslim?
Do you believe in God and the Prophet Mohammad?
Do you believe in Ghiamat (the Day of Resurrection)?
Do you pray daily?
Are you willing to participate in an interview?

Most of the prisoners gave negative replies to some or all of the questions and were sent to the left side; while a small number from each ward gave positive answers to all of the questions, or at least gave positive answers to the first three questions with no hesitation, and were sent to the right. These small groups were sent back to their respective wards, while the larger groups were taken away. The returnees indicated that the questioning was very religious in tone and content, the likes of which they said they had not encountered before in the Tehran prisons. This fact, combined with the observations of the last month, suggested that horrible events were indeed under way, and therefore they recommended that every one of us should be prepared to respond clearly to those first three questions. So that was it: an Islamic inquisition in Iranian prisons during the last part of the twentieth century.

4

That night no one got any sleep. Parham and I spent the night pondering the situation, the questions, and how we would respond to them. We were still waiting and hoping for more information, particularly on the fate of those leftists who had not returned. Any news of their fate would have been crucial to our decision making.

A prisoner who had been a religious activist in the past and was well-informed on Islamic issues explained to us that you had to be very cautious in responding to religious inquiries by an Islamic judge. He gave us a crash course about the concept of *mortad* (apostate) in Islam. This was really helpful in deciding how to frame our replies. Although no one had any direct evidence that the authorities were indeed killing prisoners, all indications were pointing in that direction. Therefore, we had to make some serious decisions and make them rather quickly.

There was constant consulting and exchange of opinion among different groups because we all felt a common danger. I remember walking and talking with Mehdi Hassani-pak from the Tudeh Party that day. He indicated that, as far as he knew, Tudeh Party prisoners did not have a problem with a tactical retreat, if necessary, regarding the religious inquisition. But he said that personally he was tired and did not like taking tactical positions anymore. I told him that I still had not made up my mind and advised him to keep his options open. I was hopeful that we would get more information and would be able to make an informed decision. We agreed to talk a couple of times a day from then on. I also walked and talked with others in the ward that day.

August 26 passed and no more prisoners from Wards 7 and 8 returned to their wards. That night, the returnees of Wards 7 and 8 were ordered to pack and store the belongings of everyone else, except their own, in the small *far'i* wards. The returnees tried to write the names of prisoners on their bags as much as they could, hoping that when and if they returned they would be able to locate their belongings. The guards had insisted that writing names on the bags did not matter anymore. Late that night, the prisoners in Ward 7 were transferred to Ward 8, where there were now about fifty to sixty prisoners altogether. Where had the rest of the prisoners been taken and what had happened to them?

The morning of August 27, more prisoners returned to Ward 8. Here is what they initially reported:

> A commission has been established through a fatwa[14] from Khomeini. The commission has apparently been given absolute power to decide about each prisoner. With the help of prison, judiciary, intelligence authorities, and guards, they have interrogated and dealt with the Mojahedin and other religious prisoners during the first month of the lockdown. Now, they have started dealing with the secular leftists. There has been a mass killing of prisoners under way and it is still ongoing. Apparently, they hang prisoners in different locations, one of which certainly is the prison amphitheater. Please be very careful.

Make wise decisions about how to respond to the inquisition, particularly to the first three questions regarding the principles of Islam.

There was now no doubt that everything we had observed and heard during the first month of the lockdown fit together and made complete sense. The prisoners we had seen in our yards in the early days were some of the Mojahedin prisoners from our prison, whom the guards were preparing to hang. The hand gesture over the head by the Afghani prisoner had certainly meant hanging and not a turban. The spraying behind the amphitheater by the guards was needed because of odor from the corpses due to the midsummer heat. The refrigerated and open trucks seen behind Wards 7 and 8 were indeed carrying cargoes of dead bodies. And the frequent helicopter flights we had heard must have been carrying members of the "death commission" back and forth between Evin and Gohardasht prisons.

Later that day, these recent returnees gradually reported the details of their ordeal during the two days they were gone. After they had been separated into left and right lines, prisoners in the left lines on both floors were led down the stairways to the ground floor. The returnees indicated that there was an atmosphere and level of terror down there that they had never seen before in prison. Some of these prisoners had experienced the 1981–1983 period, but they said this was something completely different: a level of terror that made you so numb that you did not know what to think and how to react anymore. These prisoners were taken in front of the commission, and most of them, sensing the danger, declared that they were Muslims. They were therefore sent to the right and later were sent to Ward 2. They witnessed some of their comrades being sent to the left and later taken to the end of the long corridor toward the prison amphitheater. They had no direct evidence about the fate of those friends but felt that they had all been hanged.

Wards 2 and 10, previously Mojahedin wards, had been turned into "transit" wards, where a few surviving Mojahedin, and those secular leftist prisoners who had said yes to the questions about their Islamic beliefs but had not claimed to pray daily or agreed to join in prayer now, were kept. They were kept in closed-door cells or rooms, and the secular leftists were flogged at every prayer time until they agreed to pray. Afterward, they were transferred to Ward 8, which was now the survivors' ward of the leftists. These returnees had encountered only a few Mojahedin prisoners on the ground floor or in Ward 2. This was very strange. What then had happened to the majority of the Mojahedin prisoners? Had they been transferred somewhere else, or had they all been massacred?

5

In the remaining leftist wards (13, 14, 6, and even 5), we had to make some tough decisions based on what we had heard from these recent returnees. We felt really lucky to have gotten a head start in dealing with this dangerous situation. Late at night on August 27, I was in the cell with Parham, discussing and trying to come up with a reasonable tactic in response to the inquisition. Iraj from the Fadaiyan Minority organization walked in and said that a prisoner who had just returned to Ward 8 had revealed this:

> I was taken in front of the "death commission" where the cleric Hossein-Ali Nayyeri presided as the judge, and afterward I was put on the left side. Many of my friends from Wards 7 and 8 were in those lines on the left as well. Later, they moved these lines toward the end of the corridor and closer to the prison amphitheater. Once there, I was pulled out and put aside in a corner. After a couple of hours,

> someone took me inside the amphitheater and removed my blindfold. I saw many hanging scaffolds erected there, even a few on the stage. Bodies of prisoners were still hanging up there. I recognized at least two of them, namely Kaku and Hossein Haji-Mohsen. It was a terrorizing and horrifying scene. The person who had taken me into the amphitheater put my blindfold back on, brought me out, delivered me to a guard, and told him that according to his list I should have been put on the right side. Apparently, I had mistakenly (or on purpose) been put on the left after my court session.

This was an unbelievable story, yet Iraj said he had known this prisoner for many years and trusted him. My first reaction—and Parham's—was to think the "mistake" was intentional: this could be a smart move by the authorities to spread fear among us, to force us into making more concessions and retreats. But then we thought, why would they need to resort to this tactic if their intention was to kill as many more of us as they possibly could? We decided that there were two possible explanations.

One was that the prisoner was intentionally taken to the amphitheater to witness the scaffolds and bodies and to transfer the information to the rest of us. Why? Because a faction of the regime, though it agreed with the extensive killings of the Mojahedin prisoners, whose organization was involved in a military campaign against the regime, was not in favor of killing the secular leftists, whose organizations for all practical purposes had been dismantled by the security services. Therefore, this prisoner had been shown evidence of the hangings so that he would return and tell others what he had seen, encouraging a tactical retreat among us to reduce the number of executed secular leftists.

The second explanation was that the commission itself wanted to show us real evidence of the killings, to scare and force us to retreat, not necessarily to decrease the number of executions but to make its screening job easier and faster.

Either way, whether this prisoner had "cooperated" with the authorities on the issue made no difference because we were pretty certain by this time that extensive killings were happening in prison. Later, we found out that, whether by mistake or by design, other people had also been taken to the solitary ward next to the amphitheater, where prisoners were asked to write their wills and leave their possessions. Some also had been taken to the amphitheater to show them evidence of the hangings. We learned much later that in fact Ayatollah Montazeri and his followers were against Khomeini's fatwa; they were against the killing of prisoners who were serving their sentences and had done nothing to deserve execution.

We were very lucky compared to those who had no prior knowledge of the killings when they were pulled out and questioned. They had responded as usual, thinking that it was just a bluff or a pressure game by the regime, and consequently they were hanged. We thought we had a responsibility to inform others, to make maximum use of the information we had gotten, to save ourselves, to survive the conspiracy killings, and try to help save everyone else.

I was not going to allow this regime to kill me based on my replies to some religious inquisition's questions. They had the power to kill me at any time, but it was not going to be because of my opinion of religion. I personally decided that we were in the midst of a grand political conspiracy for the wholesale killing of political prisoners. We were not going to win this battle by martyring ourselves *en masse*. Under the circumstances, I could not see the political or social benefits of such a suicidal act of sacrifice. I thought that surviving to fight the regime another day was the right tactic for those of us who were lucky to have found out about the mass killing.

From that early morning onward, my mind was made up. I started with Parham and continued on with anyone in our ward that I could influence, then continued to others in Wards 13, 14, and 5. I explained my position—specifically, why I believed we had to make a conscious tactical retreat when responding to the religious inquisition. My view was that we ought to retreat on the ideological issues to save our lives and neutralize the conspiracy, but be steadfast and resist on political and intelligence matters.

All the leftist wards were still in constant contact with each other, discussing what we should do if we were pulled out. In the final analysis, the decision was going to be a personal one. But the idea of a conscious retreat on the ideological questions grew quickly to become the dominant view of the remaining leftist prisoners.

6

In the early morning of August 28, the guards pulled out everyone in Ward 14, the so-called Evin ward. A few of the prisoners were still transmitting good-bye messages as the ward was emptying, but after a few minutes, no more signals were coming from Ward 14; they were all gone. An eerie quiet and emptiness had descended upon Ward 14. The killing machine had trapped many more victims for its daily torture and death operation. It was fairly clear from the pattern that Ward 13 would be next, and then it would be our turn in Ward 6. Ward 13 had the *mellikesh* (serving without sentence) prisoners.

Later that day, news from them indicated that some new returnees had arrived in Ward 8. The new returnees recommended that, based on what they had experienced, it would be better if the remaining leftist prisoners retreated on the ideological issues from the very beginning, so that they would have some control over their fate and would not put it in the hands of the prison authorities, the guards, or the "death commission."

In the evening, some forty prisoners were called out from Ward 13. Nothing more happened during the rest of that night and the following day. The death commission had enough prey to continue their inhumane hunting game for a couple of days. But for us in Wards 13 and 6, it was a tough wait, especially because we knew we were next. At first, we anticipated that we would be pulled out sometime on August 29, and therefore we prepared ourselves all night for the ordeal. When nothing happened that day, we could not get any sleep the following night either. This made it a few nights in a row that we had not been able to rest. We all looked like zombies.

I remember spending most of August 29 walking and talking to different people. I was hoping to be able to convince as many people as I could about their response to the inquisitor. By the end of that night, an absolute majority of prisoners in our ward had reached a similar conclusion: to retreat on the ideological issues by replying positively to the religious questions regarding the principles of Islam (belief in God, the Prophet Mohammad, and Ghiamat). On the issue of praying, we thought we would resist as much as we could and then would decide individually.

We reached a certain level of calm and resignation, but none of us slept at all that night. Everyone was preparing for the following morning. We packed our bags and labeled them, just in case someone looked for them later on. Each of us dressed in clothing that we thought would be practical for any possible outcome. I packed and labeled not only my own bags, but also those of my comrades Tababati and Farzin. I prepared myself for solitary by hiding essential items like a needle, some thread, some salt, the head of a toothbrush, and a pen in my clothing. I also wore two layers of everything including underwear, shirts, and pants. According to what had happened in the previous wards, we knew that after they pulled us out they would bring some prisoners to store our belongings in the *far'i* ward.

7

In the early morning of August 30, the guards pulled out the remaining prisoners of Ward 13. For a couple of hours afterward, nothing more happened. Our contact with Ward 8 had been completely disrupted because there was no one left in the middle building to connect us and to relay our communications.

It was about eleven o'clock when our ward door opened and Lashgari, along with some strange-looking guards, ordered all of us to line up blindfolded in the ward hallway. Lashgari ordered the Baha'i prisoners to stay in their cells. They then led the rest of us into the *zir-e hasht*. Though we had known about the process for almost a week now, it was still terrorizing and nerve-wracking. After a few minutes, the guards led the line to the stairs going up toward the third floor. It was totally dark in the stairway. The guards ordered us to sit down on the steps from top to bottom. Then they closed the doors to both floors and left us sitting there in darkness and eerie silence. They had packed us into that small space to crack our nerves and to increase our anxiety.

After a while, the door to the second floor opened, and a few people from the front were pulled out. Minutes later, they took a few more people. After ten to twelve people had been taken out, nothing more happened for a while. When the door opened again, the rest of us were ordered to walk out. We were led to the second-floor main corridor and placed apart from each other on both sides of the corridor, facing the walls. We were left there shivering in absolute terror.

Lashgari, Naserian, or whoever else was conducting the initial screening had decided after questioning the first ten to twelve people that our replies were conciliatory and did not match our previous positions at all; therefore, they had concluded that we had coordinated our response to their ideological questions. They had lost the element of surprise and secrecy that had helped them to classify the prisoners from the initial wards. Without it, they could not classify us that easily. That was why they had stopped the screening; to make decisions and maybe to resort to a new tactic or method.

It was about two o'clock when we were all ordered to move slowly toward Ward 8. In front of Ward 8, a person whom we did not know but later learned was a member of the death commission questioned each of us. He asked the religious questions and separated out only two of us to be sent to "the Haj-Agha," which meant to the Islamic judge and the death commission. Both of these people were from the Tudeh Party: Mehdi Hassani-pak and an ex-navy captain named Mohsen Bidgoli. I was not surprised about Hassani-pak, who had indicated to me the night before that he might defend his beliefs, being tired of the never-ending tactical game. Apparently, that was what he had done in the initial questioning, resulting in his segregation and trip down to the ground floor to face the death commission.

In any case, after these initial rounds of questionings, they sat us against the wall and nothing happened for another half hour. Then Lashgari walked into the corridor and toward us. I could see his legs and those of others following him. As he walked through the corridor, here and there he would pick a prisoner to address by nudging the prisoner's leg. He would then ask a few questions. Then he would either tell the prisoner to sit down again or order the guards to take the prisoner to the Haj-Agha. On what basis he was making his selections and decisions, I could not tell.

Lashgari got closer to where Parham and I were sitting. My heart was beating faster and faster as he approached us. Before reaching us, he picked someone who I thought was Iraj. I could hear a bit of the question and answer now. Lashgari first asked the three religious questions, to which he got positive replies. Then he commented, "You probably are willing to pray as well?" Iraj gave a positive reply again. Lashgari ordered him to sit down. He continued walking and then stood in front of me. He nudged my leg and ordered me to stand up. He asked me the three religious questions, to which I gave positive replies. Then he asked if I was willing to pray. I said no. He ordered the guards to take me to the Haj-Agha. While leaving, I noticed that he had come to Parham, who must have responded as I had done, because he soon joined me. We were led down some stairways to the ground floor.

Personally, I had decided the night before to take a step-by-step approach so that I could analyze the situation and decide what to do at each step. My decision was to accept the three religious principle questions first, to escape the immediate danger, and then deal with the praying issue if I got to the death commission. Whether this was a wise tactical decision, putting myself in danger by going in front of the death commission, I was not sure at the time. In retrospect, I think it was a mistake. The majority of our ward, as it turned out, had agreed in the corridor to pray, and therefore they were not sent to the death commission. Only about ten people from our ward had taken the route that I took.

8

Entering the ground level was like stepping into an underworld. It was dark, it felt damp, and it stank down there. My breathing soon became heavy and hard. I cautiously peeked from under my blindfold. Groups of prisoners were lined up, sitting or standing, in different locations; on every face I glimpsed, there was clearly fear.

The office wing of the assistant prosecutor in Gohardasht had become the operational center of the death commission. Opposite this wing was located the two-story kitchen/workshop building. There was an open space where these two opposing sections reached the main corridor, and this was where the major portion of the process was happening.

We were taken to the vicinity of the assistant prosecutor's wing and positioned by the door. Many things were happening here simultaneously. There was a line of prisoners sitting to the left of us in the main corridor. The look on their faces—a mix of disbelief and terror—reminded me of the prisoners brought to our yard in the early days of the lockdown. There was also a large group of prisoners sitting by the stairway to the right of us. Strange-looking, shaven-headed guards were moving around, shouting and abusing as they shuttled prisoners here and there. From somewhere distant I could hear prisoners screaming and the sound of flogging. Later, I figured out that the torture was being carried out in the workshop area across from where I was sitting. Every few minutes, Naserian would come out of that hallway to deliver a prisoner to the guards, announcing each prisoner's fate by means of a shouted directive: "Take him to his ward!" "Put this mister under the stairs!" "Put him on the left side!" or "This one wants to be in a Marxist ward!" The guards then put the prisoners in different locations according to the verdicts.

After a while, some of us were moved inside the small hallway where the commission room and other offices were located. The guards positioned us by the side of the wall to wait our turn. There were two rooms opposite each other, where the main activities were happening. Naserian constantly moved between the two rooms. Later, I figured out that the one on my left was the death commission's room, while the other one was where the prison files, and maybe interrogators, were located, because Naserian would go in there and would come out with a file or files in his hand. I assumed that Naserian used the files, and maybe the opinion of the interrogators, to assist the commission in assessing the responses of each prisoner who was sent inside the commission room. There was a guard standing by the commission-room door. Once in a while, Lashgari would come into the small hallway as well, but mostly I heard his voice from the "death corridor," which ended in the amphitheater.

While we were waiting, Naserian pulled a prisoner out of the commission room by his collar. He delivered the prisoner to the guard roughly and shouted, "Take him, have him lashed sixty counts, and bring him back!" Whatever the prisoner had said or done in there had earned him sixty lashes. In another instance, Naserian brought a prisoner out of the commission room while shouting and swearing at him. With the help of a few guards, he dragged the prisoner to the workshop area, shouting, "After you get some flogging, we will see if you answer the questions or not! We will beat you until you reply politely to the questions asked by the Haj-Agha!" Naserian soon returned without the prisoner and continued his work. After a half hour or so, guards dragged that poor prisoner back into the commission room. They informed Naserian that the prisoner had become "polite" and was ready to answer the questions of the Haj-Agha. A minute later, he was brought out of the commission room and Naserian, with much joy, cried out, "Take him to the left, please!"

In another instance, Naserian brought a young prisoner out of the commission room; this time both Naserian and the prisoner had big smiles on their faces. Naserian shouted, "Put him on the left side!" The young prisoner must have seen a friend of his waiting next to us, because as he passed near he said proudly, "*Zadam to cheshesh*" ("I hit him in the eye"), meaning that he had defended his beliefs and had told the judge to go to hell.

In another case, Naserian brought out a pale-looking prisoner and called the guard to put him in the "communist-ward" line. Most probably, this prisoner had been brought into the commission room directly from solitary and had been told that they were rearranging the wards and wanted to know if he preferred to be in a ward for communists or a ward for Muslims. The prisoner, not aware of the deadly inquisition happening in the prison, would have replied that he preferred to be in a "communist ward," afraid that otherwise he would be taken to a *tavvab* ward. Many prisoners who had been in solitary for punishment had a similar fate. The authorities had brought them directly from solitary and had confused them with misleading questions to make sure that they got hanged.

After a couple of hours, a guard came and asked if I was Jafar son of Bashir. He took me and delivered me to Naserian, who was standing by the commission-room door. Naserian led me to a chair in the middle of the room and then removed my blindfold. It took me a minute or so to notice people sitting in front of me behind a long table. I recognized the mullah sitting across from me, Hossein-Ali Nayyeri. To his right was the prosecutor of Tehran, Mortaza Eshraghi, and then to his right again there were a couple more civilian officials. There were also a few people sitting to the left of the judge. I was facing the death commission. Later on, we learned that Khomeini's fatwa authorized this commission to eliminate those prisoners who were determined as *monafegh*, *mohareb*, or *mortad* and that the fatwa gave decision-making authority on each prisoner to the majority vote of three members of the commission: Nayyeri, Eshraghi, and a Ministry of Intelligence representative.

Nayyeri started by asking my name and my father's name. Then he asked, "Are you a Muslim? Do you believe in God?"

"Yes."

"Do you believe in the Prophet Mohammad and his Prophecy?"

"Yes."

"Do you believe in Ghiamat, the Day of Resurrection?"

"Yes."

"Do you pray?"

"I have not prayed since I was a kid."

"So, what kind of a Muslim are you that you do not pray?"

"My parents never encouraged me to pray."

"But now we are telling you that if you are a Muslim, then you have to pray."

"That is something that I have to decide on my own."

Eshraghi jumped in and said, "Haj-Agha, I am sure he will pray, now that he says he is a Muslim. He seems sincere." And then, looking at me, he continued: "Get up and go start praying."

Nayyeri had the final word; he told me that if I did not pray, they would bring me back and he would then render his final verdict. Naserian put the blindfold back on, delivered me to the guards outside, and ordered them to put me by the stairs.

A group of guards were roaming around and abusing the prisoners. The guards knew which group was going to survive, and they had been given a free hand in terrorizing and abusing them, to keep them under control and demoralized. After a couple more hours, around five or six o'clock, the death commission apparently stopped their daily activity. Suddenly, it became very quiet. Naserian and Lashgari walked along the main corridor, directing the guards on what to do with different groups of prisoners. Lashgari ordered the guards to move our group. We were led through the death corridor toward the amphitheater, which was terrifying given what we knew about the hangings there. Many prisoners had walked that same path to their final destination. Though we knew we were a group who had probably escaped execution at this point, we also knew nothing was certain in this place. Therefore, until we got to a ward in the vicinity of the amphitheater, we were petrified. It was a *far'i* ward with just a couple of rooms. They pushed us all in; I was in a small room with maybe thirty other prisoners. We stood waiting in shock and in fear of the unknown. The guards locked the doors and left.

I looked around from under my blindfold but could not recognize anyone in the room. A few minutes later, a prisoner who had recognized me got closer and started talking. He was a prisoner from our own Ward

6. We were able to exchange a few words before the door opened again. He said he had been taken to interrogation before going in front of the commission. He added that they knew everything about our activities in the ward during the lockdown period.

When the door opened again Lashgari entered with his guards. He said, "You have to start praying, per court orders. If you don't, we are going to administer five lashes for each *rak'at* (prayer cycle) of each prayer, eighty-five lashes daily, and this will continue until you agree to pray." Then he added, "Whoever is ready to start praying can come out, go to the ward, and join the others in the prayer."

Some raised their hands and were taken out of the room, apparently returning to Ward 8. The rest of us stayed in the room. Minutes later, the guards returned and lined us up in the main corridor behind some other prisoners. It soon became a fairly long line. We were then moved toward the amphitheater. At that point, I thought to myself that I might have taken a huge unnecessary risk again, because there was no guarantee that they would not hang us right then and there. We got closer to the amphitheater, then were stopped. After a few minutes, the guards started taking prisoners one by one inside the amphitheater, where they were lashed and then brought out. There were torture beds set up in the middle of the amphitheater, and there were maybe fifty or more guards there. Prisoners were put face-down on the beds. Some guards kept prisoners restrained while others took turns flogging. Each of us got fifteen lashes for the evening prayers. We were returned to the small ward to wait for the next round, which was going to be in an hour or so for the night prayers, and this time it was going to be twenty lashes.

Lashgari came back after a half hour or so and said, "All of you are going to have to accept praying one way or another. Just accept it and go to the ward." There was no reason for me to get myself tortured anymore. There was no way that we could last for long if they continued flogging. It made sense to acquiesce, to go to the ward and be with the other surviving prisoners awaiting our fate collectively. If there was going to be any forced praying, then we were going to pretend to pray together, and it would mean nothing as far as we were concerned. It was pointless to be tortured over this issue, because all of us had to accept the forced praying to survive. Most people raised their hands this time, including me. A small group still stayed behind to be lashed some more.

A long line of people being returned to the ward had formed in the main corridor. We were soon moved to Ward 8. All the secular leftist survivors, except the Ward 5 prisoners and those still in the pipeline of the inquisition and killing machinery, had been gathered in Ward 8. There were about one hundred fifty prisoners already there, and with our group of about fifty it became close to two hundred prisoners, among which were ten or twelve from our organization. In Ward 8, the guards and authorities made sure that everyone was in the ward salon at prayer time. Under the circumstances, the majority of us pretended to pray, because we wanted to survive. In community praying, there is usually a prayer leader who stands in front of the rows of people to conduct the worship. Now the same people who were judging and hanging prisoners downstairs would come up and stand in the front of the survivors to lead their prayers.

There was a strange mood and situation in the ward. No one had any belongings, and there were up to ten people in each small cell. The prisoners looked pale and edgy, and no one dared to protest or resist anything anymore. No one wanted to eat, smile, laugh, or do anything for that matter. The inquisition and mass killing had temporarily broken our morale. This must have been one of the lowest points for the combative prisoners. Most of these prisoners had experienced something similar during the 1981–1983 period and had gone through forced praying for a while then as well.

One certain change among the survivors was that no one cared anymore who their cellmates were. People who just hours ago were not willing to even say hello to their political rivals, let alone live with them, now not only did not mind sharing a cell with them but actually preferred it to living with their own organizational comrades, so that they would not raise suspicion in the authorities. The principle of survival sometimes dictates new behaviors. I also randomly went into one of the cells. There were eight people in that cell, and soon it went up to ten people.

9

We were so edgy that we would jump each time the ward door opened. None of us assumed for a minute that we were safe. If you were called or taken out for any reason, other prisoners assumed you were going to be hanged. Some believed that the executioners were going to come for us bit by bit until none of us was alive, particularly now that we knew what had happened in the prison. There was no order or organization in the ward, and no one really cared. We tried to rest on the cell floor, with nothing under or over us, but no one could really close his eyes. You wanted to be awake when and if the authorities came for you, even if it was in the middle of the night.

It was just before sunrise, and we were finally falling asleep from stress and exhaustion, when suddenly the guards poured into the ward like barbarians, hitting the cell doors with metal and wood clubs and with *kubl* (flogging cable). We all jumped up and stood looking like zombies. It was the call to morning prayer.

No one from Ward 5 was among us, which meant that either they had not been questioned at all or they had been questioned in their ward and had all accepted the conditions. We had no way of communicating with them, because the wards between our two buildings were now empty. There were no Baha'i prisoners among us either, and we did not know what had happened to them. Political discussions had ceased at this point, but those who trusted each other wondered out loud together about the numbers. There had been maybe six hundred (more or less) secular leftist prisoners in this prison before the lockdown. At present only about two hundred of us were alive in Ward 8 plus, possibly, a hundred in Ward 5. What had happened to the rest? Had they all been massacred during the last week—just one week? And what about the Mojahedin prisoners, who had numbered maybe eight hundred or more before the lockdown? We were wondering how many of them were alive and where they were being kept.

We were given a bit of bread and feta cheese for breakfast and then we sat in our cells waiting. It was about eleven o'clock when we were all ordered to sit down on the ward hallway floor while the guards paced back and forth shouting and abusing us. It reminded me of scenes from World War II movies, where occupying German soldiers gather the population of a small town or a village in the main square, then they either select some to take away or shoot a random few on the spot. We were seated in rows from the ward entrance to the end of the ward. Then the ward door opened, and a man in a nice suit entered with his own strange-looking special guards behind him. He walked through the rows without saying a word, picked some prisoners seemingly at random, and took them away, exactly like the scenes from those movies. This strengthened the view of those prisoners who believed that they were going to come for us bit by bit, eventually finishing us all.

Nobody talked about their personal ordeal yet, because people were in survival mode and naturally very self-preserving. There were some, a few extremely optimistic and simple-minded prisoners, who still, in the back of their minds, thought that the whole thing was a ruse by the authorities, meaning that there was no real mass killing. They thought that the regime had outmaneuvered and outsmarted us and that they had been able to segregate the "problem" prisoners from the "non-problem" ones by creating an atmosphere of absolute terror. According to them, the disappeared prisoners, maybe hidden somewhere, were going to be kept under pressure for a long period; the inquisition had managed to pacify the rest of us. The majority of the survivors, on the other hand, knew well what had happened and understood the magnitude of the tragedy.

The following morning, at around ten, a guard read a short list of names of prisoners to go out. This one was not a random list; it was clear that the authorities wanted these particular people out. My name was on that list. We had a minute or so to leave. I said good-bye to a couple of my organizational comrades. I told them that if I did not make it and they survived, they should send a message to my family that I loved them to the end. Everyone on the list currently had or previously had had a family member as a top cadre or leader of one of the many different Fadaiyan organizations. I was the only exception to that rule, but I did have the longest sentence for our organization in this prison among the survivors, which might have been the reason for my name being on the list, representing our group. We had most probably been selected because prison authorities or the death-commission members had decided that we ought not to escape punishment that easily.

The guard led us down the stairs to the ground level near the amphitheater. We were taken to the solitary ward below Ward 8, where death-row prisoners were asked to write their last wishes. Each of us was positioned facing the wall in a spot in the hallway. Those minutes lasted a lifetime. Under the circumstances, waiting for the unknown was the worst.

It took a half hour before someone approached from behind and whispered in my ear, asking if I was Jafar son of Bashir. He grabbed my hand and walked me into a cell. It was completely empty, except for a school chair in the middle. He put me in the chair, reminded me not to look back at any time, then left.

Again, it was the waiting game and the anxiety of the unknown. I examined the arm of the chair to see if there were any messages written or carved on it. But there was nothing. Many had probably sat on it in the last few weeks and had been asked to write their last wishes. Many prisoners probably even then did not believe they were really going to be hanged. They probably thought it was a mock execution, staged to scare and force them to retreat from their ideological or political position.

10

It was cold, damp, dark, and very quiet in the cell. I tried hard to concentrate on potential issues that could come up soon. I was thinking about these when I heard steps approaching. My heart started to race. Someone entered, stood behind me, and very calmly said, "Mr. Yaghoobi, you thought you had escaped the Islamic judgment that easily, did you not? Those were some serious lies you told the commission about your being a Muslim and a true believer now! You think we are stupid or something?"

Then, while putting an interrogation page on the chair's arm, he said, "Remember that your life now depends on how you answer these questions. The lies you delivered before matter no more. It is my evaluation that will assist the commission and the judge to render a final verdict on your fate. So answer honestly and carefully. I will be back in an hour."

Then he left the cell. I took a look at the question written on the page: *Describe your belief system and explain through what process how and since when you have become a religious person.* As soon as I read the question, I realized it was going to be hard to maneuver around it, particularly in a written format. I had to make a fundamental decision. I had already declared that I was a Muslim and had accepted praying. I could not go back on those declarations because that would mean *ertedad* (apostasy) and a certain death sentence. I could also further concede on the ideological and even political positions, if necessary for survival. But I decided right then and there that I would under no circumstances collaborate on intelligence issues or become a tool in the hands of the authorities against my fellow prisoners.

After making my strategic decision about the process, I wrote a short response to his question. I wrote very precisely, considering each word carefully. I did not want to put down anything in writing that could be construed as evidence of apostasy and be used to justify condemning me to death.

When the interrogator returned and took a look at my reply, he first expressed anger and said that I had written the same lies as before. He then wrote another question and left again. *What is your opinion about Marxism, and have you ever been a Marxist?*

Fortunately, I had never given the authorities any written opinions about Marxism during the initial interrogations after my arrest, as far as I could remember. Only in Evin during the last interrogation before my trial, when I was asked this same question, I had maneuvered by speaking in generalities without specifically stating anything. Therefore, I had to reply to the question in a way that would be in accord with my previous position and could not be taken as being against Islam.

When the interrogator returned and read my reply, he laughed at it but did not pursue that line of questioning any further. Finally, he entered the realm of serious issues where I had originally thought the interrogation would lead:

Before being pulled out of Ward 6 on the thirtieth of August, did you have any knowledge of what was happening in prison since the lockdown? How much and what had you found out, and how?

As I had guessed, this was where they were going to try to pressure and trap me. After he left the cell, I thought about it for a while and decided to try to figure out what he really wanted. I was sure they already knew that all wards were in constant contact. I therefore decided to admit that I had found out some of the news a day or two before we were pulled out.

Then he asked,

From whom did you hear the news?

"I do not remember; news was coming from a variety of sources," I replied.

He then said that they knew everything about the ward and what had happened during the lockdown and explained that he was testing to see how honest I was, especially now that I was claiming to be a Muslim. He asked,

Do you remember one incident where someone might have told you a particular news item in those days?

"I really don't. Sources were frequent, and things were happening constantly, but I do not remember anybody in particular. I am not going to put anyone in jeopardy to save my own skin," I replied. I was pretty sure that he had not bought any of the things I had said, but I had no other options except to stay the course.

Before he left, he said that I had not been honest and convincing, and in his opinion I had not changed at all. I had tried to walk a fine line, and now it was really in the hands of the judge—or pure luck. He left me there alone for another half hour or so.

11

It was late afternoon when a guard took me out of the cell and put me in a small line of prisoners. It was terrifying not to know what might happen next. In my heart and mind, I said good-bye to my loved ones. I truly thought it was the end of the road for us right then and there, given that after a long session of questioning we were lined up toward the amphitheater. The guards ordered everyone to grab the shirt of the person in front of him, then led the line forward. Were we being taken to the amphitheater to be hanged? Did they have something else planned for us? Maybe we were going back to Ward 8?

As soon as they led us into the amphitheater, I closed my eyes under the blindfold, with only the last vision of my wife and daughter in my mind, and I prepared to die. But we went through the amphitheater and soon emerged from the other end. We were suddenly outside of the building and in the compound grounds. I then thought they were going to hang us in the warehouse. The guards ordered us to jog. We went around the main prison building from the northwest toward the southwest. We were led into the building again from another entrance and were taken up to a solitary ward on the second floor. Guards pushed each of us into an empty cell.

I stood there, stunned motionless. I was relieved not to have been immediately hanged, but horrified, knowing where they had brought us. I removed my blindfold and started examining the cell. Through the metal window shades I saw the adjacent building, the prison clinic, and then I was certain that we were in the small solitary Ward 10, the so-called terminal solitary. In the southern half of the prison, where the Mojahedin prisoners had been kept before, Wards 2 and 10 had now been turned into terminals, where prisoners were processed during the massacre.

The cells had absolutely nothing in them. We were not even given the ugly prison blankets. There was only a small built-in metal toilet and sink in the cell. This indicated to me that they were not planning to keep us there long. Suddenly the cell door opened and two guards jumped in and started beating me mercilessly, apparently because I had removed my blindfold in the cell without permission.

That first night, an official moved me into a cell in the southern side of the ward. Later, I heard footsteps in the ward, and soon a few cell doors started opening. Minutes later the absolute silence of the ward was broken by the sound of flogging and the screams of prisoners. It seemed that they were lashing those prisoners either in the hallway or in the *zir-e hasht* of the ward. Later, I figured out that the victims were the last few secular leftist prisoners who had still not agreed to pray and therefore were being lashed several times daily. The floggings continued for the next couple of days, but gradually the number of people being lashed decreased until there was only one prisoner still being beaten; he, too, must have given in, because finally the flogging stopped completely.

12

The first night there, I was not given any food. I paced the cell constantly, pondering my fate. I was anxious and jumpy, and I thought I had to stay awake in case they came to take me for hanging. My terror of losing my life, combined with the eerie silence of the ward, was maddening. In the morning I felt like a zombie. Because of the constant stress of the last few days, and having had very little food and sleep, I had started losing weight rapidly.

I was experiencing a strange mental condition. On the one hand, I thought I had to stay awake and alert. On the other hand, not enough rest made me weak, slow, and tired. I could see the contradiction, but I was not able to do anything about it. There was nothing in the cell to keep me busy, so I paced the cell and pondered, arguing with myself, analyzing nonstop, and strategizing about different scenarios. Food and sleep—regular prison pleasures—held no appeal for me anymore.

The main struggle in my mind was about what I should do if the authorities demanded things that I could not morally accept to save my life. My interpretation of the situation was that we were in line for the final judgment. We were death-row prisoners now. Within a day or two, after I resolved the issue of life and death for myself, and after I developed clear criteria about what to do if faced with such a dilemma, I was a bit relieved. But still, I was so anxious that I jumped at any noise. I certainly was ready to have it over and done with. Human beings are interesting creatures. We can and do adapt to unimaginable conditions and circumstances as long as they do not physically destroy us. After a few days, I started to get used to living under these most dangerous and stressful conditions. I gradually calmed down. I had to overcome my internal struggle to be able to interact with my surroundings.

We were provided with very little food, no chance to shower, no soap or toothpaste, and no sleeping gear. I started focusing on the very limited things I had in my possession and tried to organize and manage my life. Since arriving there, I had not even considered the fact that I was wearing two sets of clothes. One night, during a quiet time, I took off the lower layer and kept the top, cleaner layer on. I washed the used set in the sink and hung them to dry from whatever I could find in the cell. I had brought a bit of salt and a toothbrush head with me, which I used once every night to brush my teeth. After use, I hid them so that the guards would not notice.

The window of my cell faced the southern grounds of the prison compound. Through the metal shades I could see a bit of the outside area, including a road coming to the southern tip of the main prison building. Every day, I watched outside whenever it felt safe to do so. I was hoping to see signs that could help me understand the situation. The prisoner in the next cell was taken away after he had been there for only a few days, and he did not return. I thought we would all gradually disappear as a final decision was made on each of us. After the flogging stopped, there was no activity or noise, only an eerie, deathly silence in the ward.

One week passed and nothing had happened to me yet. It seemed to me that there was a delay in the process for some reason, but I still could not get too comfortable knowing that things could go terribly wrong at any moment. One night I heard cell doors being opened and closed at intervals of a few minutes. I prepared myself for the worst. The footsteps got closer and closer to my cell. My heartbeat rose, while mentally I tried to stay strong and resolved. I was ready to face the end.

My cell door opened next. It was the criminal Naserian along with a couple of his assistants. He asked my name and my father's name and also about how I had ended up in this ward. His assistants were taking notes. Then he asked if I had any requests. I replied that it would be humane if I were allowed to take a shower and have a change of clothes. He gave me a funny look with a malicious smile, then left without a word. His demeanor made me both angry and worried, but I soon forgot about it. I thought the visit by Naserian was the final information gathering and review by the death commission before finishing up the killings. I was expecting any minute to be taken out and hanged. But nothing happened for another few days. I had been there for ten days already, so I concluded that we would be taken to Evin prison for the final decision.

Then one day, the cell doors started opening and closing again. I prepared myself to go. My cell door opened, and this time it was the evil Lashgari with his entourage. He asked his assistant who I was and some other information about me. He looked at the cell and me, then they all left. As I have said many times before, often their actions made no sense to us. It could have been just a ploy, a mind game.

Since arriving in this hellhole, I had been thinking a lot about my wife and daughter, about the fact that I had not seen them for four years and that I might never get a chance to see them again. But this also gave me the resolve to resist, to maneuver, and to use any morally acceptable tactic to survive. I had prepared to die, but as long as I was alive, I was hopeful that one day I would be able to see them again.

After ten days, my mind was busy with the following: Why didn't they finish us off in the first couple of days after they brought us here? Could this mean that the mass killing had stopped? Could it mean that we had to be transferred to Evin prison because the killings in Gohardasht had stopped? Another possibility, I thought, was that all the surviving prisoners except us had been transferred to Evin, and Gohardasht had returned to being a purely solitary prison, as it had been from 1981 to 1984. That would mean the authorities had decided to keep us in solitary for a long period.

This new round of mind struggle was destroying me, and I could not escape it because I was not convinced of any of my explanations. I would pace the cell for hours, to the point of exhaustion. I would be motionless for hours in a semiconscious state. I would then be suddenly startled out of that state by any noise.

13

I think it was after about fourteen days in death-row solitary when one morning after breakfast, as I was sitting on the floor in no mood for anything, I heard very loud and strange noises coming from the outside area. I jumped up, went to the window, looked out, and listened. It was like a religious procession, chanting, or like a ceremonial greeting of some sort. Then I heard "*sale ala* Mohammad, *yar-e imam khosh amad*" (a slogan commonly used after the Islamic Revolution to welcome Khomeini appointees and pupils in gatherings and ceremonies), which I interpreted to mean that a Khomeini pupil or representative might be visiting the prison. This was important, from any angle that I looked at it. Finding out bits of news in solitary, especially during a dangerous period like this, was priceless. The noise and chanting continued for some minutes and then subsided. It seemed that the procession had gone inside the building. I could see the southern tip of the building, but nothing more. Whatever was happening was in that part of the building. I analyzed what possible effect this visit—if indeed there was such a visit—could have on the current situation. I thought it could turn our situation either way: for the better or for the worse. But my gut feeling was that the lack of action taken against us during the last two weeks, combined with this new event, could indicate a shift to normalcy.

At noon that day, when the guards opened my cell door to deliver my lunch ration, I could sense a clear change in their behavior. They gave me good food, in a plate with a spoon, and a cup of tea with sugar cubes for the first time in two weeks. They were also smiling for the first time in more than two months. One of them even asked me if I wanted extra food. After I ate a few spoonfuls, I continued with my analysis, adding in these new factors.

Then suddenly my mood changed completely. I got very upset at myself for letting my guard down so quickly and so optimistically. Although in my heart I wanted things to change for the better, I had to be prepared for the worst and stay mentally strong. I tried to relax in a corner of the cell for a few minutes. I must have dozed off from mental exhaustion. I was dreaming that the prison radio was on and the afternoon news program was about to start. The radio had not been turned on in Gohardasht since the start of the lockdown.

When I woke up, I realized it was no dream; the radio was indeed on, and for the first time in two months the prison authorities had started broadcasting the news. I immediately thought if the radio was on in the terminal solitary ward, then it must be on for all the other prisoners as well. I was so excited that I literally jumped up and down in the cell. Not only did it mean that conditions in general might have started to change and normalize, but it further meant that the danger might have passed us by. In any case, the news program started. I will never forget the top news of that day. It was about the passing of Mohammad-Hossein Shahriar, a famous contemporary poet from Iranian Azarbaijan who had composed poetry in both Farsi and Azari. The rest of that day, I had a very saddened but relieved feeling.

Late in the afternoon, a guard ordered me to blindfold myself and come out. I felt weird—hopeful and worried at the same time. He put me in the middle of the hallway and went to get a few other prisoners. Finally, he brought all of us into a line and moved us toward the ward door. One of the prisoners, encouraged by the changes in the prison conditions and the behavior of the guards, asked where we were going. The guard replied very politely that we were not going too far. The fact that he even answered the question showed an important change as well.

We were led into the main corridor on the second floor and continued walking. The guard stopped the line and took a couple of people out and away. He returned after a few minutes and moved the line until he stopped again. He then separated me and someone else from the line and took us toward a ward door and delivered us to another guard. This new guard asked us where we had been before. We both replied that we had been in Ward 8 before solitary. I recognized from his voice that the other prisoner was Iraj. The guard asked where we had been at the start of the lockdown. We replied that we had both been in Ward 6. He then walked us through the *zir-e hasht* and into a room in the *far'i* ward, where he asked us to remove our blindfolds. He ordered us to look for our own bags and said he would return in a few minutes.

Iraj and I embraced, happy to see each other alive again. This was a solid indication that conditions had truly changed and that maybe we had survived for certain. We noticed that most of the items belonging to

Ward 6 prisoners had already been taken away, but there were still some left behind. We tried to locate our own bags first. Afterward, we looked around to see what else was left there. Some of it did not belong to Ward 6 and might have belonged to the Mojahedin prisoners who used to live in this *far'i* ward. In any case, most of what was left there belonged to prisoners who had most probably been hanged.

I located Mohammad-Reza Tababati's belongings with my own handwriting on them, but there was no sign of Farzin's bags. This meant that either Tababati was among the killed or he still was in solitary. We were also able to locate the belongings of some other prisoners from Ward 6, like Mohammad-Ali Pezhman, Ibrahim Najjaran, Hossein Haji-Mohsen, and Mehdi Hassani-pak.

The guard returned and led us back to the solitary ward. Each of us was taken back to our own cell. In front of my cell, I asked the guard if I could take some or all of my things inside the cell. He told me that I should take only necessary items inside and to leave the rest out in the hallway.

Although the ordeal was not over yet, there were many good signs indicating that we had indeed survived. That night, Naserian came and checked everyone against a list he had in his hand. He asked a few ordinary questions and took some notes. The next day after breakfast, a guard told me to blindfold myself once more and to come out with all my belongings. He put me in the middle of the ward, as before, and then brought someone else behind me. It was Iraj again. The guard led the two of us into the main corridor and then toward Ward 8. We got close to Ward 8, where shift guard Ne'mati was sitting behind a desk. He asked each of us a couple of questions, searched our bags, then called another guard and told him to take us inside Ward 8.

“Death does not concern us, because as long as we exist, death is not here. And when it does come, we no longer exist.”

Epicurus (341–270 BCE)

Chapter Eleven
SURVIVORS

1

September 1988

Once inside Ward 8, we removed our blindfolds. Prisoners surrounded us in disbelief. They were elated to see that we had survived. My comrades and close friends took me into a cell. They said they had lost hope a day or two after we had been taken out and did not return. I described what had happened to me during the past two weeks. It turned out that about half of the surviving leftist prisoners, including Rostam from among our comrades, had been moved upstairs to Ward 7. My comrades told me that conditions had gradually improved but that they had not had a family visit yet.

Apparently, the pressure for communal praying had persisted only for a week or so, then the authorities had declared that praying should continue individually. Only a few people had gone on praying afterward. If anyone were questioned about it, he would say that he prayed on his own time. The fact of the matter was that the forced-prayer policy had served its purpose as an ideological screening and a temporary pressure tool. We had had no choice, under the circumstances, but to accept it because of the tortures and life-threatening dangers, knowing very well that it would be short-lived. The regime used it as a means of imposing their will on us, and we agreed to it as a means of survival.

The various political groups did not care about power struggles and mind games in the ward anymore. The crisis had changed everyone and our relationships to each other at the personal and especially at the political level. This was indeed a new era in the inner politics of the opposition in prison.

After lunch the yard opened, and for the first time in more than two months I got to go to *havakhori* (recess) to get some fresh air and enjoy the sunshine. People were sitting in the sun or walking in the yard, but due to lingering fear and paranoia, no one was jogging or exercising. We had become very cautious in our way of living. We still could not accept that the killing and the danger were completely over. Full of anger and hate toward the authorities, we did not trust them in the slightest. Because the family visits had not been reestablished yet, we were worried that the authorities could still start another round of elimination. We truly believed that they had to have something else up their sleeves for the survivors.

My close friend, "Pirouz," from the Rah-e Kargar organization, was living in a cell with a prisoner from the Fadaiyan Majority group who had had some psychological issues for years in prison. Pirouz suggested, and others agreed, that I should move to that cell. Our living together in that cell did not last long, because in late September twenty to thirty prisoners were called out with all their belongings, and our cellmate was among them. The authorities had decided to gather all the *mellikesh* (serving without sentence) prisoners from both Wards 7 and 8 in one location, in a small ward across from Ward 8. What the regime was planning for them, none of us dared to speculate.

Besides Wards 7 and 8, there was now a *mellikesh* ward containing fifty to sixty people, and then there was Ward 5 with close to one hundred ten prisoners. Overall, about four hundred secular leftist prisoners were left alive in Gohardasht, approximately two-thirds of our complement before the hangings. Gohardasht had held eight hundred or more Mojahedin and other religious prisoners before the lockdown; no one had any clue about the number of their survivors yet. Assuming that there was a Mojahedin survivor ward somewhere, holding say two hundred prisoners, it meant that maybe five hundred to six hundred of them had perished.

2

It was early December when one morning the guards informed us that we should prepare for family visits. It was our first visit in almost six months. The reestablishment of visits was critical for the survivors. It was the only way we could figure out who had been executed, what the families had been told, and how the news was spreading outside. We could also let the outside world know what really had happened in prison during the last few months.

My older brother had come alone to this visit. While speaking about normal family issues through the interphone system, I tried to show him via sign language what had happened and I felt that he understood my meaning. He told me that he had recently returned from abroad and that my wife and daughter were well and safe. When they announced that the visit time was over, I could see despair and helplessness on his face. That is one of the saddest good-byes I have ever said to a family member in my life. We both felt that it might be the last time we would ever see each other.

On this visiting day, all the families, after being informed through their contacts with each other that there was going to be visiting, had gathered in front of the main gate of the prison. Some of them were told right there that the person they had come to see was not in this prison anymore and that they should contact their local Islamic Revolution Committee office to find out where he had been transferred. This was a smart ploy by the authorities to delay as much as possible the spread of the news of the executions and to scatter the worried, angry families all over the city and country. It was designed to dilute the tragedy as much as possible by only gradually releasing the news to the bereaved families, while denying it publicly. Families who were told that their family member was not in Gohardasht prison correctly took it to mean that their loved one had been executed. But the authorities never admitted in front of the prison that there had been any executions.

During the lockdown, families had come on a regular basis to put pressure on the authorities to allow them to visit and had been told that prison visits were canceled until further notice. Some family members apparently had observed unusual signs and movements around Evin and Gohardasht prisons during the lockdown. Their suspicions had been aroused by the way refrigerated and other trucks frequently entered the prisons empty and left with cargo (particularly from Gohardasht); they had followed these trucks to an area in southeastern Tehran called Khavaran. They had not been able to get inside Khavaran at night, when the trucks normally brought their cargos, to learn what they were carrying, but they were pretty certain that it had to be illegal and criminal.

Afterward, when they searched in Khavaran they discovered that dirt had recently been disturbed in some areas, and suddenly they turned up a hand and a head from a body recently buried in a mass grave. Without being caught by the security guards, they succeeded in taking some photos and left knowing for certain that there were mass graves in Khavaran. This indicated to the families that the regime must be killing prisoners in such large numbers that they had to bury them in mass graves. As soon as the security services were informed of the possibility of people digging in Khavaran, the region was secured by the regime and guards were posted to prevent access.

In our next visit, which was about mid to late December, we found out that the authorities had started informing families about the executions through local Islamic Revolution Committee offices. They took about a month or two to gradually release the information to those families. In each case, the family was given a bag containing the prisoner's belongings (sometimes, the bag did not even belong to the right prisoner) and was told that the prisoner had been killed during a riot in prison or had been executed for taking part in a riot. Families were ordered not to hold any public ceremonies for their loved ones and were threatened that they would face the same fate if they did or said anything to anyone to indicate what had happened.

Within a couple of visits, we found out that the extent of executions had indeed been massive, as we had thought. And for the first time, we got reliable news through our families indicating that most male and some female prisoners in Evin had also been eliminated. The information revealed that only a limited number of secular leftist men, most of the leftist women, and some of the Mojahedin prisoners were still alive in Evin. We also found out from the families that the surviving *mellikesh* (serving without sentence) prisoners had been transferred to Evin and that they had recently been released after agreeing to sign the self-defamation forms. I later found out that Mansoor Davaran, my friend from Ward 1 of Unit 3 in Ghezelhessar, never made it out of prison. He had left us during the summer of 1986, at the end of his sentence, supposedly to be released; he had wanted to go see my mother in Tabriz. Apparently he had become a *mellikesh* prisoner and was one of the victims of the mass killing of the summer of 1988 in Gohardasht.

3

The events of the criminal mass killing by the regime took over our lives as survivors. Two different views and tendencies shaped up among us. There were those caught up in the web of a tremendous guilt for what had happened, and psychologically they could not deal with the fact that they had survived the ordeal while others had perished. And then there were others, who, whether through tactical retreat and maneuvering or just by pure luck, had survived, and they felt fine with that. We were all under enormous pressure and felt deep sorrow for the loss of our comrades and friends. But the guilt-ridden survivors suffered from a constant internal conflict, which in some cases resulted in psychological problems for them and difficulty for others. Though a minority, this group was a serious difficulty for all of us after the so-called normalization of prison conditions. None of us was in a condition to deal with these issues at this juncture.

Morad was very worried about Mohebbi-pour's health. We talked about it and even considered contacting the authorities to get medical help for him. One day during lunchtime, Mohebbi-pour suffered what looked like a heart attack and was rushed to the prison clinic. They kept him there because he was not feeling well. But he never returned to the ward. In the next family visit, Morad found out from his family that Ali Mohebbi-pour had passed away the same day he had had a heart attack. Although thousands had been martyred just a couple of months earlier during the massacre, for us the death of Mohebbi-pour in this way and at this time was a tragedy. He had survived the murderous ordeal with his weak heart and his poor health, but then his heart stopped pumping afterward.

This period in prison corresponded with the times of crisis and transformation in the Soviet Bloc. It was more than the leftist prisoners had bargained for. Soviet socialism, in particular, and in general the entire left was in turmoil. This was a historical, existential, and ideological crisis for all of us as leftists, but it was particularly so for those whose ideology and politics depended upon the moral, political, and even financial support of the Soviet Bloc. Dealing with the ideological and political crises of the left was difficult for those not in prison, let alone us. Some in our ward got to a point where they openly declared that the era for leftist politics was over. There was a sense of pessimism and passivity among some prisoners as far as any form of struggle was concerned. Most prisoners, though, remained loyal to their ideals of freedom, justice, equality, and humanity.

4

Then everything changed for the worse. In mid-January, without warning, we were ordered to pack and be ready for transfer. Suddenly, the authorities started moving Wards 7 and 8 at the same time, under a climate of absolute terror identical to what we had just experienced during the summer. While being terrorized by the guards, we were led to a small ward on the ground level. We were ordered to leave our belongings in the hallway, then we were stuffed, in groups of ten to twelve, into solitary cells. The guards locked the cell doors and left us there. Unable to do anything else, we stood for hours in those cells. Even if you were not a pessimist, you were still horrified to imagine what might come next.

After a few hours, the guards opened the cell doors, starting at one end of the ward. They let prisoners out, ordered them to pick up their belongings, and led them blindfolded between two lines of guards wielding clubs, sticks, and *kubl* (flogging cable). The two lines—there must have been hundreds of guards—formed a tunnel that continued all the way through the stairways up to the entrance of a ward on the third floor. We all passed through the tunnel while guards shouted and terrorized us. But this time they did not strike us.

When we entered the ward upstairs, they ordered us to remove our blindfolds. It was the old Ward 1. We put our stuff down and waited to see what would happen next. After all the prisoners from both Wards 7 and 8 were inside, the guards closed the door and left without saying a word. We were surprised and relieved. The salon at the end of the ward was also open to us, and a TV set was there as well.

Pessimists thought this was the ward from where we would be taken to a new court. Others thought that they were going to close this prison down and therefore we would soon be transferred to Evin prison. This latter idea actually made more sense to me than anything else at the time. Not many political prisoners had survived in Evin and so there was plenty of space for us there, whether they were planning to keep us or to kill us. This way the regime could turn Gohardasht into a nonpolitical prison, which was very much needed with the gradual increase of crime in the country.

In this ward, we noticed a further shift in the behavior of the guards and how nice they had suddenly become toward us. It felt very strange and seemed suspicious. We were again asked to fill out a form for personal information because we were all going to have visits on a new day and the authorities needed to contact our families.

It was late January when one day the guards informed us that we were going to have our family visits the following day. We were surprised at how quickly they had contacted all our families to arrange the visits on a new date. They even gave us hot water that day to prepare for our visits. The following morning, we put on our clean clothing and waited for the lists to be called for visiting. But nothing happened until almost noon, which was very unusual. They even gave us our lunch.

At about one thirty, the guards told all of us to get ready to go for the visit. Visits had never happened this way in prison—never did all prisoners go at once, especially when some of the prisoners had not had a visit in years. We grew very suspicious and alarmed, and, again, rumors started that this was no visit and that we were being taken for another questioning or maybe even to be killed in a staged massacre. A few people even suggested that the authorities were going to take us somewhere and shoot us all, claiming later that we had rioted or were trying to escape. The next ten to fifteen minutes passed like a lifetime as we waited full of doubt, anxiety, fear, or even terror. Finally, the door opened and many guards entered the ward, ordering us out.

They led us all the way to the northern end of the prison until we reached Ward 7. Since the visiting salon was halfway between Wards 1 and 7, and we had passed it a while back, we all prepared ourselves for the worst, especially when we were led down to the ground level near the amphitheater, a route that many prisoners had taken during the summer, and from which they had never returned. When we got to the ground floor, we were all gathered in the vicinity of the amphitheater. We waited there for a few minutes until Naserian, Lashgari, and their entourage appeared. Naserian gave a short speech, which absolutely stunned us: "We have arranged for all of you to have a collective in-person visit with your families in the amphitheater. Even those who do not have visitors will take part in this collective family visit. We request that you follow the security and administrative directives during this program."

We were shocked and amazed. The very people who had participated in the brutal elimination of hundreds of innocent prisoners in this amphitheater a few months ago now had the audacity to organize a collective in-person family visit for the survivors in the exact same location. At first it seemed odd that they would do this, but upon further examination you could see that it was an ingenious idea. They were really killing two birds with one stone. They were trying to show that the amphitheater was a nice, decorated gathering place where family visits and cultural programs were organized and to help them deny the killings by deluding the public into thinking that this location could not have been filled with hanging scaffolds only months earlier, and at the same time they were trying to create a rift among the families, between those who had lost prisoners in the mass killing of last summer and those whose family members had survived.

The door finally opened and we were ordered to remove our blindfolds and enter. The amphitheater was decorated with bouquets of flowers, and its floor was covered with colorful rugs and blankets. We were each asked to sit on a blanket to wait for our families. The authorities explained some rules before bringing the families in from another door. It was an unbelievable scene. Emotions were running high. Families were hugging anyone in their path to get to their own prisoner. There was sadness, happiness, crying, laughter, and anxiety, all in one gathering. It took about half an hour for everyone to find their prisoners and to settle down. Those prisoners who did not have visitors sat down with another prisoner and his family.

My brother "Mateen," who had never come to visit me before, had come to this visit along with my sister "Akhtar" and her youngest son, "Nima." We hugged, kissed, cried, and laughed together. I immediately started telling them what had happened in prison during the summer. I thought I should tell them whatever I knew about the massacre, in case this was my last chance to see and talk to someone from the outside world. My brother said they had found out a bit about the events, but no one knew the magnitude of it and how extensive it had been. Then he made a surprising declaration. He said he believed there was a good chance that all the surviving prisoners could be released soon. Disagreeing with him, I told him that supposition did not make any sense. He tried to explain why he thought it might really happen, but I was not paying much attention anymore.

The authorities delivered a couple of short talks. The goal basically was to influence our families. At the end, we said good-bye, and the families were asked to stay where they were, while we were ordered to leave the amphitheater the way we had entered. We were asked to put our blindfolds back on once we were out of the amphitheater, then we were lined up and taken back to our ward.

This event once again showed us that we were unable to understand the strange character of this brutal regime. When, very logically in our opinion, we thought that they were going to open up and to improve prison conditions after their acceptance of UN Resolution 598 ending the war with Iraq, they locked down the prisons and killed thousands of innocent people. When we felt they were going to kill us, they gave us a collective in-person family visit. It seems that being deliberately unpredictable enabled the regime to carry out its intentions while misleading its citizens. Whenever a window of opportunity opened up for them, they used it to the best of their ability to achieve a surprise goal.

In mid-February 1989, we were quietly sitting in the salon watching the evening news on TV. The first news of the night always was about or related to Khomeini. That particular evening, it started by saying that Khomeini had issued a general amnesty for all political prisoners in celebration and commemoration of the tenth anniversary of the Islamic Revolution of 1979.

We did not get excited. Most of us thought that as usual the amnesty would only apply to Band-e Jahad (Crusaders' Ward) and the *tavvab* prisoners in general. But some prisoners thought differently. They believed that this time around it might be different because of the new circumstances. The regime had killed half of the prisoners all over Iran, the war was over, and therefore they might release a large portion of the survivors in an attempt to cancel out the negative effect of the news spreading around the world regarding the mass killings. Although that sounded far-fetched, this perspective made sense. I also remembered my brother's analysis during the last visit, when from nowhere he predicted that the regime might release us and at the same time orchestrate a propaganda campaign to deny the killings.

A few days later, the guards told us to get ready to move out. We packed and got ready all day long. Early next morning Naserian, Lashgari, and many guards led all of us out of the ward toward the ground floor. We passed through the same spots that most of us had seen on those bloody summer days. It was like passing through a killing zone. We were led through the corridor underneath the kitchen building. That corridor ended at the main entrance gate for prison cargo. Outside, in the compound grounds, buses were waiting for us.

We felt at this point that Evin had to be our next destination, and we had mixed feelings about that. We were happy to be leaving the prison in which very recently our comrades and friends had been hanged and we ourselves had been tortured and terrorized, but we were sad and worried about the unknown fate that awaited us in Evin prison.

Part Five

NOT MANY SURVIVED HERE

CHAPTER TWELVE

KILL, RELEASE, AND DENY

1

February 1989

In Evin, we were taken to the so-called old wards. Prisoners of Gohardasht Ward 5 had been transferred ahead of us, also to one of these wards. Next to us, there were a few prisoners in another ward, whom we first saw when they came out in the yard. Among them was Kamran, my depressed friend from Ward 3 in Gohardasht. A couple of days later, these few secular leftist prisoners were brought into our ward.

They believed that nearly everyone else from the Mojahedin and the secular leftists had been killed; only some female and male prisoners who were in solitary or in Band-e Jahad (Crusaders' Ward) had survived; there were also some special-status prisoners, such as a few of the Tudeh Party or other organizational cadres and leaders, who were still alive but kept separately. This, though unbelievable, was in agreement with the news we had previously received from our families.

Kamran's mental health had deteriorated further since he had been transferred from Gohardasht to Evin more than a year ago. Whether his mental condition or another factor had helped him survive was not clear. In Evin, the buildings holding the prisoners were separate and scattered. Therefore, when the killings started in one ward, the other wards could not easily find out about it, particularly in a complete lockdown situation. The prisoners in Evin could not get the advance information that we had been able to obtain in Gohardasht before facing the initial questionings and the "death commission." In addition, because of the elevated levels of organized resistance, combativeness, and militancy among the Evin prisoners, and because they were mostly high-ranking or had longer sentences than us, they were massacred brutally. Apparently, the "death commission" started the inquisition sessions in the central office and prisoners were hanged in an open space in the parking lot of that building. Then the process was moved to a covered space in the basement of Ward 209.

The exact number of prisoners in Evin before the killings was not clear, but certainly there were a few wards for male prisoners, a few wards for the women, and many prisoners who were kept in solitary. There were always some special-case prisoners who were kept in separate wards, rooms, and cells. Then there were Band-e Jahad and other *tavvab* wards as well. Therefore there must have been about two thousand prisoners in Evin, from which only a few hundred had survived. The survivors mainly included the original Band-e Jahad and other *tavvab* ward prisoners; some Mojahedin, including men and women; and a few secular leftist men, plus most of the secular leftist women. The majority of the secular leftist men and the majority of the male and female Mojahedin prisoners had been hanged.

2

We were about two hundred prisoners jammed in an L-shaped ward, which had six or seven large rooms. Life stayed transitional, but we still organized ourselves in a limited way, both in the rooms and throughout the ward, to make our existence easier. There was a TV set in each room here.

Two events from those days are worth mentioning. First, Saied Shahsavandi, a Mojahedin leader, had been captured along with many other fighters during their early summer military campaign in the west of the country. He led a roundtable in a televised "exposé" of the leadership and policies of the Mojahedin organization. They discussed the organization's dependency on Saddam Hussein and the Iraqi regime and how the organization had turned into a cult-type group in their bases in Iraq. They then claimed that they had been forced to participate in the military campaign against their will, while being shot at from behind if they refused. They also talked about the absolute control exerted over them through torture, imprisonment, taking their family members hostage by the leadership of the organization, and other such methods. Shahsavandi claimed to have genuinely repented and defended his decisions and actions after his arrest.

He also disclosed that the leadership of the organization, especially Massoud and Maryam, had prepared their forces for the military campaign by promising them that they would be welcomed by people in every village and town on their way to Tehran. He said that, on the contrary, some of them had been arrested and delivered to the authorities by villagers and townspeople in the border areas.

The other notable event of those days was a fatwa issued by Khomeini against Salman Rushdie, the author of *The Satanic Verses*. We did not know much about Salman Rushdie or his book, but when we heard the news we felt terribly sad for the writer.

A day later, we were all taken to the Ministry of Intelligence building and in a tense atmosphere were questioned again one by one. The question asked this day was quite different: "Would you be willing to sign a self-defamation letter if we were to release you from prison?" After what we had been through and under the prevailing circumstances in prison, most of us had no problem accepting that condition—a condition that had been offered frequently to many of these same prisoners prior to the mass killings and had been rejected with certainty each time. What had seemed unacceptable to us previously seemed fine now and, in some people's opinion, even necessary at this time to escape more danger. The unspoken agreement among the survivors seemed to be that we should take advantage of this opportunity.

After we accepted the release condition verbally, it was announced that we were all going to be released as a result of the general amnesty issued by Khomeini for the celebration of the tenth anniversary of the Islamic Revolution. A list was circulated to collect family contact information again. Later, we were taken, one by one, to place a phone call to our family to ask them to post real-estate and personal collateral for our release.

It was a very strange time for us. It was like the end of a very bad dream, but this was no dream. The regime had killed thousands during the summer of 1988 and had put all of us through hell, and now in the following winter they were about to release the survivors. We were starting to feel and taste the fact that release might be a real possibility, but still we did not fully understand how and why the regime was doing what they were about to do. We were as confused now as we were when they started the mass killings.

It was two days before the scheduled date when they informed us that our release would take place collectively during a ceremony in the city. We protested that we had not agreed to this part of the deal, and for a while there was a division among us over this issue. The authorities insisted that we were not expected to do anything but just be present in the crowd of released prisoners. After a bit of discussion among us, we finally agreed. We thought of it just as a short-lived propaganda scheme by the regime, aimed mostly at the international audience, while nationally it meant nothing, given the political and social situation in the country.

The day of release, early in the morning, we were given the necessary explanations and directions. We were going to be taken to a location in front of the United Nations offices in Tehran, where there would be a short ceremony, then we were going to be taken in front of the Majles (Parliament) for another ceremony, after which we were going to be released. But the authorities revealed here that, because all the official release work had not been completed yet, we had to return to prison after three days to finish up the requirements before going home for good. This part of the bargain caused us more worry than the release conditions. How could we trust that they would really release us for good after we returned to prison? But we were now stuck. We had already committed to the plan and had involved our families by raising their hopes. We thought we had no way to change our minds.

An hour later, the authorities read a long list of names of those who were to leave the ward. We were not supposed to take anything with us. We were to leave our belongings for the final release. We were led outside of the building into the open area in the Evin compound grounds. For the first time, we were without blindfolds in Evin. While we were standing there, Noor-al-Din Kianoori, the secretary general of the Tudeh Party, and a few other prisoners were brought from another ward to join us. He said that they were being kept as a special group of prisoners in a small ward. Different groups of prisoners were being brought out from other wards as well. Overall, many hundreds of prisoners were loaded into maybe fifteen to twenty buses. Finally, the buses were allowed to leave Evin prison. The main gate opened, and the buses rolled out.

3

When our bus exited, I saw that many people were waiting outside. A few of my family members were part of the crowd. We greeted each other through the windows while the buses were moving very slowly and they could jog alongside. When the buses started to pick up speed, the families returned to their cars to follow us. The buses stopped in front of the UN building, where a short ceremony was planned. While we were walking in line, many family members joined us as well. After that short ceremony, we were loaded in the buses again and driven to the final destination. When we got there, we were ordered to sit on the ground during the ceremony in front of the Majles. First, one of the government authorities gave a short speech and then a few prisoners such as Kianoori, Babak Zahrai, the secretary general of the Socialist Workers Party, and Shahsavandi made short statements. At the end, we were told that we could go home.

We joined our families, who were waiting there for us, and we left as soon as we could. My family had come with a few cars. I was taken to one of them. Few words were exchanged in the car, but everyone was relieved and happy. My mother and the rest of the family were waiting at my brother's small, rented two-bedroom condo, where he lived with his wife and his daughter "Mina."

There was a great deal of crying when we got there, especially from my mother, who still could not believe that I had really survived the mass killings. There were more than thirty people from my family there in that little apartment. Though I looked, sounded, and behaved like a zombie for the first few hours, and even through the first twenty-four hours, we still had a good time and enjoyed each other's company after the long years of my imprisonment. By family tradition, I was being fed all kinds of food and goodies nonstop. It was as if my mother wanted to feed me enough to restore me to my normal condition in a matter of one day.

I called and talked to my wife and daughter in West Germany for the first time in almost five years. It was a very emotional moment for all three of us. They were happy and excited that I had survived the mass killings and finally been released, but we were still sad to be separated as a family. I also got phone calls from family members and friends in Europe and the United States.

4

After the first few hours in freedom, I felt overwhelmed by the commotion and constant attention and affection surrounding me. That first night, after most of the guests had left, I felt calm for the first time since we had gotten home. I needed to be in a room by myself for a while. How strange it must have looked to my family that after release from prison I wanted to be alone. The next morning, my brother insisted on staying home to keep me company, but I convinced him to go to work. During the morning hours, I was home with my mother, my sister and her family, my sister-in-law, and the little Mina. Two-year-old Mina was sweet and lovely. Her presence helped me with the emotional difficulties of adjusting to life in freedom. My wife and I had agreed to call and talk every day or every other day until we had figured out what to do about our situation.

Those three days passed fairly quickly. I knew everyone was worried about my return to prison, but they had to pretend that everything was going to be all right. My mother and I were the only ones who openly showed signs of anxiety. My family members abroad were all worried to death as well, knowing that I had to go back inside Evin again.

My family members dropped me off at Evin in the morning. The authorities received the prisoners one by one and transferred us in groups to our wards. A few prisoners who had not been released with us were still there, waiting anxiously. Within an hour or so we were all back in the ward, so happy to see each other again. The authorities later started calling people out in groups with all their belongings. We said our final good-byes to the ones called and walked with them to the ward door. We really did not know if we would see each other ever again.

I was called in a group late in the afternoon. We were transferred to the release office. The head of the office basically said that according to the amnesty issued by Khomeini we were being freed, but we should be assured that if any of us were caught fleeing the country, involved in "counterrevolutionary" activities, or doing anything against the Islamic regime, we would be brought back to Evin prison and would be hanged right here in the compound grounds. Then we were each given a form, which contained a written condemnation of all opposition and a promise of "noninvolvement" in activities against the regime. Our signing of this form was the last condition of our release. Finally, we had to sign a form declaring that we were going to appear in the designated Islamic Revolution Committee office on the indicated date, and afterward on the dates and intervals determined by that office. After all that, we were given a small slip that indicated our release to the guards by the main exit gate.

After I got the slip, I pulled my stuff to the gate and exited Evin prison. As promised, my family was all there waiting for me in the cold and dark by the side of a fire that had been set up by the waiting families. We all got in the cars and drove home.

Although "freedom" for a political prisoner in the Islamic Republic had a relatively narrow and limited meaning, at least this time when I got out I did not have the anxiety I had felt three days ago. This really was the end of an era in my life and the start of the next.

Part Six

FREEDOM

Chapter Thirteen

NEW OBSTACLES, NEW HORIZONS

1

March 1989

I was under house arrest, ordered not to leave the city limits of Tehran. I was supposed to report to the Islamic Revolution Committee office across from the University of Tehran campus a week after my final release.

My mother and sister, who had come from Tabriz, about four hundred miles away from Tehran, went back after a few days. I spent part of my daily time with little Mina in my brother's home. Afternoons, I normally went out and walked the streets of Tehran. Every other day, I would go to the public phone company office to place a call to West Germany to talk to my wife and daughter. We were stuck in a very difficult situation. All the time I had been in prison and they had been abroad, we had missed each other badly but could justify the separation and the distance. Now, every time we talked, we discussed finding a solution to overcome the geographical distance and barriers separating us as a family.

My wife, Ketty, and I were both in agreement that it was not an option for her and Bahar to return to Iran. I was prohibited from leaving even Tehran, let alone the country. Ketty was very positive and always encouraged me to be patient because, she thought, something would work out soon. Bahar had done some drawings and had made some gifts for me, which I cherished, and it encouraged me to start drawing with Mina in the house. I sent a few of those drawings to my daughter in my turn.

At my first visit to the Islamic Revolution Committee office, they blindfolded me, took me to a room, and left me there to wait. My emotions were similar to those I had had after my arrest. Finally, an interrogator came in and started by asking me some general political and personal questions. He also gave me a standard form to fill out. At the end, he asked me if I had thought about working again and what I had done about it. I told him that I had done nothing about it yet but that I was going to look for work soon. He then jokingly said, "You really do not need to look for a job. With your education and degree, you can walk into any ministry or governmental office in this country and they would beg you to work for them." I understood his meaning. He was basically telling me that he wanted to see me working next time around. I had to find a job, so as not to raise any suspicions. I had been ordered back in a week and therefore I did not have much time.

This was life for a political prisoner released into society in the Islamic regime: a weekly interrogation session, living under constant surveillance, and not being able to move or travel freely. It was like being in a larger prison, as many of us used to joke when we were in prison and as some of the guards and authorities had said.

The fastest way for me to get a job, my brother and I thought, would be to contact "Taghi," my old friend. He had been in the Majles (Parliament) when I got arrested. Now he was in the Ministry of Agriculture.

The following day I got dressed and went to see him in the high-rise building where the ministry offices were located. He took me into his office and we talked for an hour about the past, about our families, and about what he was doing. Then I told him I had a favor to ask him and

I would understand perfectly if he was not able to help. I explained to him about the requirement of the weekly visit to the Islamic Revolution Committee station and about their expectations of my finding a job quickly. I asked if he would be able to help me find something fast. Taghi, who was a very high-ranking official in the ministry, immediately picked up the phone and placed a couple of calls. He made an appointment for me for that afternoon.

I started work the following day. Now I kept busy during the day and had a good source of income as well. Best of all, when I went to the Islamic Revolution Committee office next time and told them where I was working and what I was doing, their treatment of me changed completely. After that, I was told to report every other week, and a few months later I was asked to go only once a month.

2

One of the difficulties I had during the first few weeks after my release was my inability to go to Tabriz to visit my mother. After a few weeks, we figured out that the security services did not control flights as tightly as they did travel by car, bus, or train. This showed another unique feature of the Islamic Republic of Iran, at least at that time. Although it had established one of the most effective and brutal security and judiciary systems in the world, the whole regime was still run like a chaotic complex of organizations. There were many loopholes in the system; you needed to be smart to be able to find the hole that would help you, but it was there.

We bought two tickets, and my brother and I flew to Tabriz together. It was the Iranian New Year, Nowruz, and I wanted to be with my mother for the celebrations and wanted to see my family and friends in Tabriz. I had planned the trip so that it would be after my visit to the Islamic Revolution Committee office. I had to go every other week at this time, so we had at least ten days to stay in Tabriz. I also told my work that I was going to take a few more days off besides the official New Year holidays. Those ten days I stayed in Tabriz felt great because it was a happy period and visitors came from all over to see my mother and me.

After I returned, I prepared myself for the worst in my visit to the Islamic Revolution Committee office, but nothing bad happened. After that I would routinely fly to Tabriz once a month for a few days to see my mother. Life became "normal" for me in freedom, except that I was having a hard time adjusting to being separated from my wife and daughter. I worked during the days and I spent the evenings with family and friends, taking turns in going to different households.

I wanted to find a way to join my family abroad but had no idea how I might achieve this safely. I decided first to exhaust the legal means. I was hoping that I would find a loophole in the system to exploit for my travel abroad. Through a friend, I was able to get a copy of a page from the government's list of those banned from traveling abroad. My name was in the middle of the page, and across from my name was written: "Until Further Notice." We both interpreted this to mean that the authorities were not intending to allow me to exit the country legally anytime soon. It was after seeing this that for the first time I entertained the idea of exiting the country illegally.

3

This was in the middle of the summer of 1989. I knew I would be in danger of losing my life if I was caught leaving the country. I also struggled a lot with the danger that my flight could pose to my family in Iran.

But after consulting with my wife and with no other possibilities in sight, I finally decided to go for it.

In 1989, there were not as many people risking their lives to exit Iran illegally as in previous years. Now that the war had ended, the government had more manpower to better control its borders. Based on information I had gathered, I knew I could not rely on regular human traffickers. I had to find a safe way to escape. It took me about a month and some risky contacts to conclude that it had to be done through a reliable team from outside of Iran, who could not have been contaminated or infiltrated by Iranian government security forces. I had to turn to friends and family members abroad to arrange this on my behalf. Since I had no travel documents, those taking me out of Iran had to keep me safe until my friends and family abroad would be able to arrange for my safe stay and travel.

Finally, one day my friends from Europe informed me with "code-talk" that I should travel to Tabriz to meet a guest, supposedly a merchant who needed help in purchasing some rugs. A week later, I went to Tabriz. On a Friday, the doorbell rang and two strangers were behind the door. After we exchanged contact codes, I let them into the house. I found out that one of them, "Sharif," was a Kurd from Turkey. His partner and childhood friend, "Ildrim," was an Iranian Azari from the town of Maku, close to the border region of the northwestern corner of Iran.

Sharif explained that they were professional commodity smugglers between Turkey and Iran but had never done human trafficking. He added that he had agreed to take me because of a favor he owed my friends. He assured me that he and Ildrim were clean, they were not human traffickers, and they had never been arrested. He said they knew I had been a political prisoner and it was very risky and dangerous for them and me, but he added that they were ready for it if I was.

I asked them about their relationship, their work style, their families, what they thought about political prisoners, what they thought about the Iranian regime, and how they were planning to take me out of Iran. Sharif explained that their families had lived on opposite sides of the Iran-Turkey border in the mountains of Maku for decades. He said he and Ildrim had grown up together and their two families were basically like relatives. Then he explained that I would have to get to Maku on my own, where I would meet with Ildrim, who would take me to the border area on the Iranian side. There, Sharif said, he would take control of me and would take me into Turkey and would keep me in the border town where he lived with his family. He said I could stay with them until it was possible for me to move safely inside Turkey with the help of my own contacts. In the end, he assured me that I had nothing to worry about and they would take me safely to Turkey.

This was the best possible chance I would have to get out of the country, I thought. Sharif did not want to return to Iran anymore because he did not want to arouse any suspicion. He said Ildrim would come back to Tabriz only once more, to set up our meeting in Maku. He added that the crossing should be within the next few weeks, before it got colder and started snowing in the mountains of Maku. Before their departure, for our safety, I emphasized the importance of the secrecy of this relationship and what we were engaged in, which they completely understood and agreed with. We decided that we would tell everyone else that we were engaged in the rug business together.

The last week of September passed, then one day I was informed that Ildrim was arriving on October 2 to buy some rugs. I returned to Tabriz; Ildrim came to my mother's home and we talked in private. He said they had chosen October 17, a Friday, for the operation. That was good timing for me, because my Islamic Revolution Committee office visit date was on October 14; I could return to Tabriz on the fifteenth and be ready to leave on the seventeenth.

Ildrim gave me a meeting time of 2:00 PM on that Friday at a historic tourist attraction called Kakh-e Sardar (Sardar's Palace or Baghcheh Jug Palace) just outside of Maku. Sardar's Palace dates back to the end of the Qajar dynasty (1794–1924) and was built by a Qajar commander. Ildrim said he would check to make sure that I was not being followed and then he would make contact with me if it were safe. He emphasized that I had to make sure to get safely to the meeting location on my own. I was also supposed to carry a rolled-up magazine in my right hand, as a safety sign. If there was any problem, I was going to carry the magazine but not rolled-up and not in my right hand. He was going to check the sign before making the contact. He also emphasized that I should not bring any documents along. Finally, he added that it was going to be pretty cold in that area and I should wear proper clothing and shoes, and I also should be prepared to run and hike up and down the mountains for a few hours.

We also had to invent a reason for our relationship, in case we were arrested during the meeting or afterward. I suggested that I would become a rug merchant who had shops in the Tabriz bazaar and in Europe. I also suggested that the reason for our get-together could be that he was going to take me to see his father, whom I knew from previous rug business deals. We agreed that I would be going to his father's village to buy local rugs. He told me what his father's name was, and I told him the name that I was going to use as a businessman. We agreed on all the necessary information and then he said good-bye and left.

It was October 2 and I had fifteen days before the meet date in Maku. I stayed in Tabriz for a few more days and then returned to Tehran.

4

I had to make final preparations for my departure. I did not want to involve my family in Tehran, and therefore I thought I would say goodbye to them as though I were going to Tabriz for a regular visit; in Tabriz I would ask a friend to drive me with his family to Maku for an outing on that Friday. Maku not only is located in a beautiful mountainous region but also has many historical attractions.

The date for my appointment with the Islamic Revolution Committee office had arrived. I went there in the morning, as I had always done. The agent asked me a few routine questions, then he asked if I socialized with anyone. I replied that I socialized only with my family members. He asked if I had done any traveling. I replied without any hesitation that I could not do any traveling because I was not permitted to leave the city limits. But I got very worried when he asked that question. However, he asked nothing more, just made some small talk.

I left the station with much suspicion. Had they found out about my travels to Tabriz? If they had, then I was vulnerable and the plan was at risk. Was this line of questioning coincidental? I spent the next couple of days in Tehran in complete anxiety and stress. Wednesday night, all my siblings were supposed to gather for a dinner party at my brother's house. I told them that I had to go to Tabriz for a week or so. I thought that would give me enough time to take care of my business without involving any of them.

On Thursday, I flew to Tabriz and arrived at my mother's home. With the help of a friend, I exchanged money to get one thousand US dollars. Then I told him that I would like us to go on an outing to Maku on Friday. I also explained to him that for security reasons I would have to pretend to be a rug merchant on that trip, which he understood because of my situation. He said he would explain it to his family as well, since they were coming with us too. We went over everything and decided on believable reasons for our Friday drive to Maku.

I said good-bye to my mother and told her that I was going to spend the night in my friend's home. We got ready to leave around eight in the morning. I had allowed my beard to grow for a few days so that I would look like a religious *bazaari* (a bazaar shopkeeper or merchant). I put on a suit with enough clothing underneath to protect myself from the cold in the mountains. I hid the dollar bills in a safe place in my friend's car without his knowledge. I was carrying only a set of worry beads and a silk handkerchief. My friend's car was a dark blue 1962 Mercedes-Benz. I was sitting in the front passenger seat, my friend's wife and their two kids in the back seat. We had our lunch and picnic gear in the trunk of the car. It was about three hours' drive from Tabriz to Maku. Our plan was to get to Maku by lunchtime and have a picnic lunch outside the town before going sightseeing.

The road was the main transit route connecting Iran to Turkey and to Europe, and so it was one of the major escape routes in the country. The Revolutionary Guards had many stations and roadblocks all along it. The main roadblock station was located at an intersection where another road turned off toward the city of Khoy. The majority of the people who escaped from this part of the country passed through this intersection on their way either to Khoy or to Maku. From these towns, they would be taken to the border area and then into Turkey or Iraq. The border police officially controlled the border regions, but the Revolutionary Guards were all over them as well. The highway police controlled and checked cars and trucks until they got to the Khoy intersection, where the security services had their roadblock and searched cars and questioned people. This was the location where anybody who seemed suspicious would be arrested.

We drove for about two hours and passed a few highway police stations, until we reached the Khoy intersection. The advantage we had was that we were local and spoke the native language of the people from Azarbaijan. It was tough for a Farsi-speaking Iranian to pass through this checkpoint easily because the language discrepancy automatically aroused the suspicion of the authorities.

At the checkpoint, my friend stopped the car and waited. The armed guard came from the driver's side, looked inside the car, and examined it from the outside as well. Then he came to the window and said hello to us. We looked like a religious family. My friend's wife was wearing a black *chador* (shapeless cloak) and had two children with her in the back seat, and my friend and I looked like two religious men. The guard asked my friend only a few trivial questions. Then he asked where we were going and what our aim was in traveling in that direction. We said we were just on a day outing to Maku. He asked my friend about his job. He then asked me what I did and who I was. I said I was "Hedayat" and I was in the rug business. I think not knowing the real purpose of our trip helped my friend and his family to behave very naturally.

The guard asked my friend to open the trunk for inspection. It was basically empty except for our picnic gear. The guard checked it out and then closed it. He returned and took another look at us inside the car, a psychological profiling, to see if we had become more nervous. Then he ordered us to move on. We had cleared a major hurdle. We drove a bit farther, until we neared Maku.

I asked my friend to drive to Sardar's Palace to check it out. There was a very nice green area close to the compound and we set up our picnic there. It was a beautiful sunny day. Around half past one, I talked privately with my friend and explained to him that I was supposed to meet another friend in the palace at 2:00 PM. I explained to him that if I did not return in one hour, it would mean that I was staying with the other friend for a few days, and therefore he and his family should continue sightseeing on their own and later should return without me. I thanked him and we said good-bye.

Then I walked toward the palace compound. I waited outside and checked to make sure everything was safe. Then I rolled up my magazine in my right hand and entered Sardar's Palace like a typical tourist. A few minutes later, Ildrim approached me from a corner in the building. We greeted each other like two friends and then continued to stroll around, talking casually. He led me out of the building and toward his car, and we drove off. I did see my friend and his family for a last time, but I was not sure if they noticed us leaving.

Ildrim explained that we were first going to his home in Maku, to prepare for our trip to his father's village by the border. His younger brother soon joined us in his Jeep. We had fruit and tea and rested a little bit. The two brothers were busy reviewing our trip to the village. Then Ildrim asked me what I was carrying with me. I replied that I had nothing important with me, except a thousand US dollars. He explained that if we got searched and they found those dollars on me, it would ruin the whole plan. He asked to have them and told me that he would deliver them to me as soon as we got to the border where we would meet Sharif. I agreed with his logic. I gave him the US dollars, and he immediately gave them to his brother to hide in his Jeep. Ildrim explained that we were going in his car and his brother would follow us in his Jeep.

5

The transit highway continued after Maku for about half an hour until it reached the main border station between Iran and Turkey, called Bazargan. We were going to drive out of Maku toward Bazargan on the main highway, but after about five minutes' drive we were going to turn left onto another road, which would take us to the mountains between Iran and Turkey. Ildrim explained that the main danger for us would be at that intersection, where the security agents and the Revolutionary Guards had a roadblock. They knew him and his brother because they were locals and drove frequently to the village and back. But he said because of my presence, we could be stopped and questioned. There was more than an hour's drive after the intersection until the village, and there were a few border police stations along that route, but he said they had a business arrangement with those border police agents.

We left Ildrim's home around three thirty. A few minutes after we left Maku, Ildrim signaled that we were approaching the intersection. I started fingering my worry beads. I took a few deep breaths and closed my eyes for a few seconds. When I opened my eyes, I felt as relaxed as I could ever be. We reached the intersection. Armed guards were in the middle of the road and ordered us to stop. A guard came to the driver's side window and as soon as he greeted Ildrim, he recognized him. He asked him a couple of trivial questions and then came to my side. We greeted each other. He asked where I was from, what my profession was, and where I was going. I replied that I was from Tabriz and was visiting Ildrim's family and that I also wanted to buy some local rugs with the help of his father. The guard checked me out for a few seconds, then with a hand gesture he ordered us to move on.

We entered the side road and drove off. We were both excited and relieved, Ildrim more so than I. We drove toward the mountain range, passing a couple minor border-police stations in the first half hour, where the guards waved Ildrim on as soon as they recognized him. Then we got to the foothills where there was a major border-police station. They stopped us and asked me a few questions, but soon we were on our way up the beautiful green hills.

The mountain range was picturesque. There was even some snow on the summits of a few high mountains in the range, but they were to either side of where we were heading. Ildrim explained that we were going to drive up the hills, to where his father's village was located close to the summit of one of the small mountains. We drove through winding roads, along a small valley, and up the mountain again. It was gorgeous. Suddenly, at the end of the winding road, directly ahead of us, a tall border-police tower outside a village appeared in our view. Ildrim explained that the officer and the guards in that station were like family members to them and I did not need to worry at all.

We entered the village, which was located in a sort of valley on the slope of the mountain. We stopped in front of Ildrim's family home, where his elderly father greeted us and kindly welcomed me inside. Ildrim's brother arrived soon as well. We sat in a room facing the mountain where from the windows you could see the summit, which looked and felt very close. The old man was in charge here. He told me that I should relax and enjoy my stay in his home. He said he would let us know when the time was right for us to start moving up the mountain. It was obvious that the sons respected his experience and judgment on the matter.

We had some food and tea and socialized. I was a bit anxious, wanting the journey to be under way, but they were relaxed, laughing, and enjoying themselves. At about eight in the evening, I went to use the bathroom, which was located in the yard. When I returned to the room, both brothers were preparing to move out. The old man was watching through the window, using a small telescope. He then ordered Ildrim to go to the border-police post. Ildrim returned after about ten minutes and whispered something in his father's ear. Most probably, I thought, he went to inform the border police of our moving up the mountain, and maybe even paid them their dues.

The father was continuously checking the mountaintop. Soon, he ordered us to move out. He explained to me that the fog had taken over and so conditions were favorable for crossing the border. We said good-bye to the father and the family and went out into the yard. There, before leaving the house, I asked Ildrim how he was going to find Sharif under the circumstances. He explained that they had a name, number, and vocal signal corresponding to each section of the border in that area. That was their code map for the region. He said they had agreed to meet in a certain location. Given the foggy conditions, he doubted that they were going to be able to find each other easily. But he added that when we got closer to the boundary line, he would decide what to do. He explained that though the summit looked very close, it was going to take us a couple of hours of jogging and hiking to get up there. I was in good physical shape, as were he and his brother. He asked me jokingly if I was up for running to the border, and I replied that I was. He then explained what was going to happen.

> I will be moving in the front, and you are going to follow me a few steps behind. My brother will follow a few steps behind you. We will be jogging as soon as we leave here, until I give the stop sign by raising my hand. There will be absolutely no talking and no noise of any kind. When I stop, you stop a few steps behind me, and my brother will do the same. You should not fall behind at any point; if you do, my brother will push you to go faster. If for any unforeseeable reason you get separated from us, which should never happen, just hide behind a large tree or rock and do not move or make any noise, only wait for us, because we will find you. We will run to the top of the mountain, where we will reach a sandy path, which works as the border demarcation in our region. Sharif should already be waiting for us up there in the agreed section, where he will take delivery and take you to the other side. Are you ready? Do you have any questions?

I replied that I had no questions and was ready to go. In my mind and in my heart I talked to myself as I had done hundreds of times in solitary, saying to myself, "This is it; either I am going to be freed from this oppressive, brutal regime or I am going to die." I was ready and I had made my decision to go through with it, hoping for the best.

6

Ildrim opened the yard door and started running into the dark night while I followed him and his brother followed me. It was exactly 8:39 PM when we left the yard. We made a half-circle around the village, then passed through a small valley, and finally turned up toward the top of the mountain. Ildrim was jogging slowly but steadily. We jogged and hiked for an hour and a half, during which we passed through a wooded area, through green valleys, over streams, and across rocky regions. There were no other settlements on this route to the border. Around ten thirty, we reached the top, close to the border. There was a light rain or a heavy mist, and it seemed darker because of the thick fog.

Soon, we were in the location where we were supposed to meet Sharif. We got behind a large rock and the two brothers scanned the area, sounding the agreed vocal signal, which was like the hooting of an owl, but there was no sign of Sharif. Ildrim pointed to the sandy path on the top and said that we could reach and cross it in no time but that we should wait for Sharif. Some minutes passed, and there was still no sign of him. To ease my mind, they promised that if Sharif did not show up by midnight we would cross the border and would go to a safe house on the other side, where we would wait for him.

Suddenly we heard a gunshot in the distance. We gathered ourselves and the two brothers conferred for a minute or so, then Ildrim announced that they were going to take me to the other side. For the last time, he hooted the contact signal but did not hear any response. Then he told me that we were going to the home of Sharif's father-in-law, which was in the nearest village on the other side. Ildrim set out, and we followed him. In a few minutes, we reached the sandy path and crossed it.

On the Turkish side, we ran downhill nonstop. We finally reached a plateau where we could see lights from a village. We stopped at a distance to make sure it was safe to go in. It was still foggy and misty, which helped us avoid detection. Ildrim sent his brother to check the path to the house in the village. He returned a bit later and said all was fine.

At first we ran again, but as we got closer to the village we slowed down and walked to the outskirts until we reached a house. Ildrim knocked on the door. A large, middle-aged man in Kurdish clothes opened the door. As soon as he saw Ildrim, he let us in, asking about Sharif. Ildrim and his brother explained the situation. The father-in-law said that Sharif had left around ten o'clock to meet us at around eleven. Ildrim described the foggy and rainy conditions higher up the mountain and said that Sharif had been nowhere to be found.

The father-in-law welcomed us into his home. He took us inside the large room where all of his family members were present, who were very kind to us. They all knew Ildrim and his brother, of course, so I was the only stranger. We sat down to dry out and warm up. They gave us food and tea, and we talked a bit about the situation. The father-in-law spoke Azari and the brothers could speak Kordi. I could not speak Kordi, and therefore, we all spoke in Azari. The father-in-law told me that I should relax because the danger was over for me and I was safe in his home. Ildrim and his brother, after a bit of rest, wanted to go back to see what had happened to Sharif, but the father-in-law prevented them from doing so. He wanted them to wait a bit longer, saying that Sharif would soon show up.

It was warm and nice in there. I was happy that I was on this side of the border now, though I knew the danger was not over yet. For the first time in more than twenty-four hours, I felt a bit relaxed and safe. I was gradually getting sleepy. Suddenly, the door opened and Sharif walked in. It was about one in the morning. He was worried and soaked. As soon as he saw us there safe and sound, he jumped up and down with joy and excitement. We embraced, and he sat down to dry and warm up. He said when he heard the gunshot, he thought that we might have gotten arrested or even shot.

We were happy we had been able to pull it off successfully and safely so far. Sharif explained that it was not wise to move me down to his home in town at night, and therefore I should stay and sleep at his father-in-law's tonight. He added that he had to drive back to town because his wife and child were alone at home. He said he would be back early in the morning to fetch me. The brothers initially intended to return to their village, but then Ildrim said he wanted to go to town with Sharif in the morning. Finally, they decided that the younger brother would go back so that their father would not be worried, while Ildrim would stay in the house with me. Sharif left for his home in Turkey; the younger brother left for his village in Iran; and Ildrim and I slept in the house in the border region as guests of the father-in-law.

It was around six in the morning when Sharif woke us up. He had returned so early. We washed up, and during breakfast he explained to me that the three of us were going to drive down in his car to the border town called Dogubeyazit, which was the most eastern Turkish settlement by the Iranian border, the equivalent of Maku. He was going to keep me in his home until my contacts could take safe delivery of me. I thanked his father-in-law and the family for their kind hospitality.

Sharif drove downhill through some beautiful scenery on a small, winding mountain road. Finally, we got to an intersection, where we turned left onto the main transit highway heading toward Dogubeyazit.

As soon as we turned, Sharif stopped on the right side of the road. I noticed a Turkish border-patrol car parked on the opposite side. Before getting out of the car, Sharif took a German currency note out of his pocket and went quickly toward the police car. He talked to the police, gave them the money, and soon returned.

He said they jokingly had asked if he was smuggling people into the country. Then he explained to me that most police officers in the region knew him and they had a business arrangement, plus he paid them regularly. The understanding between them was that Sharif would do his commodity-smuggling business and pay them their dues, but with one condition: that he would never get involved in human trafficking. I felt bad that I had put Sharif in a position of danger, where he could lose his livelihood if we were caught.

During the rest of our drive to Dogubeyazit, Sharif assured me that I was safe as long as I was with him. Spread out in a valley ahead, the town of Dogubeyazit came into view. Sharif explained that the people who lived there were in the smuggling business or were with the Turkish army, security services, and border patrol.

After our arrival, Ildrim went to take care of some business in the town before he returned to Iran. I thanked him for all of his help, kindness, and support. Before leaving, he gave me back my one thousand US dollars. We hugged warmly and said good-bye. I asked him to thank his brother, his father, and all his family as well.

Sharif provided me with a furnished room and invited me to feel like I was in my own home. After I rested a bit, we called Europe and I talked to my family there, letting them know that I was safe and sound in Turkey. My family made arrangements with Sharif to come and get me in a week or so. I also called my mother in Iran and surprised her by letting her know that I had left the country and had arrived safely in Turkey. She was, I am sure, relieved to hear this.

I had thought that if I got safely to Turkey, I would be relieved and relaxed, and all my worries would disappear. But now that I had gotten here and was safe, I was going crazy with anticipation, anxiety, and excitement. I stayed awake pretty much the whole night, thinking about how I was going to be able to move around in Turkey without any documents and how I was going to get to Europe to join my family.

I stayed with Sharif and his family for a few more days. During this time, Sharif and his family extended to me a degree of respect, hospitality, and kindness that an uninvited guest would receive nowhere else in the world. I will never forget their kindness and compassion. Not only did they take me into their home and give me everything I needed there, but Sharif took me out to dinner almost every night.

7

The morning of October 22, my brother called from Ankara informing us that he, my wife, and my daughter would arrive in Dogubeyazit that afternoon. I was excited and anxious at the same time. I had not seen my wife and daughter for five years. When I was arrested, my daughter was one and a half years old, and now she was six and a half and in first grade in West Germany.

The bus finally arrived and they got out. I rushed to them and we all hugged, kissed, and cried. Five years to the day, we were reunited. The last images of them from before my arrest that I had kept and cherished those long and hard times in prison had to give way to their real presence. My wife was as beautiful and strong as before, and our daughter was quiet, innocent, and lovely. There was plenty of love, excitement, and also anxiety in our reunion. Through five long and difficult years of separation we had each grown apart, in a sense, but our mutual bond, commitment, and love was strong enough to hold us together.

Readjusting to the new situation as a family turned out to be easier for my wife and me than for our daughter. In prison I had never considered this possibility. My wife had tried her best to bring up Bahar in a way that she would recognize me, through my photos, as her father. But for a six-year-old child who had always been attached to her single mother, an intruding strange man, though he was her father, turned out to be difficult for her to accept. I was not prepared for this twist. It was a complicated situation for all three of us, but with patience, love, and understanding we were able to overcome this tension during the following months.

Sharif drove all of us to a hotel at my brother's insistence—we did not want to impose any further on him and his family. We all had dinner together and then Sharif said good night and went home to his family, but he invited us to lunch at his house the following day. The next morning, Sharif came and took us to his home. After lunch, my brother opened one of the suitcases he had brought; it was full of gifts for Sharif and his family, and some for Ildrim and his family. Later, I learned that Sharif and Ildrim had helped me not for money, only for friendship. That was truly noble of these professional smugglers, who could have lost their livelihood, at the very least, if they had been caught crossing the border with me. In return, my brother and my friends who knew Sharif had decided to offer as many gifts as they possibly could.

My friends in Europe had sent an Iranian passport for me, so that I could be safe in Turkey and maybe could even use it to get out of Turkey. It was just a passport of an Iranian man. It did not have my photo or my information on it. My family, through connections, had had the passport stamped for entrance in the Istanbul airport by paying some bribe money to the airport police. There was no visa requirement between Iran and Turkey. But if the Turkish police anywhere inside Turkey questioned me, I needed to show legal Iranian documentation. We were hoping that this passport would at least help me in such a rare case, but we were doubtful it was going to work for leaving Turkey, let alone entering West Germany.

We said good-bye to Sharif. Separation from Sharif, who had been so helpful and supportive, was very difficult for me, triggering memories of separations in prison. We took a bus to Ankara, where we bought plane tickets and flew to Istanbul. Waiting for us in the airport were "Zia," my brother's son, and "Ghani," his uncle on his mother's side, both students in Turkey. They took us to their one-bedroom student apartment. For a couple of days we really enjoyed ourselves in Istanbul. It was my first time ever in the city. Here, for the first time since leaving Iran, I felt safe and had fun. During the day, we went sightseeing, and at night we would gather, talk, and plan what we should and could do about my situation. Personally, I thought my best legal option was to go to the US consulate in Istanbul. Since my wife was a US citizen, I thought she would be able to apply for a visa for me to travel to America. We all agreed that this should be our first move. Going to the German consulate to apply for a visa on that fake Iranian passport was another possibility, which I thought we would try if for some reason the US option did not work out.

One day we went to the American consulate in Istanbul and made an appointment to talk to one of the visa officers. My wife, our daughter, and I went in, and after my wife explained her situation and mine, the officer told us that under international law and bilateral agreements with Turkey, they would not be able to provide me with a visa if I was in Turkey illegally. He asked me if I could go to the Turkish police to get a letter indicating that I was in the country legally. I explained to him that that would be out of the question, because firstly I was not legally there and secondly Turkey and Iran had a bilateral security agreement to exchange illegals; going to the Turkish authorities would certainly put my life in danger. The officer told us that the US delegation could not break any laws and could not jeopardize their relationship with Turkey, a close ally. He said if I could get myself to a European country and apply for asylum there, then the United States might be able to help me out. We came out of the American consulate very disappointed and depressed.

We then decided, out of desperation, to try the German consulate visa application, knowing pretty well that it would not work. As I had predicted, they said that the only way to get a German visa was for me to go to the Turkish police to register with them and obtain a letter indicating that I was legally in their country. Since this was out of the question, we knew that there was no legal way for me to get to Europe or America from Turkey.

I could have registered with the UN refugee office in Ankara to seek political asylum as an ex–political prisoner. But I did not want to become a political refugee. I wanted to enter America with my wife and become a permanent legal resident. Disappointed, we gathered at home that night and discussed other options. There were plenty of illegal ways and means, which thousands of people, including Iranians, had used over the years to get from Turkey to Europe. They cost a lot, but they were available. My brother suggested that we should not rush, and I agreed. After going through the most dangerous part of the escape plan—crossing the Iranian border illegally—I did not want to be arrested in Turkey or while I was being smuggled out of the country. That would have been a real disaster, to come so close only to lose everything again.

After about a week, I felt that my brother needed to go back to his business in West Germany, Bahar to her school, and Ketty to her work. I thought I could stay with Zia and Ghani and enjoy myself in Istanbul while we figured out what to do. We all agreed. My brother, my wife, and my daughter left for West Germany. We were separated again, though, we hoped, only temporarily.

8

During the day, Zia and Ghani attended their university classes and I was on my own. Gradually, I learned my way around the city, and I enjoyed visiting different parts of it. I stayed in Istanbul for about four weeks, during which we pondered different ways of getting me out of Turkey and into West Germany. We had exhausted all avenues and basically were about to conclude that maybe the only real option left was to pay a smuggler to take me to West Germany, when one day my wife called from West Germany saying that she was sending someone to see me soon. When this person arrived in Istanbul, he said they had figured out how to get me to Europe. He pulled out a passport from a European country I will not mention, declaring that it was my key to the continent. I looked at the passport, which belonged to an Iranian man a few years my junior. The idea was that I would use it to return to Europe after a supposed weeklong vacation in Turkey. As soon as I looked at the passport and heard the plan, I knew that it was an ingenious idea.

This was a genuine European passport, and we were not going to alter it in any way. The only thing we needed to do was to have it legally stamped for entry and be entered in the computer system in a Turkish airport. Then, I would simply fly "back" to Europe on it. The photo on the passport looked very much like me. I was positive that the Turkish immigration and airport police officers would not be able to tell the difference between the real passport owner and me.

My nephew thought differently. He agreed that this was the best option so far, but at the same time he was worried that the police would know I was not the person in the photo. I worked hard to convince him that, because he was my nephew and had known me since his birth, he was able to differentiate between the photo and me. A policeman in a foreign country would not be able to do so because we all looked alike in their eyes. This was especially true because in many cases a passport photo does look different from the person holding the passport, as a result of time having elapsed, and that is normal and understood.

After a couple of days of discussion, we finally agreed that this passport was the best shot I had of entering Europe. Then the friend who had brought the passport revealed that we would travel to West Germany together, not the country that had issued the passport. That was smart thinking as well because it would be less dangerous for me to enter West Germany with that European passport than to enter the other country. In West Germany I could speak English to get through immigration and customs, while in the other European country things could go wrong if the officials started questioning me in their own language. Also, my wife had already contacted a German lawyer who had said that even if there was a problem on arrival at the German airport, he could help keep me in West Germany because I had been a political prisoner in Iran.

Another smart move by my wife and the others helping me was that they had bought a round-trip ticket for the European passport in West Germany. I was going to use the return portion of that ticket for my travel to West Germany. My wife's friend contacted friends of his in Turkey, and through them the European passport was sent to an officer in the Istanbul airport, where it was stamped and entered into the system. They paid two hundred deutsche marks to the officer for this. After we got the passport back and everything looked fine, we were set to fly to Hamburg, West Germany. My friend and I decided not to fly from the Istanbul airport but rather from a coastal city in the southwest of the country.

On the day of the flight, my nephew took us to that airport. We agreed that as we neared the immigration and security checkpoint my friend would fall behind me to allow a few people in between us before he joined the line. My nephew would stay to watch to make sure that we both got past the checkpoint. If I had any problems, my friend would stay back to get help from his contacts in the Turkish police. If there were no problems, then he would go through the checkpoint as well and we would fly out together.

Being relatively fluent in English was a big help for me from this point on. I got to a gate and to the immigration officer. I handed over my passport and ticket, saying hello to him with a big smile. He looked at me and at the passport for a couple of minutes. I kept my cool, which was easy for me to do after all the experience I had gained during interrogations in prison. He asked me a few questions. Then he entered something in his computer and did some more checking. Afterward, he stamped my passport for exit and said *bon voyage*! I was so excited that I wanted to scream out loud, but I just walked quickly into the transit area. My friend also passed through after a few minutes. We hugged each other and were very excited and relieved. Then, we sat waiting and pondering about the arrival in Hamburg.

My travel companion had a business in West Germany and had many contacts, plus there was the lawyer who was waiting for my wife's call in case of emergency. Therefore, I was not too worried, but I was still tense and would be until I had passed German immigration. The flight lasted a few hours, and then we landed at Hamburg airport. Our agreement again was that I would go first, but this time he would be right behind me. Since there was no visa requirement between European countries, I should have had no problem entering West Germany.

I went to the first available passport control kiosk while my friend watched from behind. I gave my passport to the officer; he asked in English where I had traveled and why. I replied that I had gone for a week's vacation to Turkey with my friend, who was a German resident. He asked why I had not returned to my own European country but had come here instead. I said that I had some business to take care of with my friend and then I was going to pick up my car and drive to my own country. The officer said good luck and good-bye and sent me through.

I walked inside the transit area, where family and friends were all waiting. They hugged me, kissed me, and otherwise showered me with their love and affection. My friend soon got through and joined us. We all drove to my brother's home. Now, it was a happy time for all of us, and particularly a time for me to relax and enjoy everything and everyone. My younger brother and his family had come from France to be with us at this reunion.

I had to become legal in West Germany, so that my wife and I could go to the US consulate in Frankfurt and apply for a US visa. Ketty contacted her German lawyer friend. He said that he would submit paperwork on my behalf and would apply for political asylum for me in the German court system. He explained that this way he could get a letter that should be satisfactory proof of my legality for the US officials. He called a few days later and said that I should stay with my wife until the day of a court hearing on my case. Meanwhile, he was able to get a letter from the German court system indicating that I had applied for political asylum in West Germany. We took this letter and went to the US consulate in Frankfurt. After many interviews, a pile of paperwork, and clearance from the FBI, I finally got my visa to travel to the United States. This process took about two months, during which time I lived with my wife and daughter in their tiny condo in Offenbach, near Frankfurt.

After spending three months together in West Germany and having obtained my US visa, we decided to move permanently to America. Early in 1990, we said good-bye to all our family and friends in West Germany, and the three of us flew to Honolulu, where my wife's family lived.

EPILOGUE

Since my release from prison, two important issues beyond my own direct experiences have occupied my mind: first, what our families went through while we were in prison; second, the continuing deplorable state of human rights in Iran and the world, and what can be done to improve it.

THE FAMILIES

While we political prisoners were subjected to the horrific physical and mental torture described in my memoirs, our families outside of prison went through a different, no less excruciating hell. Political activists are highly motivated and, generally speaking, are mentally prepared for the possible consequences of their actions, such as imprisonment. After the initial shock of arrest and interrogation, the majority of prisoners gradually pull themselves together; in communal settings in particular, they strive to maintain their morale in the face of continuous prison pressures and get through their prison ordeal in a reasonably stable frame of mind.

Prisoners' family members (other than those who are politically active), on the other hand, generally are not prepared to deal with this situation. In the immediate aftermath of arrest, the shock of what has happened, the sudden destruction of hope and stability in life, and the loneliness that follows can destroy them. If they can withstand this initial stage, they must cope with unrelenting pressures from every side.

My wife's description of her acute loneliness, helplessness, and sense of terror when I did not come home that first night still haunts me today, more than twenty years after she first described it to me. I had never stayed away at night without telling her in advance where I would be, so she knew by late that night that something alarming must have happened to me. Filled with dread, she had to care for our one-and-a-half-year-old daughter alone; deal with the hepatitis she was recovering from at the time; decide how to dispose of the valuable but incriminating equipment, paper, and documents I had stored in our home; resist being overwhelmed by anxiety over my fate; and more. We were fortunate that two of my friends from work agreed to help when she called and explained the situation to them. They risked their lives by coming to our home and disposing of the incriminating items.

From that night forward, Ketty's life was changed irrevocably. As soon as they found out that I was missing, most friends and relatives distanced themselves from her. Whether or not their actions were justified, the fact of the matter was that she was left utterly alone.

The day after my disappearance, she took our daughter, Bahar, and went from one governmental agency to another, making inquiries. All denied any knowledge of my whereabouts; no one even acknowledged I had been detained. After many days of fruitless inquiries, she decided she must resort to desperate measures to make herself heard.

She went to the office of Ayatollah Khomeini's personal representative in charge of prisoner affairs and arranged to see the official in charge. With Bahar in her arms, she told him that she had been born and raised abroad and had no relatives in the country and that she had to find out about the fate of her husband so that she could decide what to do. The official took down her name and mine, and he asked her to return the next day. When she did, he finally confirmed that I had been detained but said I would not be allowed any visits for a long while. Our car had disappeared along with me; Ketty told the official it belonged to her and was the only valuable possession she owned. She threatened to leave Bahar with him if the car wasn't returned to her because she was unable to care for the child on her own anymore. He promised to look into the issue. A few weeks later, they returned the car, which Ketty took as the first sign of hope that I might still be alive.

We were extremely lucky that Ketty wasn't arrested. Many spouses of political prisoners were arrested at the same time as their partner. Others were taken hostage after their family member managed to escape: a friend's wife languished in prison for four years after he managed to flee.

Both Ketty and my older brother tried hard through various channels to secure a visit with me, without success. Finally, about three months after my arrest, we were allowed a monitored phone conversation, during which she told me in code that she had decided to leave Iran with Bahar. Shortly thereafter, without being able to see me first, they left for Europe.

Ketty was lucky to be able to leave the country and even luckier to be allowed to take our daughter with her. Just hours before my arrest, I had finalized the legal paperwork required for Ketty to travel abroad and to have power of attorney over Bahar. Without those documents, they would not have been allowed out of the country.

Other members of my family, like all prisoners' families in Iran, went through hardship and humiliation at the hands of the authorities when they came to visit us in prison. Many, like my elderly mother, traveled long distances from all over Iran and often braved extreme weather conditions to visit loved ones in Tehran prisons. After months or years without any word of a loved one's fate, many parents finally were rewarded with the joy of finding their tortured son or daughter still alive. Others were not so lucky, struggling for long periods to remain hopeful, only to be told that their loved ones had been executed.

Not knowing was the worst torture for the families. Even when a visit was allowed, anxiety returned as soon as the visit ended. Would another visit be allowed? Would their loved one be moved to another prison without them being informed? Would the prisoner be tortured, deprived of essential medical treatment, or executed? Helplessness and ceaseless anxiety took a terrible toll.

Unfortunately, just like war veterans, political prisoners who survive their ordeal often suffer from post-traumatic stress disorder (PTSD), which frequently remains undiagnosed and misunderstood. Many marriages broke down during or in the aftermath of imprisonment. Some couples simply grew apart; other individuals went through such a tough time that they developed psychological problems and could not remain in the relationship; a few had "political" or "moral" difficulties with their partners.

Since the crackdown on opposition forces some thirty years ago, families of political prisoners have remained integral to the struggle for justice, freedom, and democracy in Iran. Once again, in the aftermath of the 2009 postelection turmoil in the country, families of arrested democracy movement activists practically lived in front of the gates of Evin and other prisons, campaigning for the release of their loved ones. Meanwhile, families of prisoners executed during the bloody massacres of the 1980s gather weekly in Park-e Laleh (a city park in Tehran) and in Khavaran cemetery (where some of the mass graves are located) to keep the memory of the victims alive and to continue the struggle for freedom and justice.

epilogue

HUMAN RIGHTS AND THE POLITICS OF POWER

I was one of the first survivors of the mass killing of the summer of 1988 to make it out of Iran. As soon as I reached Europe in autumn 1989, I contacted Amnesty International, the United Nations Human Rights Commission, and other human rights organizations, reporting to them in detail what I had experienced and witnessed in the prisons of the Islamic Republic. Though news of these horrors had already reached them by then, little had happened. I was hoping that eyewitness accounts from a survivor like me would initiate a storm of condemnation of the Islamic Republic and action against their barbaric crimes against humanity. But no serious action on this particular issue has taken place then or since.

More than sixty years have passed since the Universal Declaration of Human Rights. But according to Amnesty International's 2010 Annual Report, these rights are violated daily around the globe, and in 2009 "torture and other ill-treatment remained endemic and, for the most part, were committed with impunity." In many countries, "state authorities have shown themselves either reluctant or downright unwilling to honor their international treaty obligations to protect and promote human rights."

Since its inception in 1979, the Islamic Republic of Iran has had no regard for the fundamental human rights of its citizens. The leadership's extreme abuse of power, all in the name of Islam, has at times risen to crimes against humanity, in which tens of thousands of people have been seized, tortured, and killed.

How is it that a regime that twice within a decade massacred thousands of its political prisoners has been able to escape any serious review or punishment from the world?

The answer lies, at least partially, in the fact that the United States, the

European Union, and other powerful countries like Russia and China have consistently prioritized their political and economic short- and long-term interests over human rights concerns. And it is also partially because the West, and the United States in particular, has insisted upon pressuring the regime in ways that strengthen rather than weaken its grasp on power.

Iran often is portrayed in the West, particularly in the United States, in a way that mainly serves the purpose of those bent on military action against Iran, whether for the destruction of Iranian nuclear facilities or for regime change engineered by the West. But is Western military intervention the way forward to promote human rights in Iran and a more peaceful world? The millions of Iranians who flooded the streets in June 2009 to oppose the regime are perhaps the most graphic illustration of why this picture and "solution" are so terribly flawed. Given the horrors of the recent experiments in regime change elsewhere in the region by the West, and taking into account the presence of a growing democratic movement within Iran, the answer to the above question must be a resounding no. Regime change is needed in Iran but must be done by Iranians in their own interest, in their own time, and in their own way, rather than imposed by foreign powers.

The fact is that under the surface, change has been the only constant in Iran over the past thirty years, both within the regime and, most crucially, among the population at large. Within the regime, fierce infighting and deep divisions have resulted in the gradual consolidation of power in the hands of a conservative faction that increasingly is dominated by the Revolutionary Guards Corps and is supported by a powerful reactionary element of the religious establishment.

Hope for reform of the regime from within was crushed when the popularly elected, reform-minded President Khatami and his faction, who controlled both the administrative and the legislative branches of government, proved to be powerless against the conservative faction. This faction controls the military, the police and militia, the judiciary, and a large portion of the economy, and, crucially, it has the full support of Supreme Leader Khamenei, who holds absolute power over all internal and foreign policy matters. It was during Khatami's presidency that vigilantes broke into student dormitories and threw protesting students out of windows, to their deaths; many other students were abducted, tortured, and killed. Khatami's government proved itself powerless to intervene.

The gradual domination of power by the Revolutionary Guards, which began in the 1990s, was accelerated following Mahmood Ahmadinejad's election as president in 2005. This set the stage for their seizure of power in June 2009, when they stole the presidential election.

Within the population at large, however, change has been in the opposite direction. In the beginning, the majority of Iranians supported the Islamic regime; this is no longer true. Most crucially, the children of the Islamic Republic—those who have grown up knowing nothing else—want nothing to do with the Islamists and their despotic theocracy. Instead, over the years a strong democratic movement has taken shape in Iran with young women and men, students, both secular and religious intellectuals, and others at its forefront. This is the democratic force that came out in 2009 to reform the system through the election process, was outraged by what happened, and consequently seriously challenged the system in the streets of Iran. For the first time in the thirty-year history of the Islamic Republic, the authority of the supreme leader and the unity of the regime were shattered. Iran's so-called Green Movement, the product of this era, is a democratic social movement that includes all those who are struggling for freedom, peace, and justice in Iran. Though the movement lacks organization and strong leadership at this stage, it provides all Iranians with hope that democratic change in the country, in the long run, is possible.

Western powers, led by the United States, have done very little to help the cause of democratic change in Iran. Instead, their menacing, transparently hypocritical approach to the nuclear issue has drawn many Iranians to rally around their national leaders, greatly weakening unity around demands for democracy and providing the regime with an excuse to crack down on its internal opposition. The international community must move to rid the world of nuclear weapons. It is a double-standard practice for some countries to decide what countries should or should not have them. It would be suicidal for the Islamic Republic, even if they had nuclear weapons, which they do not, to use them against Israel or the United States, countries that have an arsenal of nuclear weapons and would destroy Iran in retaliation.

The Islamic Republic's principal claim to legitimacy is as the embodiment of Muslim purity and justice on earth. By exerting only occasional, token pressure on the Islamic Republic's weaknesses—namely its contravention of human rights, rampant corruption, and lawlessness—the United States and other powerful countries ignore the regime's greatest vulnerability. Exposing the regime's horrific contraventions of the most basic human rights threatens its internal unity and shatters its reputation and honor internationally. Moreover, compromise on the regime's human rights record, whether by opposition forces inside Iran or by the international community, compromises the development of the democratic movement.

Internationally, the double standard on human rights issues practiced by the West, particularly by the United States, which maintains one standard for friendly countries and another for all others less sympathetic to their interests, together with America's own record of human rights crimes at Abu Ghraib prison and Guantanamo Bay, has scarred the hearts and minds of millions around the globe. It has also provided brutal regimes and dictators around the world, including in Iran, with an extra excuse to justify the torture and murder of their opponents.

epilogue

The mass killings of political prisoners during the summer of 1988, most of whom were serving sentences handed down by the regime's own Islamic tribunals, must be considered one of the most outrageous crimes committed by the Islamic Republic. Both in scale and brutality, it is unparalleled in contemporary Iranian history. Though the Islamic regime in Iran is known for its brutality and abuse of human rights, there is not much public awareness in the world about the mass killings of political prisoners in 1988.

As a survivor of these mass executions, I am hoping to play a small role in educating people around the globe about the regime in Iran, the status of human rights, and particularly the mass killings of political prisoners in the summer of 1988. Increased international awareness of this atrocity must lead to investigation and prosecution of those responsible by the world community, which would exert pressure on the regime where it is most vulnerable. In this regard, independent pressure groups, whose motives cannot be confused with the self-interest of governments, have a particularly important role to play.

Instead of concentrating on counterproductive pressure on the nuclear issue, the West should support Iran's internal democratic movement by exerting international pressure on the regime's weaknesses—contravention of human rights, corruption, and lawlessness. That is the best way to aid the deeply rooted, strong democratic opposition in Iran; the best way to guarantee human rights in Iran; and the best way toward a more peaceful world.

I am very hopeful that the growing democratic social movement in Iran will one day be able to bring to justice those in the Islamic Republic who have been responsible for the torture and killing of Iranians.

—Jafar Yaghoobi
San Francisco, California
October 27, 2010

NOTES

1. Sepah-e Pasdaran-e Enghelab-e Eslami (Army of the Guardians of the Islamic Revolution, a.k.a. Islamic Revolutionary Guards Corps; Iranian Revolutionary Guards Corps [IRGC], as it is known in the West; or simply the Revolutionary Guards, Pasdaran, or Sepah) is the largest branch of the Islamic Republic's military. The IRGC was formed in May 1979 as a militia group loyal to Ayatollah Khomeini. It now has its own ground forces, navy, air force, intelligence, and Special Forces, and it also controls the Basij militia force. The IRGC became a full military force separate from and parallel to the *artesh* (army) during the Iran-Iraq War. From the beginning, the IRGC functioned as an army of the Islamic faithful. As one of the first institutions of the postrevolution, it helped legitimize the new regime and provided an armed base of support to Ayatollah Khomeini. Since its formation the IRGC has actively been involved in intelligence gathering, security operations, and destruction of the opposition forces. It was also actively involved in Lebanon's internal affairs and with the Hezbollah organization. The Qods (Jerusalem) Force of the IRGC is responsible for extraterritorial operations. Since the end of the Iran-Iraq War and the death of Khomeini, the IRGC has increased its involvement in Iran's politics and economy, and currently, particularly during and after the 2009 presidential election turmoil, it has become the major power center in Iranian political and economic affairs.

2. Middle-class university students in Tehran founded the revolutionary organization Sazman-e Mojahedin-e Khalgh-e Iran (the People's Mojahedin Organization of Iran [PMOI], a.k.a. the Mojahedin-e Khalgh [MEK], the Mojahedin-e Khalgh Organization [MKO], or just Mojahedin) in 1965. Ideo-

logically, the group combined a unique interpretation of Islam with aspects of Iranian nationalism and Marxism. Before it could undertake any military operations, a raid by SAVAK resulted in the arrest of all of the group's leadership and most of its cadres. All but one of its leaders was executed. Other members were kept in prison for many years. The remaining members and sympathizers continued to reorganize, and after 1971 they engaged in armed struggle against the shah's regime. During the revolution of 1979 their veteran members were released from prison and joined the ranks of the organization, which expanded to become a considerable force in Iran. Massoud Rajavi became the leader of the PMOI. Ayatollah Khomeini and his followers, based on their prior knowledge and understanding of the group's Islamic interpretations, did not trust them and would not give them any acknowledgement, but in the early postrevolution years the Islamic regime exploited all the support that the MEK extended to them. Mojahedin organized and trained a militia to confront the Islamic regime at an opportune time, which came in early 1981 when Abolhassan Banisadr, who had been elected the president of the Islamic Republic with support from Khomeini, fell in opposition to the clerical leadership of the country. Mojahedin rushed to Banisadr's help with the hope of joining their forces in confronting the clerical regime. Khomeini denounced both Banisadr and Rajavi, forcing them to go into hiding and later escape the country. On June 20, 1981, the MEK organized massive demonstrations all over Iran, which resulted in armed confrontation with the forces of the regime in the streets of major Iranian cities. Hundreds of MEK followers were killed and thousands were arrested. This was a turning point in postrevolution Iran. The clerical regime, waiting for an opportunity to put their repressive plans into action, exploited this adventurous climate and cracked down on all opposition, arresting in the streets anyone they deemed suspicious. Soon, prisons were filled with tens of thousands of mostly young men and women. On June 28, 1981, bombs exploded in the headquarters of the Islamic Republic Party, killing 72 high-ranking government officials. Two months later, another bomb exploded in the office of the new president, killing him and his prime minister. The MEK accepted responsibility for these actions. In retaliation, thousands of

MEK prisoners were rounded up and killed in the summer and fall of 1981 through summary questioning and execution procedures. A Koranic term, *Monafeghin* (hypocrites) was extensively used by the Islamic Republic against Mojahedin to discredit them. After the June 20, 1981 crisis, thousands of Mojahedin followers were forced in prisons to admit that they were *Monafeghin*. Whenever they were questioned about their organizational affiliation, they were not allowed to declare Mojahedin, but rather they had to say *Monafeghin*. Gradually all leading cadres of the MEK left the country and gathered in France. In exile, by 1987 Mojahedin, once a massive popular organization, had shrunk to more like a cult. The new marriage for Rajavi and the launching of a so-called "Ideological Revolution" within the Mojahedin were factors in its decline. Rajavi married Azodanlu, the former wife of Mehdi Abrishamchi, his prison and organizational comrade. Following this, there was a consolidation of the leadership of the organization. Many "voluntarily" gave up their positions, and others were raised to higher ranks. The Islamic regime exploited the marriage to the fullest and exposed the contradictions inherent in the Mojahedin organization. The organization was active in France until 1986, when they moved most of their forces to Iraq. This was in the middle of the long Iran-Iraq War (1980–1988), and therefore the Islamic regime exploited this move as an act of treason to discredit the MEK. With the help of Iraqi President Saddam Hussein, the MEK built an army with the goal of overthrowing the Iranian regime. In return they collaborated with the Iraqi regime both on intelligence issues and also by interrogating and controlling the Iranian POWs. They also took part in suppressing the uprisings and revolts of the Iraqi Kurds and Shiites against Saddam's regime. At the end of the Iran-Iraq War, following the acceptance of the cease-fire by both countries, MEK forces attacked western Iran. During this operation, the Mojahedin were defeated by the Islamic Republic forces, and some were arrested while many lost their lives. The regime had an advance plan for the mass execution of political prisoners at the end of the war, and once again they exploited the daring action of the MEK leadership to justify the lockdown of all prisons, where they secretly killed thousands of prisoners all over Iran during the summer and fall of 1988. The

MEK is currently in sorry circumstances. Since the 2003 invasion of Iraq and the overthrow of Saddam's regime by a US-led coalition, MEK forces in Iraq—ranging in number from 3,000 to 30,000, according to different sources and estimates—have been held up in their camps, where they are being safeguarded, for now, from both the Iraqi and the Iranian governments. Iraq wants to put the Mojahedin on trial for their collaboration in suppressing the Kurds and the Shiites. Iran wants the Mojahedin extradited to be put on trial for terrorist activities. For this reason, the United States is holding on to the Mojahedin as a valuable bargaining chip in its dealings with Iran.

3. Vezarat-e Etela'at Va Amniyat-e Keshvar (VEVAK) (Ministry of Intelligence and Security, a.k.a. Ministry of Intelligence or MI) is the primary intelligence agency of the Islamic Republic. The ministry was officially formed on August 14, 1984, from the merging of many small intelligence agencies that had been established in different governmental organizations, with the condition that the minister be a cleric. The main cooperation in shaping the ministry was provided by the security apparatus of the Revolutionary Guards, while the main challenge to the formation of the ministry was produced by the intelligence services of the Islamic Revolution Public Prosecutor, headed by Assadollah Lajavardi. With a large budget and extensive organization, the Ministry of Intelligence is one of the most powerful agencies in the Iranian government. Traditionally it has operated under the control of the supreme leader apparatus of Ayatollah Khomeini in the beginning and Ayatollah Khamenei currently. Since its formation, the ministry has been involved not only in destroying the internal opposition to the regime but also in terrorist activities, including the assassination of Iranian political dissidents inside and outside of the country. In 1998, after the infamous serial murders of dissident writers and intellectuals by the MI agents, an overhaul of the agency took place.

4. Sazman-e Cherikha-ye Fadai-ye Khalgh-e Iran (Organization of Iranian People's Fadai Guerrillas [OIPFG], a.k.a. Cherikha-ye Fadai, Fadai, or Fadaiyan) was officially formed in early spring of 1971 from the union of two revolutionary leftist groups. Their decision to resort to armed struggle was in part due to the inability of traditional parties to bring about any changes

through peaceful means. It also was the result of the repressive rule of the shah and the secret police, SAVAK. Soon after the formation of the organization, most of its leading members were killed by the regime, either in prison or in shootouts, but the organization survived and pursued armed struggle against the shah's regime. From 1971 to 1979, nearly 300 members of the Fadaiyan lost their lives. Other members and followers were in prison serving long sentences. Just before the revolution of 1979, the shah was forced to release political prisoners, among them some of the veteran members of the Fadaiyan, who rebuilt the organization. During the revolution, the Fadaiyan became the largest secular leftist organization in the country and was instrumental in the overthrow of the shah's regime in 1979. The Fadaiyan had suddenly been transformed from a small guerrilla group to a massive political organization facing complex issues, most noticeable of which was dealing with a theocratic Islamic regime. But the leadership of the organization, the majority of whom had just been released from prison, were unable to deal with the ideological, theoretical, strategic/tactical, and practical issues facing them. Immediately after the revolution in 1979, veteran member Ashraf Dehghani and some others left the organization, accusing the Fadaiyan leadership of deviation from its principles regarding armed struggle. In 1980, following an internal dispute in the leadership of the Fadaiyan regarding its political line, its analysis of the nature of the new regime, and the tactics employed in dealing with it, the organization split in two, a "majority" and a "minority." "The Fadaiyan Minority" took a more radical position in dealing with the regime. "The Fadaiyan Majority," which was still the largest secular leftist organization in the country, gradually transformed itself into a political organization, putting aside any military or radical actions. Fadaiyan Majority leadership gradually followed a policy of unity with the pro-Soviet Tudeh Party and its policy of defending the regime against "its enemies." This unification process and particularly the policies followed by the Fadaiyan Majority during the spring and summer of 1981, when the regime was brutally killing or arresting and torturing thousands of opposition members, eventually caused another split in the Fadaiyan Majority. Thus the Fadaiyan Sixteenth of Azar emerged from the Fadaiyan Majority in December

1981. The Fadaiyan Sixteenth of Azar was against the regime's suppression of the opposition, and it was particularly against the Tudeh Party political line and unity with the Tudeh Party. All organizations stemming from the original Fadaiyan were gradually crushed by the Islamic regime from 1981 to 1986. Many of the leadership cadres, and some members and followers, escaped the repression and settled in Europe to continue their struggle from exile. At the same time, hundreds were killed in the streets fighting the regime or were arrested, tortured, and imprisoned and/or executed.

5. Komiteh-ye Moshtarak (Joint Committee, a.k.a. Komiteh, Ward 3000, or Towhid), near Meydan-e Tupkhaneh (Cannon Square) in central Tehran, was built in 1937 as the first modern prison in Iran. It later became the site of the Tehran Central Jail, officially known as the Zendan-e Movaghat (Temporary Detention House). Initially, in the shah's time, it was used as a prison for women. SAVAK and the intelligence division of the urban police, when they formed a joint "antiterrorism and antisabotage" task force in 1971, used it as a detention center. From then on it became known in Iran as Komiteh-ye Moshtarak. SAVAK later took over and used it as its main interrogation and torture center of the opposition forces. During the revolution of 1979, the Komiteh was captured and the new regime declared that it would never be used as a place of torture. But shortly after the establishment of the Islamic Republic, the new regime secretly started using it, first to keep some of the American hostages captured by the student followers of Khomeini. Later it was used to interrogate and torture the regime's opponents. It has been called Komiteh-ye Towhid or Ward 3000 in the Islamic Republic, but prisoners, in general, still refer to it as Komiteh-ye Moshtarak. Many prisoners of the Islamic Republic have spent some time in this notorious detention center. Its main structure consists of a round four-story building with a round courtyard in the middle and other facilities attached to it. It has recently been turned into a museum (Muse-ye Ebrat) by the Islamic regime.

6. The Iran-Iraq War (1980–1988), or the "Iraqi-Imposed War" as it is called in Iran, was the longest and bloodiest war since World War II. On September 22, 1980, Iraqi troops invaded Iran and captured the Arvandrood

(Shatt al Arab) and seized a forty-eight-kilometer-wide strip of Iranian territory. Iran's resistance at the outset of the Iraqi invasion was neither well organized nor equally successful on all fronts. But the majority of Iranians, regardless of their political differences, rushed to defend their country. Iran stopped Iraqi forces on the Karoun River and resorted to "human wave" assaults using thousands of Basij volunteers. Iran gained its first major victory when the army and the Revolutionary Guards put aside their rivalry and cooperated to force Iraq to lift its long siege of Abadan in September 1981. By 1984 it was reported that some 300,000 Iranian and 250,000 Iraqi soldiers had been killed. The following years of war saw increased use of chemical weapons from the Iraqi side, shelling of more and more population centers, oil tanker war in the Persian Gulf area, and many military operations from both sides. Iranian military gains inside Iraq after 1984 were a major reason for increased involvement by powerful countries like the United States, France, and others in the war, though they had supported Iraq from the outset. By the late spring of 1987, the superpowers became more directly involved because they feared that the fall of Basra might lead to a pro-Iranian Islamic regime in largely Shi'a-dominated southern Iraq. To avoid defeat, Iraq resorted to all kinds of weapons. During a period of six weeks some 190 missiles were fired at Iranian cities in 1988. The Iraqi missiles caused great destruction and forced almost 30 percent of Tehran's population to flee the city. Four major battles were fought from April to August 1988, in which Iraqis effectively used massive chemical weapons to defeat Iranians. The Iran-Iraq War ended when both countries accepted United Nations (UN) Security Council Resolution 598, leading to an August 20, 1988, cease-fire. Casualty figures are uncertain, though estimates (both military and civilian) suggest more than 1.5 million war and war-related casualties, perhaps as many as 1 million dead. The war also turned millions of people into refugees.

7. Veteran socialists and communists, some of which had recently been released from prison after allied forces entered Iran and ended the rule of Reza Shah Pahlavi, founded Hezb-e Tudeh-ye Iran (Tudeh Party of Iran) in 1941. From the beginning, the Tudeh Party was always dependent on Soviet policy and never acted as an independent organization on major issues. Within the

first two years of its existence the Tudeh Party grew to become a formidable force in Iranian politics. After an assassination attempt on the shah in 1948, the Tudeh Party was declared illegal by the regime and many of its leaders were arrested. The party survived, arranged the escape of its leaders from prison, and continued to organize its activities as a semi-underground force. The party had a great deal of influence in the workers' trade union organizations, in the student and women's organizations, and particularly in the armed forces. By the start of the oil nationalization campaign under the leadership of Dr. Mohammad Mossadegh in 1951, the reaction of the Tudeh Party toward this movement and its leader was contradictory and basically followed the interests of the Soviet Union rather than the national interests of the Iranian people. In the summer of 1952, following disagreements with the shah, Mossadegh resigned from the post of prime minister. Iranian people in support of Mossadegh revolted against the shah and forced him to reinstate Mossadegh to his post. This time the Tudeh Party supported Mossadegh in his struggle with the shah, and from then until the coup of 1953 the Tudeh Party took a policy of "conditional" support of the Mossadegh government. The Tudeh Party was ineffective in confronting the coup of 1953 guided by the CIA against the democratically elected government of Iran, and the party leadership stayed inactive waiting for Mossadegh to lead its actions. The coup changed the history of modern Iran forever. From 1953 until 1958 the coup-regime forces, supported by the CIA, destroyed the Tudeh Party and the democratic forces in Iran. Hundreds were put in prison and many lost their lives, while the majority of the leadership of the party escaped to the Soviet Union. From then until 1979 the Tudeh Party was a small group in exile in the Soviet Union and later in East Germany. The revolution of 1979, in which the Tudeh Party had almost no role, created an opportune time for the Soviet Union and the Tudeh Party to exert their influence. For the first time since the coup, the Tudeh Party found opportunity to be active in the lives of the people and to reorganize its followers. From the beginning, even before returning, the Tudeh Party under the leadership of Noor-aldin Kianouri had adopted a strategy of unconditional support of Khomeini and his Islamist regime. This political line and strategy, and its consequences for the opposition in general and the secular leftist movement in Iran in particular, must be one of the most destructive political events of postrevolution Iran. Not only did it result in the collaboration of the Tudeh Party with the brutal Islamist regime, but also it caused divisions within the opposition forces and facilitated their destruction, including the destruction of the Tudeh Party itself, by the Islamic regime. Khomeini and his regime exploited the Tudeh Party's help and strategy. The Tudeh Party directed its members to spy on the opposition and to share their intelligence with the government security and intelligence agents. The party helped, directly or indirectly, in the suppression of the opposition forces. When, in early 1983, the Islamic regime security forces arrested the Tudeh Party leaders, no one was more surprised than the Tudeh Party and its backers. Except for a fraction, which still exists outside of Iran, within a few months the party was completely destroyed—even the underground sector and the secret organizational divisions within the armed forces of the Islamic Republic were rooted out. During the later months of 1983, having been pressured and tortured, the leadership of the party appeared on TV and admitted to crimes including spying for the Soviets and preparing to overthrow the Islamic regime.

8. Rah-e Kargar (Worker's Path) was a Marxist-Leninist group formed exclusively by some of the freed political prisoners soon after the revolution of 1979. This group and the trend they represented became known as the "fourth line" because of their theoretical and political positions, which differentiated them from the Tudeh Party (known as the "first line"), followers of the guerrilla-style armed struggle (the "second line"), and the Maoist currents (the "third line"). The founders of the group published their views analyzing and criticizing Soviet revisionism, Maoism, and also the guerrilla-style armed struggle of revolutionaries separate from the masses. More important than these ideological distinctions, it was their unique analysis of the revolution of 1979 and the regime resulting from it that gave rise to a distinct political trend in Iran. They described the Islamic regime as "Bonapartist," composed of the representatives of the traditional petit bourgeoisie, the bazaar bourgeoisie, and the semi-proletariat masses led by the clerics. They also announced that

although the insurrection had succeeded in overthrowing the shah's regime, the revolution had failed. During and after the events of 1981, many of the members of Rah-e Kargar were arrested, tortured, and executed in prisons. Later they changed the name of their group to "Organization of Revolutionary Workers of Iran."

9. Assadollah Lajavardi (a.k.a. the Butcher of Evin) was an active fanatic in religious circles in the 1960s, when the shah of Iran announced his "reform" program known as the "White Revolution." Clergy opposed the reforms, particularly those relating to "women's rights," the "land reform," and others. Lajavardi, a bazaar draper, supported Ayatollah Khomeini in his opposition to these reforms. In 1963, the shah's army and police massacred followers of Khomeini during demonstrations; many more were arrested and Khomeini was sent into exile. In 1969, SAVAK arrested Assadollah Lajavardi and tortured and imprisoned him. Lajavardi remained a fanatic Muslim and devout follower of Khomeini in prison. He did not like any association with the secular leftist prisoners. In 1971, after the start of the armed struggle against the shah's regime by the Fadaiyan and the Mojahedin, prisons in Iran were soon filled with members and followers of these two organizations. Lajavardi did not participate in the *komon* formed by the two organizations in prison, and on many occasions he declared that he would rather collaborate with SAVAK than be in a *komon* with nonbelievers. On many occasions in prison he had privately declared to other Muslim prisoners, who later became secular leftists, that if some day the Muslim forces took power in Iran he would destroy all nonbelievers. His prison days had shown others how ruthless and vengeful he was toward modernity, freedom, nonbelievers, and even the Muslim Mojahedin. He was a fanatic believer of the Islamic rule and a ruthless man. Torturing and killing people who thought differently was a way for him to get closer to his God. The revolution of 1979 and the establishment of the Islamic Republic with the leadership of Khomeini provided the historical opportunity for people like Lajavardi to put their vengeful desires into action. Khomeini soon appointed Lajavardi as the Islamic Revolution Public Prosecutor in Tehran. Lajavardi settled in the notorious Evin prison, along with the Islamic judge

Ayatollah Gilani, who was also appointed by Khomeini, and together they killed thousands from 1981 to 1983. Lajavardi and his gang tortured detainees inhumanely and forced a large group of prisoners to break down and collaborate with them. They then exploited the services of these broken and repented detainees (*tavvab* prisoners) to control and abuse the combatant and resistant prisoners. He forced prisoners to give public interviews and recantations, whether in prisoner gatherings or in TV broadcasts. Because of his criminal acts he basically never dared to leave Evin prison as long as he was working as a prosecutor. When Ayatollah Montazeri and his followers in 1984 forced Lajavardi out of his position, he still remained involved in Evin prison in other capacities. Finally when he dared to come out of Evin and return to his business, gunmen assassinated him in the Tehran bazaar. The Mojahedin took responsibility for the assassination, but many have doubts about that. It could have been an inside job to eliminate the "butcher" who knew too much about the criminality of the Islamist regime.

10. Interrogation and torture became more sophisticated and systematic after the regime's June 20, 1981, conflicts with the Mojahedin. In Tehran, both Evin prison and the Komiteh were soon filled to capacity. Most of the interrogations and torture took place in these two facilities, though the local Islamic Revolution Committees and the secret detention houses of the Revolutionary Guards, or the prosecutor's office, and those of the Ministry of Intelligence (MI) were also used for these purposes. Gradually the Komiteh became the interrogation and torture place for the MI and the Revolutionary Guards, while the prosecutor's office under Assadollah Lajavardi concentrated its actions in Evin prison. In Evin, the interrogations were carried out in different branches of the Sho'beh and in Ward 209. There were different interrogation branches in Sho'beh, specializing in different opposition groups. By this time the Islamic tribunals were in full action, and a new judiciary system based on Islamic law, sharia, had been developed. The use of torture did not abate. Torture was readily used in interrogations to extract the identities of leaders, members, and sympathizers of opposition groups and information about their activities, assets, and organizational structure. It was also used to force confessions,

public interviews, collaboration, and cooperation. A leading form of torture in the Islamic Republic was and still is long isolation in solitary confinement under constant pressure—whether ideological pressure, political pressure, or life-threatening danger. It has been one of the most effective tools in forcing prisoners to make false confessions and agree to interviews. But the main form of torture, particularly for extracting intelligence quickly, was physical torture by lashing with a *kubl* (flogging cable) under the soles of the prisoner's feet. Torture by *kubl* delivered a continuous and intense form of extreme pain. This pain could drive a prisoner mad. In my own experience, after each blow of the *kubl* I felt like something was moving through my body and forcing itself to exit out of my ears and temples. After being lashed with a *kubl*, prisoners were not able to put any weight on their feet for days without agony. In the case of continuous *kubl* lashing, feet were bruised and torn and the bleeding created ongoing problems for the prisoner. First aid or other medical treatment was needed to prevent infection. Prisoners were forced to walk or even jump on their injured and tortured feet, for two reasons: it was used as an extra form of torture, and it was also helpful in promoting blood flow and preventing blood clotting, which could have caused kidney, heart, and brain damage. Other methods of torture included suspension by the legs or arms (*ghapani*), sexual threat or assault in the case of women prisoners, taking family members hostage and torturing them in front of the prisoner, punching and kicking, sleep deprivation, crushing the hands and fingers, pulling out or inserting sharp objects under the fingernails, electric shocks or burns to the genitals, mock execution, burning with a cigarette, and forcing the prisoner to stand in one place for hours or even days.

11. Haji Davoud Rahmani, a former blacksmith from the Tehran bazaar and a follower of Khomeini, became the warden of Ghezelhessar prison in 1981. He was a large, violent, sadistic man of low-level education, with a feeling of inferiority and hatred toward those opposing the Islamic regime. Rahmani set up a system of torture, brutality, inhumane pressure, and criminality never seen in modern Iran prison history. His goal was to convert every single prisoner into a follower of the Islamic regime. This was only possible through

absolute pressure to break down the resistance of the prisoners. He set out to do just that and succeeded to a large degree by putting the resistant prisoners through what he called his *dastgah* (apparatus). Many prisoners came out of it broken, paranoid, and even insane. Finally, in 1984, pressure by the prisoners' families and documentation by the followers of Ayatollah Montazeri convinced Montazeri to make some changes in the prison system. As a result of this, Montazeri was successful in removing Assadollah Lajavardi and Davoud Rahmani from their posts. Rahmani's brutal legacy in the Iranian political prison system will never be forgotten.

12. Grand Ayatollah Hossein-Ali Montazeri, born in 1922, was one of the leaders of the Islamic Revolution. He was once designated successor to Ayatollah Khomeini. Montazeri studied with Khomeini at the Faiziyeh Theological School in the holy city of Ghom, and after the shah forced Khomeini into exile in 1963, Montazeri continued his opposition of the shah's rule. Montazeri was put in prison in 1974 and was released in 1978. In 1979, following the overthrow of the shah, Montazeri played a key role in establishing the theocracy. During this time he also served as the Friday prayer leader of Ghom and as a member of the Islamic Revolution Council. In 1980 Supreme Leader Khomeini began to transfer some of his powers to Montazeri, who was later officially declared Khomeini's future successor. Montazeri's troubles began with his association with Mehdi Hashemi, the brother of his son-in-law. Subsequent to the Iran-Contra Affair, Mehdi Hashemi was arrested on charges of "counterrevolutionary" activities and executed in 1987. The real reason for his execution was that he had exposed the secret dealings of Khomeini and his aides with the US administration during the Iran-Contra Affair. Montazeri later criticized the views and actions of the Islamic regime, including Khomeini himself, on a variety of matters, particularly the mass killings of thousands of political prisoners in the summer and fall of 1988. On March 26, 1989, Khomeini strongly denounced Montazeri and his actions, and two days later it was announced that Montazeri had resigned his post. In addition to losing his position to be the next supreme leader, Montazeri temporarily lost his title of Grand Ayatollah, and any reference to him on the state radio and television stopped. Khomeini died in

June 1989 and a junior cleric, Ali Khamenei, was selected by the Assembly of Experts to be the new supreme leader. Some ayatollahs, including Montazeri, disputed Khamenei's legitimacy as supreme leader. In October 1997, Montazeri was placed under house arrest for openly criticizing the authority of the Supreme Leader Ayatollah Khamenei. This punishment was lifted in 2003 after more than 100 Iranian legislators called on President Khatami to free Montazeri. Montazeri's freedoms were still limited by the security services, however. Montazeri understood the role he had played in the establishment of the theocracy, was critical of his own past actions, and tried hard to reform the system. He remained strong as a main supporter of the reform movement until his death in 2009. Tens of thousands of Iranians participated in his funeral, in spite of threats by government authorities against doing so.

13. Komite-haye Enghlab-e Eslami (Committees of Islamic Revolution, a.k.a. Committees) sprang up autonomously in every neighborhood in late 1978. Committees were originally organized in mosques, schools, and workplaces to mobilize people and organize strikes and demonstrations during the revolution. In Tehran alone, there might have been fifteen hundred of them. Their main role was to exert the power of the Islamist movement during the revolution and to establish the authority of the new regime later. After the revolution the committees arrested people deemed "counterrevolutionaries," controlled neighborhoods, and were the face of the Islamic regime. Committees were charged with gathering weapons, organizing and training followers of Khomeini, and generally establishing order in the wake of the collapse of the shah's security forces. They were involved in many arbitrary arrests, executions, and confiscations of property. In 1991, they were merged with the conventional police in a new organization known as the Niruha-ye Entezami (Forces of Order) and were put under the supervision of the Ministry of the Interior.

14. Ayatollah Khomeini issued a fatwa (religious edict) sometime in July 1988 just before the mass executions, ordering the historic criminal act. Following is a translation from the Farsi text of his fatwa. (Arabic phrases in the text have not been translated. Sentence structure in the translation is based on the original text structure.)

> In the name of God, the Compassionate and the Merciful. Since the treacherous *Monafeghin* have never believed in Islam, and whatever they say is based on their hypocrisy and lies, and according to the confessions of their leaders indicating their apostasy from Islam, and since they are *Mohareb* based on their classic wars in the north and west of the country in collaboration with the Iraqi Ba'th Party and their spying for Saddam against our Muslim nation, and with attention to their collaboration with the world arrogance and their unjustified strikes against the Islamic Republic since its foundation, those prisoners all over Iran who have insisted and are still steadfast on their positions of *Nefagh* are *Mohareb* and condemned to death. In Tehran, the evaluation and judgment on the matter shall be with the majority vote of Misters Hojjatoleslam Nayyeri-Damat Efazateh- (as Islamic judge) and Eshraghi (as public prosecutor) and a representative from the Ministry of Intelligence, though unanimity is preferred. Also in central prisons of the provinces, the majority vote of the public prosecutor or his assistant and the representative of the Ministry of Intelligence should be followed with no hesitation. Showing any compassion for *Mohareb* is naive. Resolve of Islam against the enemies of God is among the unquestionable principles of the Islamic system. I hope that you can gain God's satisfaction with your revolutionary anger and hatred toward the enemies of Islam. Misters who have responsibility of judgment on the matter should not hesitate at all and should try to be Ashadan al-alkoffar. Hesitation in the revolutionary Islamic judiciary issues is like ignoring the spilled pure blood of the martyrs. Val-Salam. Ruhollah al-Mussavi al-Khomeini.

Because the content of the fatwa was not clear even to some of the closest aides of Khomeini, Ahmad Khomeini, the son of Ayatollah Khomeini and his closest aide, in a short letter asked his father to clarify some of the ambiguities. Ahmad wrote:

> . . . Ayatollah Mousavi Ardabili has some doubts about your recent fatwa regarding the *Monafeghin*, which he relayed over the phone in three questions: 1. Does the order relate to those prisoners who have been in prison for a while, have been in the courts, and have been condemned to death, but so far have not changed their positions and their sentences have not been carried out yet? Or, it includes those prisoners who have not even been to the court yet. 2. There are *Monafeghin* prisoners who have been given a prison term and have already served a part of it but are steadfast in their position of *Nefagh*. Are they condemned to death? 3. In administering the fatwa, should those towns in the country that have judicial independence send their files of the *Monafeghin* to the provincial capitals or they could deal with these files on their own?

In response, Ayatollah Khomeini wrote a supplement to his original fatwa:

> . . . In the Name of God, in all of these cases if anyone in any stage is steadfast on his *Nefagh*, he is condemned to death. Quickly eliminate the enemies of Islam. In dealing with the files, any which way that the fatwa can be carried out faster is what we had in mind. Ruhollah al-Mussavi al-Khomeini.

GLOSSARY

aash: a thick, flavorful soup containing a variety of herbs, vegetables, beans, dried fruit, rice, and meat. There are many types and regional varieties of this "meal in a bowl."

abgusht: a stew of lamb meat, made with onions, turmeric, salt and pepper, saffron, beans, potatoes, tomatoes, and tomato paste. Traditionally, it is cooked in a clay pot over low heat and served with copious amounts of bread.

Alborz: a mountain range north of Tehran.

ammameh: the turban worn by Shiite clerics.

amoozeshgah: literally, a learning or training center. In Evin prison, Amoozeshgah was the name given to the largest prisoner-holding cellblock compound.

assayeshgah: usually the term associated with a psychiatric ward. But in Evin prison, Assayeshgah was the name given to the largest complex of solitary cells.

Ayyaran: a small group that belonged to a Sufi dervish order from western Iran. Part of their leadership lived in a small town near Karaj called Sorkhe Hessar. Many of its leaders and members were arrested in 1986, and later most of them were executed by the Khomeini regime.

Azari: the language of the minority ethnic Azari people, who live all over Iran but mainly in the northwest (Azarbaijan). About 25 percent of the Iranian population is Azari.

Baha'i: a religion founded in nineteenth-century Persia. Baha'i emphasizes the spiritual unity of all humankind. Baha'ullah, the founder of Baha'i, claimed to be the personification of the twelfth Shiite imam, the "Hidden Imam." This claim, considered as heresy by the Shiite clergy, has since put the Baha'i people under continuous persecution in Iran.

Basij: a volunteer paramilitary force founded by Ayatollah Khomeini in November 1979, with branches in almost every Iranian mosque and an official membership of 90,000 regular soldiers and 300,000 reservists. The regime claims that the Basij force has a potential strength of eleven million. The Basij force currently is subordinate to the Revolutionary Guards.

bazaar: a traditional marketplace typically found in Middle Eastern countries. A *bazaari* is a merchant, guildsman, or artisan who works in the bazaar. Historically, as a group, the *bazaaris* have been tied to the clergy, and they played a major role in the Islamic Revolution of 1979.

carevan-e shadi: "joy caravan." Conditions permitting, prisoners would hold open or secret "happy hour" gatherings, during which they would sing, tell jokes, imitate the authorities, and entertain themselves. These events took a variety of names in different prisons, one of which was *carevan-e shadi*.

Chomaghdaran: plainclothes, club-wielding vigilantes, organized by the regime, who attack headquarters, gatherings, and other activities of opposition groups.

Confederation: international federation of Iranian students studying in Europe and America, formed in 1960. The Confederation of Iranian Students Abroad was a politically autonomous organization financed by dues and contributions from members and supporters, fundraising events, and sales of its publications. Through public protests and demonstrations, and through close cooperation with human rights, legal, and other student organizations, the Confederation spearheaded an international campaign exposing the shah's regime as a repressive dictatorship.

dabirkhaneh: the headquarters of a political party, where the secretary general and other party officials have their offices.

Dadgah-Haye Engelab-e Eslami: the Islamic Revolutionary Courts, founded immediately after the Islamic Revolution of 1979. In practice, they are religious tribunals operating summary judicial processes and focusing primarily upon "crimes against national security" and narcotics smuggling.

Daftar-e Azadi: the prisoner release administration office in Evin prison.

dahi: a snack regularly served at ten in the morning by the Mojahedin prisoners in their rooms or to all prisoners when the Mojahedin were in charge of a ward.

du'a: an Arabic word meaning "call out" or "summon." In Islam, it means "supplication." *Du'a* is essentially an expression by the faithful of submission to God and of one's dependence on Him. There are various forms of *du'a* in Islam. Du'a-ye Komeyl is one for the expression of repentance and remorse. In Iran, the vocalist performing the *du'a* is called a *du'a-khan.*

Eid-e Fetr: a day of celebration at the end of Ramadan, the Muslim month of fasting.

enzejar nameh: a letter of repentance and self-defamation, which political prisoners were required to sign before their release and in which they condemned their own activities, and those of others, against the regime.

ertedad: apostasy; the rejection of Islam and the Muslim community. In Islam, rejection of the faith is equal to treason, punishable by death for men and life imprisonment for women. *Mortad* (plural *mortaddin*) refers to a person who has committed *ertedad.*

Esfahan: the capital of Esfahan (Isfahan) province; the third largest city in Iran. Located 340 kilometers (227 miles) south of Tehran, Esfahan was once one of the largest cities in the world. It is famous for its Islamic architecture and has been designated by UNESCO as a World Heritage Site.

Fadaiyan: the largest secular leftist opposition group. See the "Notes" section for a detailed explanation.

far'i: minor. In Gohardasht prison, *far'i* ward referred to the small prisoner-holding unit attached to each main ward.

Farsi: the official language of Iran; the language of the majority Persian ethnic group.

fatwa: a religious edict or decree issued by a senior Islamic cleric, such as the one Ayatollah Khomeini issued in 1988 ordering the mass killing of the political prisoners in Iran, or the one he issued against Salman Rushdie, the author of *The Satanic Verses.*

Ghiamat: the Day of Resurrection. One of the principal beliefs in Islam is that there will be a final judgment day when God will judge everyone for their actions throughout their lives.

***ghossl* (or *ghusl*)**: obligatory baths; ritual washing required of Muslims before religious worship or prayers, particularly after sexual activity.

Grouh-e E'zam: a secret internal committee in charge of smuggling leading members of the Fadaiyan Sixteenth of Azar to safety abroad.

Grouh-e Vizhe: the reorganized security and emergency action committee of the Fadaiyan Sixteenth of Azar, previously known as the Special Commission for Security, by the executive committee of the organization in Tehran.

Haj-Agha: the title bestowed on a Muslim man (*agha*) who has made a *hajj,* a pilgrimage to Mecca. More generally, it is an honorific title of respect. In prison, the expression was used both by the authorities when they addressed or referred to each other and by the prisoners when they referred to the authorities.

hakem-e shar': an Islamic judge (a cleric) in the Islamic court system, who wields unlimited powers over those who appear before him.

havakhori: recess; in prison, a yard or place where prisoners could get fresh air. The frequency and the length of *havakhori* varied depending on the prison, the particular era of the Islamic Republic, and the whim of the authorities.

hejab (in the West, usually "hijab"): veiling, the obligatory Islamic covering of a woman's entire body other than the face and hands. Depending on the strictness of the religious interpretation and enforcement, the form and degree of covering varies across societies and times. Traditionally, Iranian *hejab* consists of wearing a *chador*, a shapeless cloak draped over the head so that the face is visible but the rest of the body is covered. All women prisoners were forced to wear the *chador* whenever they left their cells, rooms, or wards.

hosseiniye: literally, a mosque or place of worship, particularly in Shi'a Islamic society. In Evin prison it specifically referred to the erstwhile dining facility, which under the Islamic regime had been converted into a mosque and gathering place and was called Hosseiniye-ye Evin.

imam: a religious title given to Khomeini by his followers during the Islamic Revolution of 1979. In Shi'a Islam, it specifically refers to the twelve infallible leaders who led the Shiites and were all descendants of the Prophet Mohammad.

jahad (commonly "jihad" in the West): a struggle or crusade conducted by a Muslim for Islam and his personal faith. In prison, Band-e Jahad (Crusaders' Ward) referred to a ward where *tavvab* prisoners, who had repented and were cooperating with the authorities, lived and worked.

jan: a term of endearment following a person's name, meaning "dear."

kafar: a nonbeliever; an infidel. Any Muslim who apostates from Islam and rejects God (Allah) is also considered a *kafar* (or *kafir*). In Shi'a Iran, people of the scripture (Jews, Christians, and Zoroastrians) are not considered as *kafar*.

Karaj: a city near Tehran with a population of more than a million. Both Ghezelhessar and Gohardasht prisons are located on the outskirts of Karaj.

Kayhan: a daily newspaper in Iran.

Khavaran: a cemetery in southeastern Tehran, where prisoners hanged in the mass killings of 1988 were buried in mass graves.

khoresht: a refined type of stew combining meat with herbs or vegetables, fresh or dried fruits, and sometimes grains or nuts, seasoned with spices and simmered slowly. There are many types and varieties of *khoresht*.

Kohkilouye and Boyer-Ahmad: an encompassing part of the Zagros mountain range, inhabited mostly by nomadic tribes speaking the Lur language.

komon: literally, a collective or a commune. In prison, it referred to the communal organization of the prisoners' lives, which took a variety of forms and degrees, depending on the time period and the prison. The way of life in prison varied from totally communal to completely individualistic.

Komouleh: an Iranian Kurdish organization founded in 1979 adhering to Maoist ideology. Komouleh (or Komalah) joined forces with several other small non-Kurdish Iranian Maoist groups in 1983 to form the Iranian Communist Party. Many of its followers died in conflicts with the regime or in prison.

Kordi: the language of the minority ethnic Kurdish people, who live mostly in western Iran (Kordestan) in the Zagros Mountains. About 8 percent of the Iranian population is Kurdish.

Kordestan Conflict: refers to the conflicts that took place soon after the establishment of the Islamic Republic between the Iranian Kurds, who were organized and led by the local Kurdish organizations and the Fadaiyan, against the Islamic militia and the Revolutionary Guards.

kubl: a rubber-encased metal cable used to flog political prisoners to extract information and confessions; the most effective tool of physical torture in the Islamic prison system.

lavash: traditional flat, thin bread that, once dried, can be stored for a long time.

Majles: Iranian Parliament.

mass'oul-e band: ward representative; a person appointed, elected, or who volunteered to take responsibility for any contact with the guards on behalf of the prison ward. Frequently, the authorities appointed their own choice of prisoner, typically a *tavvab*, to be in charge of a ward; otherwise, they never officially acknowledged the person elected by prisoners to the position.

mass'oul-e otagh: room representative; the person elected or who volunteered to take charge of the prison cell and represent its occupants in dealings with the authorities on matters relating to the whole room.

mass'oul-e senfi: food service representative; the person who was elected or volunteered to be in charge of the food-related and spending issues for a cell or ward.

me'dei: an expression used in prison to refer to a prisoner with any digestive illness or problem. *Me'de* means "stomach" in Farsi.

melli: literally, national. In prison, anything that was public, for the community, free, or extra would be labeled *melli*. For example: prisoners serving time without a sentence or serving extra time after the end of their sentences were referred to as *mellikesh* (serving without sentence) by other prisoners. Community work organized and carried out on Fridays on behalf of and for the good of all prisoners was called *kar-e melli*.

mohareb: a person warring against God, Islam, or Islamic governance. The punishment for a *mohareb* could include execution, crucifixion, amputation of limbs, or exile. *Moharebin* is the plural form.

Mojahedin: an Islamic leftist opposition group. See the "Notes" section for a detailed explanation.

mokh: literally, brain. In colloquial Farsi it refers to a person of high intelligence.

monafegh: hypocrite (plural *monafeghin*). The Islamic regime refers to the Mojahedin organization as *Monafeghin*, meaning nonbelievers masquerading as Muslims, in order to discredit them. In prison, Mojahedin followers were forced to call themselves *monafegh*; if they did not, they were brutally tortured and eventually killed.

mullah: in Iran, Islamic clerics are commonly known as mullahs. In some Muslim communities around the world, mullah is the title commonly given to the mosque leaders or local Islamic clerics. It is generally used to refer to a Muslim man educated in Islamic theology and sacred law.

Mullah Nasreddin: a satirical Sufi figure who supposedly lived during the thirteenth century. The mythical mullah's parables have been passed down via word of mouth around the globe.

Nowruz: Iranian New Year, celebrated on the first day of spring. In modern Iran, people celebrate the New Year for thirteen days, visiting friends and relatives, exchanging gifts, feasting, and consuming sweets. The Nowruz festival and celebration has survived for thousands of years because it represents a celebration of life.

panji: a snack regularly served at five in the afternoon by Mojahedin prisoners in their rooms or to all prisoners when the Mojahedin were in charge of a ward.

Peykar: the commonly used short name for "Organization of Struggle for the Freedom of the Working Class," a Marxist-Leninist-Maoist organization, which emerged from the Islamic Mojahedin after a change of ideology by some of the leaders in 1975. The Peykar organization was completely destroyed by the Khomeini regime, and many of its leaders, members, and followers were tortured and killed.

Pich-e Tobeh: "Repentance Turn," the name given to a turn in the road approaching Evin prison. Assadollah Lajavardi coined the term to emphasize that anyone arrested and brought to Evin prison started to entertain thoughts of *tobeh* (repentance) as soon as they rounded the bend and the prison came into view. Lajavardi maintained that this change of heart took place because of the power of Islam and the Islamic forces working in prison; in fact it was because of the fear the notorious Evin prison and its torturers instilled in detainees.

porze: lint. In prison *porze* specifically referred to the lint produced by the ugly, gray prison blankets.

Rah-e Kargar: a Marxist opposition group. See the "Notes" section for a detailed explanation.

rak'at: Muslim prayer sequence. The prayer that Muslims perform five times a day involves repeating this sequence. The required daily observance is seventeen *rak'ats*: two before sunrise, three at noon, four in the afternoon, four in the evening, and four before midnight.

Ramadan: the ninth month in the Islamic lunar calendar, during which all healthy adult Muslims are required to fast from sunrise to sunset.

Ranjbaran Party: in the 1960s some members of the Tudeh Party split off and formed a group that called itself the "Revolutionary Organization of the Tudeh Party of Iran." This group was active abroad mainly among Iranian students. It adopted a Maoist ideology. After the revolution of 1979, it returned to Iran and changed its name to

"Ranjbaran Party of Iran." Later, many of its leaders, members, and followers were arrested and killed in Khomeini's prisons.

Razmandegan: a small Maoist group formed after the revolution of 1979. After many attempts to unite with other small Maoist groups, Razmandegan (Organization of Fighters for the Freedom of the Iranian Working Class) finally dissolved itself in 1981 to escape the coming repression. Even so, many of its members were arrested and killed in Khomeini's prisons.

Salone: any of the six wards in Evin's Amoozeshgah compound.

sar-e moze'i: a term used by the authorities in reference to a combatant prisoner who remained steadfast in his views.

SAVAK: an acronym in Farsi for the Shah's State Organization for Security and Intelligence; the secret police force of Iran.

senfi: literally, guild-related. In prison, it was used in contrast to *syasi* (political) and referred to issues that were supposed to be nonpolitical.

Shiraz: the capital of Fars province and one of the most beautiful and historic cities in the world. With close to a million in population, it is located in south-central Iran, about 200 kilometers (133 miles) from the Persian Gulf. It is known as the city of poets, wine, and flowers.

Sho'beh: *sho'beh* means "branch" or "division." In Evin prison Sho'beh referred to a building housing various interrogation branches.

sofreh: dinner cloth. Traditionally, in Iran, food is served on a cloth spread on the floor. In prison we used whatever was available: a newspaper or a long plastic sheet, if not a cloth.

Sufi: a practitioner of Sufism, a system of esoteric philosophy commonly associated with Islam. "Islamic spirituality" or "Islamic mysticism" is modern reference to the same practice. The central concept in Sufism is "love," which Sufis believe to be a projection of the essence of God in the universe.

ta'zir: a category of crime and punishment in sharia (Islamic law). *Ta'zir* usually refers to corporal punishment, which can be administered at the discretion of the Islamic judges. *Ta'zir* crimes are crimes against Islamic society. In the Islamic Republic, *ta'zir* is an ideological cover for physical torture.

Tabriz: the capital of East Azarbaijan province; the fourth largest city in Iran. With a population of close to two million people, it is located at an altitude of 1,350 meters (4,430 feet) in northwestern Iran. It has proven to be very influential in the country's recent history. It is a summer resort and a commercial, industrial, and transportation center. Tabriz is also famous for its cuisine, its rugs, and its bazaar, one of the largest covered markets in the world.

tavvab: literally, a person who has repented. In prison, *tavvab* referred to prisoners who under pressure had repented of their political and ideological positions and collaborated with the authorities in controlling non-*tavvab* or combatant prisoners.

Tehran: Iran's national capital, the largest city in the Middle East, and the sixteenth most populous city in the world, Tehran has a daytime population of twelve million to fifteen million. It is located on the slopes of the Alborz Mountains.

Tudeh Party: the pro-Soviet communist party in Iran. See the "Notes" section for a detailed explanation.

Vajebi: a depilatory paste.

zir-e hasht: the entrance hall, lobby, or foyer of a building. In prison, this was where the ward guards were stationed, where the admission or discharge of the prisoners took place, and where punishment of prisoners by the guards for any violation of ward rules took place.

RESOURCES

Though the main body of my memoirs is based on my own observations and experiences, or those of other prisoners who have shared them with me, I have benefited greatly from reading books, reports, articles, and interviews. Following are some of these resources, for those interested in further reading:

Abrahamian, Ervand. *The Iranian Mojahedin*. New Haven: Yale University Press, 1989.

Abrahamian, Ervand. *Tortured Confessions: Prison and Public Recantations in Modern Iran*. Berkeley: University of California Press, 1999.

Agha, Azadeh, Sousan Mehr, and Shadi Parsi. *We Lived to Tell: Political Prison Memoirs of Iranian Women*. Toronto: McGilligan Books, 2007.

Amirahmadi, Hooshang, and Manoucher Parvin, eds. *Post-Revolutionary Iran*. Boulder, CO: Westview Press, 1988.

Amnesty International. *Amnesty International Report 2010*. Available for purchase at http://thereport.amnesty.org.

Amnesty International. *Iran: Election Contested, Repression Compounded*. London: Amnesty International Publications, 2009. http://www.amnestyusa.org/pdf/mde131232009en.pdf.

Amnesty International. *Iran: Preserve the Khavaran Grave Site for Investigation into Mass Killings* (press release). January 20, 2009. http://www.amnesty.org/en/library/info/MDE13/006/2009/en.

Behrooz, Maziar. *Rebels with a Cause: The Failure of the Left in Iran*. London: I. B. Tauris Publishers, 2000.

Dabashi, Hamid. *Iran: A People Interrupted.* New York: The New Press, 2007.

Esfandiari, Haleh. *My Prison, My Home: One Woman's Story of Captivity in Iran.* New York: HarperCollins Publishers, 2009.

Khalili Batmanglij, Najmieh. *New Food of Life: Ancient Persian and Modern Iranian Cooking and Ceremonies.* Washington, DC: Mage Publishers, 2005.

Levi, Primo. *Survival in Auschwitz.* New York: A Touchstone Book Published by Simon & Schuster, 1996.

Majd, Hooman. *The Ayatollah Begs to Differ: The Paradox of Modern Iran.* New York: Doubleday, 2008.

Nafisi, Azar. *Things I've Been Silent About.* New York: Random House, 2008.

Rejali, Darius. *Torture and Democracy.* Princeton: Princeton University Press, 2007.

Saberi, Roxana. *Between Two Worlds: My Life and Captivity in Iran.* New York: HarperCollins Publishers, 2010.

Seng Z. Brang, ed. *Life in Burma Military Prisons: A Prison Memoir of Nang Zing La.* Pittsburgh: RoseDog Books, 2005.

Shamlu, Ahmad. "In this Dead-end." Shamlu.com, http://www.shamlu.com.

Sofer, Dalia. *The Septembers of Shiraz.* New York: HarperCollins Publishers, 2007.

Timerman, Jacobo. *Prisoner Without a Name, Cell Without a Number.* New York: Vintage Books, 1988.

Ulloa Bornemann, Alberto. *Surviving Mexico's Dirty War: A Political Prisoner's Memoir.* Ed. and trans. Arthur Schmidt and Aurora Camacho de Schmidt. Philadelphia: Temple University Press, 2007.

Ward, Terence. *Searching for Hassan: A Journey to the Heart of Iran.* New York: Anchor Books, 2003.

Weschler, Lawrence. *A Miracle, a Universe: Settling Accounts with Torturers.* Chicago: University of Chicago Press, 1998.

Many prison memoirs have been published in Farsi over the years. The following are just two examples for the interested reader:

Aslani, Mehdi. *Kalagh va Gol-e Sorkh (The Crow & the Red Rose): Memoirs of Prison*. Koln, Germany: Arash Books & Magazine, 2009.

Mesdaghi, Iraj. *Neither Life nor Death: Memoirs of Prison.* Four volumes. Stockholm, Sweden: Alphabet Maxima Publishing, 2004.

A list of the names of those executed during the mass killings of 1988 can be found at: http://asre-nou.net/1386/shahrivar/6/koshtar/m-liste-koshtar.html

Following are Web sites of Iranian electronic journals and magazines and the Web sites of some of the opposition groups:

Asr-e Nou, an electronic newsmagazine:
asre-nou.net

Iran-e Emrooz, an electronic newsmagazine:
iran-emrooz.net

Prison's Dialogue:
dialogt.org

Roozonline, an electronic news journal:
www.roozonline.com

Balatarin, a Web 2.0 Web site:
balatarin.com

Akhbar-e Rooz, an electronic newsmagazine:
iran-chabar.de

Khabarnameye Gooya, an electronic news journal:
news.gooya.com

Jonbeshe Rahe Sabz (Jaras), an electronic newsmagazine:
www.rahesabz.net

The Union of People's Fedaian of Iran organization:
etehadefedaian.org

Rah-e Kargar organization:
rahekargar.net

Association of Iranian Political Prisoners (in Exile):
kanoon-zendanian.org

The Iranian People's Fadai Guerrilas:
siahkal.com

Fadaiyan Minority organization:
fadaian-minority.org

Fadaiyan Majority organization:
fadai.org

Komouleh (Komala) organization:
komala.org

National Council of Resistance of Iran:
www.ncr-iran.org

Democratic Party of Iranian Kurdistan:
pdki.org

Ranjbaran Party:
www.ranjbaran.org

Tudeh Party:
tudehpartyiran.org